Codex Alimentarius

The End of Health Freedom

by Brandon Turbeville

Codex Alimentarius -The End of Health Freedom
by Brandon Turbeville

Cover Illustration: Whitney Limehouse
Contact Whitney for graphic design at: WhitLimehouse@yahoo.com

Distributed by False Flag Publications.

Printed by The Book Patch at www.thebookpatch.com

ISBN 978-0-615-38842-7

Trademark Acknowledgements:

Starlink® is a registered trademark of Aventis Crop Science.

Roundup® and Roundup Ready® are registered trademarks of Monsanto Company.

Nutrasweet® is a registered trademark of Nutrasweet Property Holding Inc.

Quest® is a registered trademark of Vector Tobacco Ltd. Company.

FDA DISCLAIMER

This book and the statements in it have not been evaluated by the Food and Drug Administration. This book is not intended to diagnose, treat, cure or prevent any disease. One should only make health-related decisions after consulting with a doctor. The author of this book is not a doctor and has no medical training whatsoever.

Author's

Disclaimer

The previous statement is the result of living in a country where free speech is now severely limited for the benefit of the corporations and eugenicists that run its' government. The FDA is one of the most corrupt government agencies in existence and one should take any statement made by the FDA with a grain of salt. After all, the public position of the FDA is that only a drug can cure disease. As will be explained later in the book, the previous FDA DISCLAIMER is required by both law and regulation to be added to anything espousing the use of natural healthcare, herbs, vitamins, minerals or pointing out the dangers of pharmaceuticals and invasive surgeries. Only as an attempt to comply with a ridiculous law was the disclaimer added.

Acknowledgements

Thanks to my family and friends for their continued support for my efforts in writing this book.

Special thanks to William Raines for his aid in proofreading the first manuscript and to Julius Foxworth who, without his suggestion for an article topic, the task of writing this book would never have begun. Also thanks to Dr. William Ramsey for his advice and direction throughout the publication process.

Thanks to Whitney Limehouse for her creation of the cover illustration.

Contents

Introduction

When I first heard about Codex Alimentarius, the news was shocking. According to some very loud voices, Codex would be implemented on December 31, 2009. On that date, all of our natural food supplements would disappear and we would be required by law to consume only food and drink made of poisonous chemicals. Naturally, this concerned me deeply. Especially since I found out about this "law" only a few months before the end of 2009. I subsequently embarked upon a crusade to discover what this "law" was and how it could be stopped. Knowing full well the power of the elite world controllers over the mainstream media, I nevertheless wondered how such an imminent issue would fly under the radar of natural health community. Why weren't all the health freedom organizations screaming at the top of their lungs? Why wasn't the supplement industry up in arms? Why had no one even heard of Codex? Why hadn't I heard of it? As a result of these questions I found myself on the websites of some of the more vocal opponents of Codex and, from there, I found a small group of individuals who were attempting to engage the general public in a fight against the tyranny of the Codex guidelines. I then went to Codex's' own site, a virtual indecipherable maze of unhelpful information. In the end, like in any search, much of the information I found was solid. Some of it was not.

Those reading this book should now be fully aware that Codex Alimentarius guidelines were not implemented worldwide on December 31, 2009. While we are undoubtedly fortunate that this is the case, it is quite unfortunate that, because of the misinformation regarding dates, many individuals may have been persuaded that the fight against Codex is merely a scam or conspiracy theory. It is neither. The threat that Codex poses to our natural supplements, food supply, and national sovereignty is very real. As will be mentioned throughout this book, it is unlikely that we will see a sudden and total implementation of Codex guidelines worldwide. Rather, we will witness more of a gradual incremental implementation under the guise of domestic legislation or national regulatory policy. Over the course of this book you will receive an introduction to the secretive history of Codex, an explanation of how it works, its implementation and how it can be stopped. There will be a fairly detailed discussion of its guidelines on vitamin and mineral supplements, genetically modified food, food irradiation, rBGH, pesticide residues, and persistent organic pollutants. In the course of these discussions, it may seem at first as if the book strays from its original topic of Codex Alimentarius. However, keep in mind, it is often important to understand more than just the position of Codex on a particular issue in order to understand the gravity of it.

As a disclaimer, it should be mentioned that this book should not be considered as all-encompassing when it comes to information about Codex Alimentarius. Unfortunately, there are many topics that are not covered here simply out of contextual and length concerns. Therefore, all of the claims made against, for, and by Codex could not be addressed. The purpose of this book is to deal with some of the most important and widely discussed issues regarding Codex and the impact its guidelines will have on the natural health and natural food communities the world over, particularly in the United States. Also, as with any book, a certain amount of reliance upon the research of others has been utilized. Original source documents are used whenever possible but in some instances, for different reasons, they may be unavailable. In this sense, it should be taken into consideration that, as is the case in all forms of research, this book depends upon the honesty and accuracy of the sources it utilizes.

One can only imagine the effects on health that the implementation of Codex Alimentarius guidelines would have on the global population. The deaths resulting from the subsequent cancers, chronic illness, and malnutrition would be staggering. This is not even taking into account the effects on animals and the environment. Yet this is nevertheless the goal of those who control international organizations like Codex Alimentarius, as will be demonstrated throughout the course of this book.

Pay careful attention to players in this game. They will reappear in the plots of many other international "movements" not necessarily related to Codex and will play important roles in many of the geopolitical realignments currently taking place the world over.

Chapter 1

The History and Workings Of Codex Alimentarius

The History and Workings of Codex Alimentarius

Contrary to popular belief Codex Alimentarius is neither a law nor a policy. It is in fact a functioning body, a Commission, created by the Food and Agricultural Organization and the World Health Organization under the direction of the United Nations. The confusion in this regard is largely due to statements made by many critics referring to the "implementation" of Codex Alimentarius as if it were legislation waiting to come into effect. A more accurate phrase would be the "implementation of Codex Alimentarius guidelines," as it would more adequately describe the situation. As will be made clear throughout the course of this book, Codex is merely another tool in the chest of an elite group of individuals whose goal is to create a one world government in which they wield complete control. Power over the food supply is essential in order to achieve this. As will be discussed later, Codex Alimentarius will be "implemented" whenever guidelines are established and national governments begin to arrange their domestic laws in accordance with the standards set by the organization.

The existence of Codex Alimentarius as a policy making body has roots going back over a hundred years. The name itself, Codex Alimentarius, is Latin for "food code"[1] and directly descended from the Codex Alimentarius Austriacus, a set of standards and descriptions of a variety of foods in the Austria-Hungarian Empire between 1897 and 1911.[2] This set of standards was the brainchild of both the food industry

---

[1] Tips, Scott C. "Codex Alimentarius: Global Food Imperialism." FHR. 2007. P. ii.

[2] "Opening Statement by Dr. B.P. Dutia Assistant Director-General Economic and Social Policy Department, FAO to the Nineteenth Session of the Codex Alimentarius Commission." Food and Agricultural Organization. July 1, 1991. http://www.fao.org/docrep/meeting/005/t0490e/T0490E04.htm
See also,

and academia and was used by the courts in order to determine food identity in a legal fashion. Even as far back as 1897, nations were being pushed toward harmonization of national laws into an international set of standards that would reduce the "barriers to trade" created by differences in national laws.[3] As the Codex Alimentarius Austriacus gained steam in its localized area, the idea of having a single set of standards for all of Europe began to pick up steam as well. From 1954-1958, Austria successfully pursued the creation of the Codex Alimentarius Europaeus (the European Codex Alimentarius). Almost immediately the UN directed FAO (Food and Agricultural Organization) sprang into action when the FAO Regional Conference for Europe expressed the desire for a global international set of standards for food. The FAO Regional Conference then sent a proposal up the chain of command to the FAO itself with the suggestion to create a joint FAO/WHO programme dealing with food standards. The very next year, the Codex Alimentarius Europeaus adopted a resolution that it's' work on food standards be taken over by the FAO. In 1961, it was decided by the WHO, Codex Alimentarius Europaeus, Organization for Economic Co-operation and Development (OECD), and the FAO Conference to create an international food standards programme known as the Codex Alimentarius.[4] In 1963, as a result of the resolutions passed by these

---

Taylor, Paul Anthony. "Codex Guidelines for Vitamins and Minerals – Optional or Mandatory?" Dr.Rath Health Foundation. http://www4.dr-rath-foundation.org/features/codex_wto.html

[3] "Codex Alimentarius: how it all began." Food and Agricultural Organization. http://www.fao.org/docrep/v7700t/v7700t09.htm Accessed April 23, 2010.

[4] "Understanding the Codex Alimentarius." World Health Organization. Food and Agricultural Organization. 2006. P. 7 http://www.scribd.com/doc/25710873/WHO-Understanding-the-Codex-Alimentarius Accessed April 23, 2010.

organizations two years earlier, Codex Alimentarius was officially created. [5]

Although created under the auspices of the FAO and the WHO, there is some controversy regarding individuals who may or may not have participated in the establishment of Codex. Many anti-Codex organizations have asserted that Nazi war criminals, Fritz Ter Meer[6] and Hermann Schmitz[7] in particular, were principal architects of the organization. Because many of these claims are made with only indirect evidence or no evidence at all, one might be tempted to disregard them at first glance. However, as the allegations gain more and more adherents, Codex has attempted to refute them. In its' Frequently Asked Questions section, Codex answers the question, "Is it true that Codex was created by a former war criminal to control the world food supply?"[8] It then goes on to answer the charges by stating,

> No. It is a false claim. You just need to type the words "Codex Alimentarius" in any search engine and you will find lots of these rumors about Codex. Usually the people spreading them will give no proof but will ask you to send donations or to sign petitions against Codex.

---

[5] Tips, Scott C. "Codex Alimentarius: Global Food Imperialism." FHR. 2007. P.ii

[6] "The History of the 'Business With Disease.'" Dr. Rath Health Foundation. http://www4.dr-rath-foundation.org/PHARMACEUTICAL_BUSINESS/history_of_the_pharmaceutical_industry.htm Accessed April 26, 2010.

[7] Minton, Barbara. "Codex Threatens Health of Billions." Naturalnews. July 30, 2009. http://www.naturalnews.com/026731_CODEX_food_health.html

[8] "FAQs – Rumours" CodexAlimentarius.net http://www.codexalimentarius.net/web/faq_rum.jsp#R1 Accessed April 26, 2010.

Truthful information about Codex is found on Internet
(www.codexalimentarius.net) - there is nothing to hide from
our side - we are a public institution working in public for the
public - we are happy if people want to know more about our
work and ask questions. There is an official Codex Contact
Point in each member country
(www.codexalimentarius.net/web/members.jsp) who will be
pleased to answer your questions on Codex.[9]

But, as one can see from the statement above, Codex's
response does very little to answer this question beyond simply
disagreeing with it. While it is true that many individuals who make this
claim provide little evidence for it, the presentation of the information
does not necessarily negate its truthfulness. In fact, Codex offers its own
website as a source for accurate information about the organization, yet
beyond the FAQ section, there is nothing to be found that is relevant to
the "war criminal" allegations. Furthermore, the codexalimentarius.net
website is virtually indecipherable, almost to the point of being
completely useless. In the end, this response raises more questions than
it answers. This is because Codex, if it wanted, could put these rumors
to rest by simply posting a list of the individuals and organizations that
funded or played an integral role in its' creation. However, it does
nothing of the sort. Beyond mentioning the FAO and the WHO, we are
completely unaware of who or how many other individuals and
organizations participated in the creation of Codex Alimentarius.

The "war criminal" claims center around the chemical
conglomerate known as I.G. Farben. I.G. Farben was made up of several
German chemical firms including, BASF, Bayer, Hoechst and AGFA,[10]

---

[9] Ibid.
[10] Behreandt, Dennis. "The crimes of I.G. Farben: during
WWII, I.G. Farben, a synthetic-fuels manufacturer for the
German war machine, was a major supporter of the Nazi
regime and a willing co-conspirator in the Holocaust." The

that merged together. It was essentially the manufacturing wing of the Third Reich and was the engine behind the Nazi war machine. The company provided the vast majority of explosives and synthetic gasoline used for the military conquest and murder of millions. It also manufactured the now infamous Zyklon-B gas used in the gas chambers. Not only that, but it was influential in the conducting of experiments on concentration camp victims. Indeed, camp victims were often purchased outright at the behest of the company for the express purposes of testing by several different branches of the company, particularly Bayer and Hoechst. Without I.G. Farben, the German wars simply could not have been sustained. During the Nuremberg war trials, the tribunal convicted 24 board members and executives of the company and dissolved it into several different daughter companies. Namely, BASF, Hoechst (later to be known as Aventis), and Bayer. By 1951, virtually all 24 of these executives were released, including Fritz Ter Meer and Hermann Schmitz. Ter Meer had been a member of the I.G. Farben executive committee from 1926-1945 and also a member of the working committee and the technical committee as well as a director of the infamous Section II. He was also the ambassador to Italy given full power by the Reich Minister for armaments and war production and was the industrialist most responsible for Auschwitz. Schmitz was also a member of the I.G. Farben executive committee from 1926-1935, and was chairman of the board and "head of finances" from 1935-1945. He was also head of military economics and a member

---

New American. November 27, 2006. http://findarticles.com/p/articles/mi_m0JZS/is_24_22/ai_n24 996865/ Accessed April 26, 2010.
See Also,
"The Documentation About 'Codex Alimentarius.'" Dr. Rath Health Foundation. http://www4.dr-rath-foundation.org/PHARMACEUTICAL_BUSINESS/health_movem ent_against_codex/health_movement24.htm Accessed April 26, 2010.

of the Nazi party. Both men were found guilty by the Nuremberg war tribunal in 1948, yet Schmitz was released in 1950 and Ter Meer in 1952.[11]

After all this, Schmitz was appointed board member of the German bank of Berlin West in 1952 and in 1956, the honorary chairman of the board of Rheinish steel plants. Ter Meer, however, was even more successful. Upon his release, he was appointed board member of Bayer in 1955 and, in 1956 was appointed chairman. In the years following, he would take on many additional roles such as chairman of the board of Theodore Goldschmidt AG, deputy chairman of the board of Commerzbank and Bank-Association AG, as well as a board member of the Waggonfabrik Uerdingen, Duesseldorger Waggonfabrik AG, the bank association of West Germany, and United Industrial Enterprises AG.[12] These are documented connections for both of these men. Indeed, Ter Meer's' connections to the pharmaceutical firm Bayer earned him a foundation named in his honor, the Fritz Ter-Meer Foundation.[13] Through all of this however, this author could not confirm that either Ter Meer or Schmitz had direct connections to the creation of Codex Alimentarius. This is why this book will not take one position over the other regarding this particular issue. There is no hard evidence (encountered by this author at least) that proves Ter Meer or Schmitz were integral to the creation of the organization.

---

[11] "The History of the 'Business With Disease.'" Dr. Rath Health Foundation. http://www4.dr-rath-foundation.org/PHARMACEUTICAL_BUSINESS/history_of_the_pharmaceutical_industry.htm Accessed April 26, 2010.

[12] Ibid.

[13] Weimbs Lab: Molecular, Cellular and Developmental Biology University of California, Santa Barbra. http://www.lifesci.ucsb.edu/mcdb/labs/weimbs/people/weimbs/index.html Accessed April 27, 2010. Dr. Thomas Weimbs received a scholarship from the Fritz ter Meer Foundation in 1988.

However, Codex does nothing to dispel the allegations besides simply disagreeing with them and the connections are not at all implausible. Codex is very secretive about it's' beginnings, as evidenced on its' website where it only states that it was created at the behest of the FAO and the WHO. It is highly unlikely that such an organization would be created without the assistance, input, and even funding of privately owned international corporations. Thanks to both the anti-Codex community and Codex Alimentarius itself, there is no evidence (again at least to this author) that documents which individuals or corporations were involved in it's' establishment. However, there are ties that lend more credence to the belief that war criminals played a role in the creation of Codex.

I.G. Farben was not isolated to Germany. Not only a conglomerate of Bayer, Hoechst, BASF and other companies, I.G. Farben was also welded to Shell Oil of Britain and Standard Oil and DuPont of the United States by 1929. This occurred after I.G. Farben discovered how to make petroleum out of coal. Subsequently, there was an agreement for I.G. Farben to stay out of the petroleum market if Standard Oil would stay out of the chemical market.[14] Hermann Schmitz, who was chairman of the board for I.G. Farben as mentioned above, had a large amount of stock in Standard Oil New Jersey and the Rockefeller Foundation likewise owned a substantial amount of stock in

---

[14] Griffin, G. Edward. "World Without Cancer." 2nd edition. American Media. 1997. P. 235-236.
See Also,
Nield, Michael. "The Police State Road Map." March 2005. http://www.bibliotecapleyades.net/sociopolitica/policestate_roadmap/policestate_roadmap.htm#Contents specifically, Chapter 2, "The Great Trust." http://www.bibliotecapleyades.net/sociopolitica/policestate_roadmap/policestate_roadmap02.htm Accessed May 25, 2010.

I.G. Farben.[15] So much stock that when I.G. Farben's holdings were completely sold off in 1962, the Rockefellers were the dominant holders involved in the transactions.[16] This is significant because the Rockefeller Foundation and the Rockefeller family in general were major supporters not just of the Nazi regime and eugenics, but the creation of the United Nations.[17] Indeed, the connections between the Rockefellers and the atrocities of Nazi Germany, Communist Russia, and Communist China are so plentiful as to preclude them from being dealt with in much detail in this book. This evidence is readily available to anyone who wishes to investigate and is made much easier because, in large part, the Rockefellers do not deny it. In addition to open support for eugenics, the Rockefellers are also committed globalists, again a philosophy which is readily admitted. The Rockefeller connections to globalist organizations such as the United Nations,[18] the Council on Foreign Relations,[19] and the Trilateral Commission[20] to name a few are

---

[15] Griffin, G. Edward. "World Without Cancer." 2nd edition. American Media. 1997. P. 235-236.
See Also,
Chaitkin, Anton. "Population Control, Nazis, and the U.N.!" Tetrahedron.com. 2002
http://www.tetrahedron.org/articles/new_world_order/UN_Rockefeller_Genocide.html
[16] Griffin, G. Edward. "World Without Cancer." 2nd edition. American Media. 1997. P. 235-236.
[17] Chaitkin, Anton. "Population Control, Nazis, and the U.N.!" Tetrahedron.com. 2002
http://www.tetrahedron.org/articles/new_world_order/UN_Rockefeller_Genocide.html
[18]National Park Service: Biographical Vignettes – John D. Rockefeller.
http://www.nps.gov/history/history/online_books/sontag/rockefeller.htm
[19] Council on Foreign Relations.
http://www.cfr.org/about/people/international_advisory_board.html Accessed on April 28, 2010.

widely documented and discussed. Indeed, it was John D. Rockefeller that donated the land on which the United Nations headquarters was built.[21] As one digs deeper and deeper into the history of the United Nations and even the concept of globalization itself, one encounters more and more of the Rockefeller family tree along the way. It eventually becomes obvious that the Rockefellers, along with other elite families, had a vested interest in the creation of an international governing body as well as a powerful hand in its' creation through organizations such as those mentioned above, specifically the Council on Foreign Relations, the Bilderberg Group, and the Royal Institute of International Affairs.[22] All of these groups and organizations exist for the stated purpose of world government and the UN in particular is a vital piece of the infrastructure used to facilitate it. Indeed, much evidence has shown definite links between these organizations and the creation of the United Nations.[23]

But eliciting perhaps even more concern, especially since the Rockefeller family has as much control as it does, is their obsession with eugenics. It seems that the Rockefeller family has been involved in the eugenics movement since the inception of it's more modern form. To be clear, eugenics is the pseudo-scientific theory that some humans are hereditarily more fit than others and that those deemed unfit should be eradicated through various means. Its' contemporary form originated with Charles Darwin's theory of evolution and natural selection but gained more steam when Sir Francis Galton, a cousin of Darwin's, began

---

[20] The Trilateral Commission: Membership. http://www.trilateral.org/memb.htm Accessed on April 28, 2010.
[21] National Park Service: Biographical Vignettes – John D. Rockefeller. http://www.nps.gov/history/history/online_books/sontag/rockefeller.htm
[22] Marrs, Jim. "Rule By Secrecy." Harper. 2000. Pp. 20-58.
[23] Ibid.

to push these theories with increased vigor. Galton also claimed that if fit or talented human beings would only marry other fit or talented human beings then the end result would be much more fit and talented offspring. At the same time Darwin and Galton's theories were being considered, the idea of heredity was being given more attention as well. Yet, in just a few years, what were mainly just bizarre theories came to be not only accepted but turned into a mass movement of eugenics that resulted in forced sterilizations, abortions, euthanasia and even infanticide in the United States. This was years before these practices were introduced and intensified in Germany. In fact, it was the United States that Hitler took as a model for his own plan to eliminate "unfits." These practices blossomed in the years before World War II due to large scale acceptance of eugenics in academia and the media as well as massive funding from hereditary elite families such as the Rockefellers and Carnegies.[24]

Though certainly not the only proponents of eugenics, these families played an immensely important role in its expansion. The Rockefeller Foundation alone funded the American Eugenics Society to the point where it's' own eugenics foundation, the Rockefeller Population Council, was virtually indistinguishable from it. The Foundation funded the Eugenics Society which eventually changed its' name to the Society for the Study of Social Biology, the name that it currently holds. Rockefeller also helped to create and subsequently fund the Kaiser Wilhelm Institute for Psychiatry and the Kaiser Wilhelm Institute for Anthropology, Eugenics, and Human Heredity.[25] The latter

---

[24] Black, Edwin. "The Horrifying American Roots of Nazi Eugenics." History News Network, George Mason University. November 11, 2003. http://hnn.us/articles/1796.html

[25] Chaitkin, Anton. "Population Control, Nazis, and the U.N.!" Tetrahedron.com. 2002 http://www.tetrahedron.org/articles/new_world_order/UN_Rockefeller_Genocide.html

was directly responsible for the coordination, funding, and implementation of the program that Josef Mengele worked in prior to his infamous experiments in Auschwitz.[26] Indeed, many of the experiments themselves were funded by the Rockefeller Foundation via the Kaiser Wilhelm Institute for Anthropology, Eugenics, and Human Heredity.[27] Through the Bureau of Social Hygiene, another Rockefeller eugenics foundation, John D. Rockefeller also anonymously funded notorious racist, eugenicist, and abortion pioneer Margaret Sanger's American Birth Control League, Birth Control Clinical Research Bureau, and Planned Parenthood of America.[28] Sanger was the initiator of The Negro Project, a concerted effort to eliminate the black race. In a 1939 letter to Clarence Gamble she wrote, "We do not want word to go out that we want to exterminate the Negro population and the minister is the man who can straighten out that idea if it ever occurs to their more rebellious members."[29] In 1939, Sanger renamed her Clinical Research Bureau to the Birth Control Clinical Research Bureau, both integral institutions to the Negro Project, which became the Planned

---

[26] Black, Edwin. "The Horrifying American Roots of Nazi Eugenics." History News Network, George Mason University. November 11, 2003. http://hnn.us/articles/1796.html

[27] Chaitkin, Anton. "Population Control, Nazis, and the U.N.!" Tetrahedron.com. 2002 http://www.tetrahedron.org/articles/new_world_order/UN_Rockefeller_Genocide.html

[28] Takeuchi, Aiko. "The Transnational Politics of Public Health and Population Control: The Rockefeller Foundation's Role in Japan, 1920's – 1950's." Rockefeller Archives. 2009. http://www.rockarch.org/publications/resrep/takeuchi.pdf

[29] "Birth Control or Race Control?" Margaret Sanger Papers Project #28, Fall 2001. New York University. http://www.nyu.edu/projects/sanger/secure/newsletter/articles/bc_or_race_control.html

Parenthood Federation of America in 1942, its' current name as it exists today.[30]

Considering the many connections of the Rockefellers to the United Nations and their role in its' creation, it would seem logical that the two would share ideals. Indeed, population control and reduction is one of the main concerns of the UN as they fund and operate a variety of different organizations under the UN umbrella to serve just that purpose most notably the United Nations Population Fund.[31] Sven Burmester, a representative of the latter organization, even stated publicly his support for the barbaric practices of China's population control programs. He said, "China has had the most successful family planning policy in the history of mankind in terms of quantity and with that, China has done mankind a favor."[32] This is only one example of the ideology that is pervasive among those intricately involved in the United Nations and, unfortunately, much of the scientific community. Due to the focus of this book, little more will be said about the elite and UN ideologies. The evidence is readily available and it should be researched in order to gain a clearer picture of the direction this system of global governance is moving. When one has a basic understanding of the connections between the Rockefellers and the UN as well as the common belief system of eugenics and population reduction, it is not such a stretch to see traces of these elitists in the architecture of Codex

---

[30] "Birth Control Organizations – American Birth Control League – About Margaret Sanger." New York University. http://www.nyu.edu/projects/sanger/secure/aboutms/organization_abcl.html

[31] United Nations Population Fund website. http://www.unfpa.org/public/about Accessed April 29, 2010.

[32] Watson, Steve; Watson, Paul Joseph; Jones, Alex. "Professor's 'Kill 90% of Population' Comments Echo UN, Elite NGO Policies." www.prisonplanet.com April 4, 2006. http://www.prisonplanet.com/articles/april2006/040406_b_depopulation.htm

Alimentarius. Codex, after all, is an organization created under the FAO and WHO, which are both under the jurisdiction of the UN. The connections between the Rockefellers and the pharmaceutical industry and medical establishments also serve as a motive for the destruction of the natural healthcare industry and natural supplement access.[33]

However, the above evidence is not presented in order to pin the goal of global tyranny and mass population reduction on the backs of the Rockefeller family alone. The Rockefellers are not the only elite hereditary ruling class family with this ideology nor are they necessarily at the top of the heap when it comes to the pecking order of those that are. The Rockefellers themselves are only agents of individuals in even higher places, but who manage to remain unseen. Nevertheless, the Rockefeller connection to Codex should not be ignored because in this case, as in many others, history predicts the future. The globalists plans of a one world state built upon eugenics were not born with Adolph Hitler and they certainly did not die with him. It is as alive today as it ever was.

While the history is important, one should also understand the structure of Codex Alimentarius in order to understand how it arrives at its' decisions. The Codex Alimentarius Commission (CAC) is the active and controlling arm of Codex. It is the main body that makes recommendations and proposals and is consulted by the FAO and the WHO regarding food safety standards and their implementation. Each year the CAC meets in Rome (at FAO headquarters) and Geneva (WHO headquarters) alternately with delegations from its 182 member

---

[33] "Medisin." Whitaker, Scott; Fleming, Jose. Divine Protection Publications. 2007. Pp. 12-14.
See Also,
Rockwell, Llewellyn Jr. "Medical Control, Medical Corruption." www.lewrockwell.com
http://www.lewrockwell.com/rockwell/medical.html

countries. The chief delegate to the commission must be a government official or an employee of that country and it is this individual that decides who will speak for the delegation. No votes are taken at these meeting as "consensus," not voting, is the method of decision making.[34] While the idea of "consensus" may seem reassuring, it is important to note that the Chairman of the Codex committee can prevent a delegate from even being heard at the meeting. If he is unhappy with the opposition he can simply declare that there is none and then that a "consensus" has been reached. This has occurred on numerous occasions, at least in the Codex Committee on Nutrition and Foods for Special Dietary Uses. In some cases, this has even taken the form of the Chairman cutting off the microphone of dissenting delegates. An example of this is provided by Ingrid Frazon, the head of the National Health Federation Delegation to the Codex Committee on Nutrition and Foods for Special Dietary Uses (CCNFSDU). Frazon states,

> One of the more interesting discussions that took place during the committee meetings had to do with fatty acids in infant formula for special needs. The Japanese delegate questioned why the proposed level of arachidonic acid in infant formula were set to be no less than the levels of DHA. He pointed out that there is exceedingly little arachidonic acid in the breast milk of Japanese mothers and opposed the addition of arachidonic acid in the formula as the proposed formula would force Japanese children to consume levels of arachidonic acid that are foreign to their race and culture.

> The U.S. delegation claimed that American research shows that the levels of DHA and AA should be the same. One can also wonder if the high levels of arachidonic acid in the breast milk of mothers from industrialized countries could be as a result of their diet. After considerable discussion, the

---

[34] "What is Codex?" American Holistic Health Association, http://ahha.org/codex1.htm

CCNFSDU Chairman Dr. Grossklaus finally came to the conclusion that the committee had reached a consensus and decided in favor of DHA and AA remaining at the same level. Although the microphone was turned off, the whole assembly could hear the voice of the Japanese delegate shouting "No, no, no, no!"[35]

It is obvious from experiences such as the one recounted above that any opposition to the pre-ordained agenda, in the rare instances that any exists, is promptly dealt with. Clearly, Codex is no democracy.

The Codex Alimentarius Commission maintains 10 general subject committees[36] that often form their own sub-committees and task forces to tackle specific issues.[37] Codex is also made up of various commodity committees, task forces, and regional coordinating committees.[38] Each of these committees deal with their own detailed product(s) and, in the end, encompass just about everything that can be physically consumed by human beings. That is, except pharmaceuticals which Codex does not regulate at all. Each works under the direction of the Codex Alimentarius Commission to which they report and who ultimately approves the work of the committees. Likewise, they all work

---

[35] Franzon, Ingrid. "Report from the Thai Codex Meeting." Codex Alimentarius: Global Food Imperialism. Ed. Scott C. Tips. FHR 2007. Pp. 199.

[36] Codex Alimentarius: Committees and Task Forces – General Subject Committees. USDA Food Safety and Inspection Service. http://www.fsis.usda.gov/codex_alimentarius/General_Subject_Committees/index.asp Accessed April 29, 2010.

[37] MacKenzie, Anne A. "The Process of Developing Labeling Standards for GM Foods In The Codex Alimentarius." AgBioForum – Vol.3 Number 4, 2000. Pp. 203-208

[38] Codex Alimentarius - USDA Food Safety and Inspection Service. http://www.fsis.usda.gov/Codex_Alimentarius/index.asp Accessed April 30, 2010.

under the method of "consensus" with no votes taken to determine the final policy. Some of these committees are listed below.

Commodity Committees[39]	
Cereals, Pulses and Legumes	Cocoa Products and Chocolate
Fats and Oils	Fish and Fishery Products
Fresh Fruits and Vegetables	Meat and Meat Hygiene
Milk and Milk Products	Natural Mineral Waters
Processed Fruits and Vegetables	Sugars Vegetable Proteins

General Subject Committees[40]	
Food Additives	Contaminants in Food
Food Hygiene	Food Import and Export Certification & Inspection Systems
Food Labeling	General Principles
Methods of Analysis & Sampling	Nutrition and Foods For Special Dietary Uses
Pesticide Residues	Residues of Veterinary Drugs In Foods

---

[39] Codex Alimentarius: Committees and Task Forces – Commodity Committees. USDA Food Safety and Inspection Service. http://www.fsis.usda.gov/codex_alimentarius/Commodity_Committees/index.asp Accessed on April 30, 2010.
[40] Codex Alimentarius: Committees and Task Forces – General Subject Committees. USDA Food Safety and Inspection Service. http://www.fsis.usda.gov/codex_alimentarius/General_Subject_Committees/index.asp Accessed April 29, 2010.

ad hoc Intergovernmental Task Forces[41]	
ad hoc Intergovernmental Task Force on Foods Derived From Modern Biotechnology	ad hoc Codex Intergovernmental Task Force on Antimicrobial Resistance
ad hoc Intergovernmental Task Force on Processing and Handling of Quick Frozen Food	

Without bogging down with too much detail, it should be mentioned that Codex uses an eight step procedure to arrive at the final Guidelines for whatever substance it is investigating. Once the eighth step is reached, the Guidelines are either approved by the Codex Alimentarius Commission or sent back to the Committee for more changes. Generally speaking, all of the dirty work and manipulation of language to suit the eugenics and corporate goals are done in the committees and their sub-committees. By the time the guidelines reach the Commission, the damage has been done and the text merely awaits the approval of the higher-ups. Nevertheless, the eight step procedure is described as follows by the FAO/WHO Codex Training Package.

Step 1 – The Commission decides to elaborate a standard and assigns the work to a committee. A decision to elaborate a standard may also be taken by a committee.

Step 2 – The Secretariat arranges the preparation of a proposed draft standard.

Step 3 – The proposed draft standard is sent to governments and international organizations for comment.

Step 4 – The Secretariat forwards comments to the Committee.

---

[41] Codex Alimentarius: Committees and Task Forces – ad hoc Intergovernmental Task Forces. USDA Food Safety and Inspection Service. http://www.fsis.usda.gov/codex_alimentarius/Ad_Hoc_Inter national_Task_Forces/index.asp Accessed on April 30, 2010.

Step 5 – The proposed draft standard is sent to the Commission through the Secretariat for adoption as a draft standard.

Step 6 – The draft standard is sent to governments and international organizations for comment.

Step 7 – The Secretariat forwards comments to the committee.

Step 8 - The draft standard is submitted to the Commission through the Secretariat for adoption as a Codex Standard.[42]

Essentially, the Commission introduces a standard to be debated, at which point the designated committee takes up the standard and creates a draft of the guidelines. This draft is circulated to member countries who comment on it. These comments are reviewed and potentially incorporated into the next draft which is then adopted by the committee. This draft is then redistributed to member countries for comment. The committee then adopts the guidelines and sends them to the Commission for final approval. Both the Commission and the committee can require that the draft guideline be pushed back to a previous step if it so desires.[43]

---

[42] "FAO/WHO Training Package – Section Two: Understanding the Organization of Codex" CodexEurope. http://webcache.googleusercontent.com/search?q=cache:eq kOsc0nYGMJ:codexeurope.ch/ppt/Section%2520Two%2520- %25202.6%2520How%2520does%2520Codex%2BEC.ppt+%E2 %80%9CFAO/WHO+Training+Package+%E2%80%93+Section+ Two:+Understanding+the+Organization+of+Codex%E2%80%9 D&cd=3&hl=en&ct=clnk&gl=us (this is the html format).
[43] "Codex Alimentarius: Global Food Imperialism." Ed. Scott C. Tips. FHR. 2007.

Chapter 2

Codex and Vitamin/Mineral Supplements

Codex and Vitamin/Mineral Supplements

Perhaps the most publicized aspect of Codex is the threat it poses to free access to vitamin and mineral supplements. While there are varying opinions on the effects the Codex guidelines would have on dietary supplements, there is little debate about the fact that these effects would be detrimental. At best, the guidelines will reduce dose levels to miniscule amounts too small to be beneficial as well as causing the prices to skyrocket for both consumers and producers.[44] However, a more frightening scenario is possible and, unfortunately, quite likely. When one examines the evidence, it is clear that the effects of the Codex guidelines will do more than reduce the level of nutrients available in supplements. It will go so far as to list vitamins, minerals, herbs and other nutrients as toxins while, at the same time, listing dangerous chemicals as nutrients. Maximum Upper Limits on vitamins will be set for the few temporarily remaining nutrients as well as the complete removal of others from multi-vitamin supplements. The ramifications for human health and national sovereignty will therefore be extremely destructive. As always, this global domination and subversion of national sovereignty will be done in the name of trade and the true aims of the perpetrators will be cloaked in flowery language, wordplay, and semantics. It will also be done right under our noses.

The committee charged with completing this task is the Codex Committee on Nutrition and Foods for Special Dietary Uses (CCNFSDU), chaired by Dr. Rolf Grossklaus until recently. In 2005, and in the face of much opposition from the informed pro-supplement and natural health community, the CCNFSDU approved The Guidelines for Vitamin and

---

[44] "Codex Alimentarius: Codex – government and corporate control of our food supply." Alliance for Natural Health Europe. http://www.anhcampaign.org/campaigns/codex Accessed May 24, 2010.

Mineral Food Supplements, the set of rules by which vitamin and mineral supplements may very well be removed from the market.[45] The Natural Health Federation (NHF) and the Alliance for Natural Health (ANH) have traditionally been the most vocal opponents of Codex's attempts. However, it appears that these organizations, as well as the many others that oppose Codex such as the Natural Solutions Foundation (NSF), are fighting a losing battle. While these groups and individuals spend countless amounts of money and energy fighting this global tyranny, their efforts amount to little more than rearranging the deck chairs on the titanic. At this point, their work focuses on lessening the blow from the Codex guidelines. Unfortunately, it does nothing to stop the blow from coming nor does it protect against subsequent heavier blows. While these statements are not meant to belittle their work, it is meant to show, as will be demonstrated later, that the battle is not within Codex itself but outside of it.

That being said, the idea that nutrients (vitamins and minerals) will be considered as toxins is not readily apparent even when reading the actual guidelines for Vitamin and Mineral Food Supplements. Nowhere in the guidelines is it stated that "nutrients will be listed as toxins." However, as with most governmental and institutional mandates, it is hidden within coded language and meticulous directives. Such a technicality exists in this instance in the form of "risk assessment," the technique specified by Codex to evaluate the safety of vitamin and mineral supplements. In section 3.2.2 (a), the Guidelines state that "upper safe levels of vitamins and minerals [should be] established by scientific risk assessment based on generally accepted scientific data, taking into consideration, as appropriate, the varying

---

[45] "Guidelines for Vitamin and Mineral Food Supplements." Codexalimentarius.net www.codexalimentarius.net/download/standards/.../cxg_055 e.pdf

degrees of sensitivity of different consumer groups. "[46] Risk assessment, while seemingly benign, is actually crucial to the ability of Codex to justify the ban of vitamin and mineral supplements. This concept works on the assumption that the item being tested is inherently dangerous and toxic. This method is completely the opposite of what should be used when evaluating vitamins and minerals. As Dr. Rima Laibow states in her article "Nutraceuticide' and Codex Alimentarius,'" "This use of risk assessment, of course, represents a major deflection from the real use and value of risk assessment, which is to make sure that people are not exposed to the dangerous industrial chemicals that have serious and sometimes lethal effects on them and their children."[47] By applying "scientific risk assessment" to nutrients and supplements, they are essentially considering them toxins as they are lumped into the same category as chemicals and poisons. There is no need to explicitly state that "nutrients are toxins." This is done by default. So, in the end, we have the categorization of vitamins and minerals that are essential to human health and life as something that is actually toxic. In this sense, we are entering the world of doublethink.

Regardless, this is the position of Codex and it was also the position of the U.S. Delegation throughout the discussion.[48] Indeed, even many alleged "health freedom" International Non-Governmental Organizations were either gullible enough to be taken in by the promise of the benefits of risk assessment or morally bankrupt enough to be bought off by the pharmaceutical industry or others who might benefit from the demise of the natural supplement industry. Yet some of the

---

[46] Ibid.

[47] Laibow, Rima. "'Nutraceuticide' and Codex Alimentarius." Alternative and Complementary Therapies, October 2005. P. 227.

[48] Tips, Scott C. "Breathe Easier – Codex Adjourns." Codex Alimentarius: Global Food Imperialism. Ed. Scott C. Tips. FHR. 2007. P. 33.

support for risk assessment methods early on seems to have been based on the fear of the implementation of maximum limits proposed by European countries like France. These limits would have reduced the potency level of each pill to no more than 15% Recommended Daily Intake (RDI), a figure that is already set much too low. [49] Yet those who favored risk assessment seemed to jump from the frying pan into the fire. As Scott Tips of the Natural Health Federation writes,

> The so-called "science-based risk assessment" for establishing Safe Upper Limits (maximum levels) for vitamin-and-mineral potencies, to which the EU has agreed, and about which the Americans are as happy as flies on cow dung, is nothing but a trap. The Americans think that they will be able to get real science to establish high maximum levels for their vitamins and minerals and then sell them to European consumers by the bushels. But by the time the Europeans get through applying their science, those maximum limits will be so low toddlers would be lucky to get any nutritional value out of Codex-harmonized vitamins and minerals. The European Union's Scientific Committee on Food has already started using its science-based risk assessment to establish laughably low maximum limits for European vitamins. And, lately, I have begun to see a growing concern, if not outright fear, in the faces of some science-based risk-assessment proponents that perhaps things might not go their way here after all. [50]

Indeed, things are not going "their" way. That is, if the general wish is that Codex would offer up new trade opportunities for American supplement manufacturers in the form of a new European market. To be sure it takes monumental ignorance to actually believe this. Nevertheless, trade associations like the International Alliance of

---

[49] Ibid.
[50] Tips, Scott C. "A Meeting Of Two." Codex Alimentarius: Global Food Imperialsim. Ed. Scott C. Tips. FHR. 2007. P. 101.

Dietary Food Supplements, National Nutritional Foods Association, and even the Council for Responsible Nutrition are proclaiming that Codex poses no threat to their access to supplements and, specifically, to the DSHEA law which was passed in 1994. In general those individuals who rely on these organizations for their knowledge of the legal and political workings of the industry take these reports as truth, trusting them as "credible" sources. It should also be noted that it is widely known that members of various natural health/supplement trade organizations are increasingly being purchased by the pharmaceutical industry themselves. Once this is acknowledged, one can understand more fully how disinformation spreads around the supplement community and encourages apathy and a false sense of security among the populace.[51]

But there are other problems with the process of risk assessment as well. First, the current methodologies are based upon the assessment of entire groups of nutrients as opposed to the individual nutrients that make up the group. This method is called the nutrient group approach, a method which depends upon the lumping of many different forms of a nutrient into one category rather than testing each individual form separately as is done for toxic chemicals.[52] An example would be assessing Vitamin B as a whole group. Assessing Vitamin B3, Vitamin B12, and Vitamin B6 as separate and individual nutrients is called the nutrient form approach and would be the more rational method to apply (even though risk assessment should not be used in the first place) because the alleged risks posed by these supplements are themselves dependent upon the form in which it occurs. For instance, Vitamin C, in the form of ascorbic acid, has been known to cause loose bowels in some people who take it in very high doses. Yet,

---

[51] Tips, Scott C. "The Maginot Mentality." Codex Alimentarius: Global Food Imperialism. Ed. Scott C. Tips. FHR. 2007. P 220.
[52] Taylor, Paul Anthony. "Nutrient Risk Assessment: What You're Not Being Told." http://www4.dr-rath-foundation.org/features/risk_assessment.html P.2

when taken as calcium ascorbate, this does not occur. Indeed, this is about the most severe side effect from a vitamin supplement that one can document. Yet under the risk assessment process using the method of the nutrient group approach, Vitamin C as a whole would be regulated based upon the "risks" associated with the ascorbic acid form of Vitamin C. Therefore, the ascorbic acid form of vitamin C would be the basis for the setting of the upper safe levels or the Maximum Upper Limits of Vitamin C. This is because this particular method takes the most "toxic" form of the tested substance and uses it for the basis of it's' regulation.[53] In this case, the nutrient group is considered only as safe as its most dangerous form. Indeed, this is the method advocated by the FAO and WHO. In a joint FAO/WHO report published in 2005 entitled "A Model for Establishing Upper Levels of Intake for Nutrients and Related Substances," reports of conclusions dealing with Vitamin C, Iron, and Zinc are all listed as the nutrient group and not the various forms in which they occur.[54]

Clearly, there is a double standard within the FAO, WHO, and Codex regarding the safety testing of vitamin/mineral supplements and that of chemicals. As Paul Anthony Taylor points out, in the process used for risk assessment of toxins, pesticides, etc., each individual substance is analyzed as a "separate chemical entity."[55] This is a recurring theme in the discussion of Codex and its guidelines for various forms of food substances and supplements and can be easily seen in its regulation requirements for GMO's as well. While GMO products are

---

[53] Ibid.

[54] A Model for Establishing Upper Levels of Intake for Nutrients and Related Substances, WHO/FAO. http://www.who.int/ipcs/highlights/full_report.pdf Accessed May 24, 2010.

[55] Taylor, Paul Anthony. "Nutrient Risk Assessment: What You're Not Being Told." http://www4.dr-rath-foundation.org/features/risk_assessment.html P.2Ibid.

allowed in the international food chain, nutrients are treated as dangerous substances. In this case, simply giving nutrients the same treatment as toxic chemicals would be an improvement over their current treatment.

A second problem with the risk assessment methodology is the fact that it completely ignores the positive health benefits of nutritional supplements and focuses only on their risks. This is especially important because when a regulatory agency determines, as Codex and other agencies apparently have, that any risk, no matter how insignificant it is, may constitute an "unreasonable risk of illness or injury" it may therefore be banned. This is actually provided for under the DSHEA law passed in the United States in 1994 which will be discussed more later. This, however, is essentially what the risk assessment procedure is all about - assessing dangers not benefits.

Not surprisingly, most of the evidence such as observational and clinical data that demonstrates a positive effect is ignored. Instead, all we are left with is "peer-reviewed" studies of isolated nutrient forms that are so varied in terms of experimental design, dosages, and even the nutrient forms themselves that they are virtually non-comparable. Not only that, but the form of the vitamin being tested is often in a synthetic form as opposed to its natural state with very little concern given to the individuals' nutritional requirements or current state of health. Even follow up times vary significantly. [56] Paul Anthony Taylor explains this in his article "Nutrient Risk Assessment: What You're Not Being Told," when he writes,

> In some areas of the world, such as the United States and the United Kingdom, supplemental nutrients have been in use for over half a century now. As a result, some doctors and practitioners have built up extensive databases containing

---

[56] Ibid.

carefully documented case histories of patients who have used high doses of vitamin and mineral supplements, safely and effectively, for many years. Similarly, research scientists have conducted numerous small-scale clinical trials that have produced impressive results providing clear evidence of the safety of high dose supplements in human beings.

Nevertheless, a serious flaw in the current regulatory approach to nutrient risk assessment is that some of the most valuable potential sources of positive scientific evidence regarding the use and safety of supplements, such as the types of observational and clinical data described above, are generally ignored. Instead, the sole source of evidence that is considered are peer-reviewed scientific studies of particular nutrient forms, which are often non-comparable owing to differing experimental designs, nutrient forms delivered, dosages given, and so on.

The net result of this is that the evidence-base for nutrient risk assessment tends to be skewed towards consideration of negative outcome studies that used a single vitamin or mineral - frequently in a synthetic rather than a naturally-occurring form – without full and proper consideration of the participants' overall state of health or individual nutritional requirements. Moreover such studies are often non-comparable owing to differences in their follow-up periods; the fact that many have been conducted on diseased rather than healthy populations; and that many were started well after disease states had already been initiated. As a result, a process that may appear rational, objective and scientific to the lay person or even the regulator, is, we discover, actually flawed and deeply unscientific. [57]

Yet the problems extend to more than just unscientific expansion upon unreliable models. There is both rhyme and reason to the madness of Codex Alimentarius. It is on the basis of the aforementioned science that Codex works to regulate nutrients as if they are industrial chemicals. This goal is achieved through the use of risk assessment

---

[57] Ibid.

methodology by setting Maximum Upper Limits (also described as Maximum Upper Levels or Upper Safe Levels), and later Maximum Permitted Levels of nutrients. There is a fine line between the two but the difference is a very important one.

To further understand the danger of using Risk Assessment to test nutrients, one must understand how the process works. Dr. Rima Laibow gives an excellent synopsis:

> First a group of test animals, mice, rats, rabbits, et cetera, are given increasing amounts of the toxin of interest. The dose is increased until half of the animals are dead. The dose at which 50 percent of the test animals die is called the Lethal Dose 50 (LD_{50}). A similar dose is extrapolated for humans.
>
> Next, the other end of the dose spectrum is investigated by giving test animals smaller and smaller doses until no impact can be indentified from the dose of the toxin to establish the Maximum Upper Limit (MUL). The MUL is divided by a safety factor, typically 100. The dosage that results is called the Maximum Permissible Upper Limit.[58]

Here of course, the "toxin" being administered is a nutrient – a vital component of human life. This in itself is a contradiction. But add to that the fact that the Maximum Upper Limit is set at the level where there is no impact, then further reduced by a safety factor division, and you begin to see the purpose of banning nutrients coming to fruition. Although the synopsis given above is admittedly a simplistic one, the end result is as described above – the dosage of the substance being tested is reduced further and further until no impact (positive or negative) is observed, this figure is then divided by another number (depending on the evaluation but usually 100) which results in the

---

[58] Laibow, Rima. "'Nutraceuticide' and Codex Alimentarius." Alternative and Complementary Therapies, October 2005. P. 227

Maximum Permissible Upper Limit. Already, at the end of such a procedure, dietary supplements are reduced to a state where they are virtually useless. Yet the insanity does not end there.

The goal of reducing nutrients to virtually nonexistent levels continues with the creation of Maximum Permitted Levels. Dr. Rolf Grossklaus, Chairman of the Codex Committee on Foods for Special Dietary Uses (one of the Codex committees that deal with nutrition) and Director of the German Federal Institute for Risk Assessment,[59] brought to the committees' attention what is labeled as the Global Expectable Average Daily Diet.[60] This is essentially what is estimated to be the average diet of all human beings in the world and their nutritional intake as a result of that diet. However, the Global Expectable Average Daily Diet does not take into consideration populations with lower nutritional intake such as third world countries. It is simply an average that everyone is lumped into.[61] But because populations with very low levels of nutrient intake are not properly included in the estimate, this leaves only those countries where higher levels of nutrient intake exists, falsely providing results that suggest the Global Average Daily Diet is higher than it is. Essentially, the levels of acceptable nutrient intake will be ratcheted down based on the populations with the highest amounts of nutritional intake. This process removes countries with low level intake of nutrition from the equation, providing Codex with a higher Global Average Daily Diet which it will then use to reduce the levels of vitamins and minerals even further. [62]

This stance is enumerated in the Codex "Guidelines for Vitamin

---

[59] Codex Committee On Nutrition and Foods For Special Dietary Uses. https://www.ccnfsdu.de/index.php?id=493
[60] Ibid.
[61] Ibid.
[62] Laibow, Rima. "'Nutraceuticide' and Codex Alimentarius." Alternative and Complementary Therapies, October 2005.

and Mineral Food Supplements" when it is stated, "Most people who have access to a balanced diet can usually obtain all the nutrients they require from their normal diet."[63] Such a statement is laughable to anyone who has studied health and nutrition because anyone who has done so knows very well that, even in the most highly developed countries in the world, we do not receive nearly enough nutrients from our daily diet. Yet Codex is working on the supposition that everyone eats the same diet (on average) and that they get all the nutrition they need from it. Nevertheless, the Global Expectable Average Daily Diet is then used to subtract the amount of nutrition we allegedly receive from our diets from the Maximum Permissible Upper Limit set by Codex. The value that results is the new Maximum Permitted Level,[64] - a value that lowers the acceptable level of nutrients even further. As Paul Anthony Taylor illustrates,

> If the upper safe level for vitamin B6 is calculated to be 10mg, as recommended by the UK's Expert Group on Vitamins and Minerals, and the average daily intake of vitamin B6 from food is calculated to be 2.9mg, as was stated to be the case for men in the UK's National Diet & Nutrition Survey in 2003, then the "maximum permitted level" of vitamin B6 in supplements could potentially be set by regulators at a mere 7.1 mg. [65]

The rationale is that, since we are already receiving a certain amount of nutrients from our food, we must take that amount of nutrients into

---

[63] "Guidelines for Vitamin and Mineral Food Supplements." Codexalimentarius.net www.codexalimentarius.net/download/standards/.../cxg_055 e.pdf

[64] Laibow, Rima. "'Nutraceuticide' and Codex Alimentarius." Alternative and Complementary Therapies, October 2005.

[65] Taylor, Paul Anthony. "Nutrient Risk Assessment: What You're Not Being Told." http://www4.dr-rath-foundation.org/features/risk_assessment.html

consideration when establishing a "maximum permitted level" for nutrients in general. Hence the lowering of the "safe" levels.

It should be noted that, while the differences between the Upper Safe Levels and Maximum Permitted Levels are slight, they are still important. One of the main and most important differences is the method by which Maximum Permitted Levels are reached with the further lowering of nutritional content using the Global Expectable Average Daily Diet mechanism. But even semantical differences play a role in the reduction of nutrients as the designation of "Maximum Permitted Level" carries with it a more authoritative and restrictive tone, an important aspect when dealing with scientific, legal, and regulatory labeling. MPL's deal with Maximum **Permitted** Levels, abandoning the cover language of safety guidelines and moving its' motives more out in the open.

The process of establishing Maximum Permitted Levels began in 2005 with recommendations made by the German Federal Institute for Risk Assessment (BfR), the first organization to carry out this task. It should also be noted that not only will BfR be instrumental in providing "scientific" information to Codex, but that Dr. Rolf Grossklaus is BfR's Director. This is the same Dr. Grossklaus that is the chairman of the Codex Committee on Nutrition and Foods for Special Dietary Uses and has become somewhat famous in the health freedom community for his tyrannical methods of conducting meetings[66] and for making the claim that nutrition is only for maintaining health, not for the prevention or treatment of diseases.[67] Indeed, Dr. Grossklaus was one of the leading

---

[66] Tips, Scott C. "Breathe Easier – Codex Adjourns." Codex Alimentarius: Global Food Imperialism." Ed. Scott C. Tips. Foundation for Health Research, 2007.

[67] Walter, Suzan. "Important News from Bonn." Codex Alimentarius: Global Food Imperialism. Ed. Scott C. Tips. FHR. 2007. P.88.

scientists of the team that conducted the studies used in BfR's standings.[68] This is particularly concerning in light of the context of the CCNFSDU as Dr. Grossklaus is the man responsible for guiding the Commissions' position on the safety of these substances. In this instance, the Chairman of the Codex committee requesting an assessment on nutrients is also the Director of the company conducting the assessment as well as one of the leading scientists in the assessment itself. True science would never allow someone with such a blatant conflict of interest to take part in these studies. This, however, is business as usual with Codex.

But the clearly unscientific manner in which risk assessment is conducted apparently knows no bounds. Dr. Rima Laibow comments on this obvious conflict of interest further by saying,

> Dr. Grossklaus uses his position to bludgeon through his own personal agenda and that of the European Union (EU) representative to Codex and CCNFSDU, Mr. Basil Mathioudakis. The two of them confer regularly as if there were no other members present and whatever the antinutrient Dr. Grossklaus and Mr. Mathioudakis agree upon is the "outcome" of the deliberations. [69]

Dr. Laibow's assessment is a fairly accurate one. The methods by which Codex reaches its "consensus" are dubious to say the least. In fact, the "consensus" as declared by the CCNFSDU bears little resemblance to any other real consensus being reached on any other board. Scott Tips, who has regularly attended Codex meetings as an observer, elaborates further:

---

[68] Taylor, Paul Anthony. "Nutrient Risk Assessment: What You're Not Being Told." http://www4.dr-rath-foundation.org/features/risk_assessment.html
[69] Laibow, Rima. "'Nutraceuticide' and Codex Alimentarius." Alternative and Complementary Therapies, October 2005.

> The Chairman was a German, Dr. Rolf Grossklaus, who ran
> the Codex meetings in an innovative (to me at least) way.
> After much discussion on a topic, and especially after the
> German government delegate did not seem to have anything
> more to say, the chairman would somehow psychically
> determine that a "consensus" had been reached or not
> reached by the delegates and the group would move on to
> the next topic of discussion. I never once saw a vote taken or
> even the slightest hint of a show of hands; the outcome was
> all calculated in Dr. Grossklaus' marvelous brain as he
> scanned the room and remembered how many had spoken
> for or against each proposal. Of course, the squeaky wheels
> counted the most; the silent ones not at all. We Americans,
> who suffer from this obsessive notion that votes must
> actually be counted before deciding upon an outcome, might
> learn much from this economical and quick means of
> "voting." In fact, stupid me, why even vote when the
> chairman could just decide for all of us?[70]

Anyone who has attended these meetings with the expectation of observing some form of democratic input by anyone except the chairman or the EU must have been seriously disappointed. Indeed, this has been the impression of virtually every health freedom advocate that has ever attended these meetings.

Nevertheless, the process of risk assessment was continued and, in 2005, BfR published "Use of Vitamins in Foods: Toxicological and nutritional-physiological aspects," its' list of recommendations for the maximum levels of nutrients in vitamin and mineral supplements. Of the many tables included in these results, Tables 3 and 4 are of particular interest. Table 3 is an overview of the BfR teams' classification of

---

[70] Tips, Scott C. "Breathe Easier – Codex Adjourns." Codex Alimentarius: Global Food Imperialism." Ed. Scott C. Tips. Foundation for Health Research, 2007.

vitamins and minerals into supply and risk categories (each of these categories being separate). Supply categories deal mainly with the status of the supply of tested materials such as their possible contamination or their potential to be contaminated during shipping as well as the intake status. However, the risk categories have to do with the potential for nutrients and vitamins to cause adverse effects. The risk category is divided into High risk, Moderate risk, and Low risk and is based on "how large the margin is between recommended/observed intakes and the defined UL" [Upper Limit]. [71] Rather, how much further than the Recommended Daily Allowance (RDA) a nutrient must go to reach the level of perceived adverse side effects (the Upper Limit).[72] Indeed, Table 2, which is a different chart showing the criteria for each risk category, is entitled "Various degrees of **probability** that a nutrient leads to adverse side effects."[73] This in itself should trigger questions as to what amount of "proof" this study actually offers. The idea that it is the probability, not a clearly defined set of risks or causes of those risks, shows that the study has not actually proven nutrients pose a threat of adverse side effects even when using the risk assessment process to begin with.

Yet BfR and subsequently Codex Alimentarius continue to use this data to create a maximum permitted level for nutrients. Vitamins A and D, Beta-Carotene, Niacin (as Nicotinic acid), Sodium, Potassium, Calcium, Iron, Iodine, Zinc, Copper, and Manganese are all added into the high risk category while the best that any other nutrient or mineral can hope for is the low risk category. None fall into a no-risk category

---

[71] " Use of Vitamins in Foods: Toxicological and nutritional-physiological aspects." Domke, A., Grosklaus R., Niemann B., Przyrembel H., Richter K., Schimdt E., WeiBenborn B., Worner B., Ziegenhagen R., Federal Institute for Risk Assessment, BfR, 2005. P.18.
[72] Ibid.
[73] Ibid.

because no such category exists in this type of study. A brief summation of the results are as follows:

Vitamins and Minerals Added To Risk Categories		
High Risk	Moderate Risk	Low Risk
Vitamin A	Vitamin E	Vitamin B_1
Beta Carotene	Vitamin K	Vitamin B_2
Vitamin D	Vitamin C	Niacin (as
Niacin (as Nicotinic acid)	Vitamin B_6	Nicotinamide)
Sodium	Folic Acid	Pantothenic Acid
Potassium	Phosphorus	Biotin
Calcium	Magnesium	Vitamin B_{12}
Iron	Molybdenum	Chromium
Iodine		
Zinc		
Copper		
Manganese		
Moderately High Risk		
Selenium		

[74]

Table 4 (as summarized below), titled "Proposed maximum levels for the use of vitamins and minerals in food supplements (FS) referred to the daily dose recommended by the manufacturer," is a tabular representation of the suggestions made by BfR for maximum permitted levels of nutrients and minerals.[75] Almost without exception these MPL's are set at ridiculously low levels compared to what is needed on a daily basis for the average adult. [76] The proposed MPL's are as listed below:

---

[74] Ibid. p.22

[75] Ibid p.23

[76] It should be noted that, in the comparison made between the suggested Maximum Permitted Levels and the Recommended Daily Intake for adults in the BfR study, the Recommended Daily Intake is that which is used in Germany, a nation under the European Union Food Supplements Directive.

Maximum Permitted Levels for Vitamins and Minerals		
Vitamins/Minerals	Proposed Maximum Permitted Level	Additional Comments by Researchers
Vitamin A	400 mcg[77]	For children aged between 4 and 10 – 200 mcg
Beta-carotene	2 mg	
Vitamin D	5 mcg	For persons over 65 – 10 mcg
Vitamin E	15 mg	
Vitamin K	80 mcg	
Vitamin B_1	4 mg	
Vitamin B_2	4.5 mg	
Niacin	17 mg	No use of nicotinic acid
Vitamin B_6	5.4 mg	
Folate equivalents	400 mcg	
Pantothenic acid	18 mg	
Biotin	180 mcg	
Vitamin B_{12}	3-9 mcg	
Vitamin C	225 mg	
Sodium	0 mg	
Chloride	0 mg	
Potassium	500 mg	
Calcium	500 mg	
Phosphorus	250 mg	As phosphate
Magnesium	250 mg	Where appropriate, break down into 2 single doses
Iron	0 mg	
Iodine	100 mcg	
Zinc	2.25 mg	No supplements for children or adolescents under the age of 18
Selenium	25-30 mcg	
Copper	0 mcg	
Manganese	0 mg	
Chromium	60 mcg	
Molybdenum	80 mcg	Maximum level not suitable for children under the age of 11

[78]

Clearly, as one can see from the chart above, the levels suggested by

---

[77] There are 1000 mcg in 1 mg.

[78] "Use of Vitamins in Foods: Toxicological and nutritional-physiological aspects,"Domke, A., Grosklaus R., Niemann B., Przyrembel H., Richter K., Schimdt E., WeiBenborn B., Worner B., Ziegenhagen R., Federal Institute for Risk Assessment, BfR, 2005. P. 23.

Codex for the Maximum Permitted Levels are excessively low. For instance, the most liberal dosage allowed is for Vitamin C at the levels of 225 mg. Yet the Upper Safe Levels of Vitamin C are nowhere near this small amount. Even according to Medline Plus, administered by the National Institute of Health and the U.S. National Library of Medicine, the Upper Safe Levels for Vitamin C is 2,000 mg for adults above 18.[79] This is a difference of 1,750 mg. set by an agency that is not considered exactly friendly towards nutritional supplements or natural healthcare. Of course, for individuals with some kind of sickness such as cancer, the limits on Vitamin C intake are much higher.[80] The limits placed on Vitamin D are perhaps the most egregious. BfR sets the Maximum Permitted Levels of Vitamin D at 5 mcg while even the Medline service lists the Upper Safe Limits at approximately 50 mcg (2000 IU).[81] A comparison of the Upper Safe Limits set by the Medline Plus system (under the direction of the aforementioned government agencies) is provided in the chart below. Keep in mind, as mentioned earlier, that the U.S. agencies who established these Upper Safe Limits are not exactly those that can be considered champions of health freedom, natural healthcare, or nutritional supplementation. Using their figures, however, provide an opportunity to see just how dramatic a decrease in the level of nutrition is caused by BfR's Maximum Permitted Levels.

In the table below, Vitamin E, Sodium, Chloride, Potassium, Calcium, Chromium, and Molybednum are not included due to the fact

---

[79] "Vitamin C." Medline Plus website. http://www.nlm.nih.gov/medlineplus/druginfo/natural/patient-vitaminc.html Accessed April 15, 2010.
[80] "Vitamin C." Oregon State University. Linus Pauling Institute. http://lpi.oregonstate.edu/infocenter/vitamins/vitaminC/ Accessed April 15, 2010.
[81] "Vitamin D." Medline Plus Website. http://www.nlm.nih.gov/medlineplus/druginfo/natural/patient-vitamind.html Accessed April 15, 2010.

that they were not listed on Medline's website. Zinc, Pantothenic Acid, Vitamin K, Vitamin B$_1$, Vitamin B$_{12}$, and Selenium are not listed because Medline has set **no** USL for them. Medline claims that there is insufficient data for Beta-Carotene to set a USL at this time. Also, where levels differ for different age groups as well as between men and women, the figures provided below are for adult males over 18 years of age for the purpose of uniformity.[82]

Comparison of BfR MPL's with Medline USL's[83]		
Supplement	BfR MPL	Medline USL
Vitamin A	400 mcg	900 mcg
Vitamin B$_6$	5.4 mg	100 mg
Copper	0 mcg	10,000 mcg
Niacin	17 mg	35 mg
Biotin	180 mcg	200 mcg
Folate	400 mcg	1,000 mcg
Phosphorous	250 mg	4 g
Iron	0 mg	45 mg
Iodine	100 mcg	1,100 mcg

Although only nine vitamins and minerals were able to be contrasted with one another, these distinctions help clarify the direction that Codex is taking with MPLs through BfR. While some of these differences are smaller in scale than others, most BfR MPLs are much more than double their Medline counterparts. The standards for Copper are quite telling as there is a 10,000 mcg difference between the two.

The problem, however, goes even deeper than the establishment of MPLs and USLs. The Recommended Daily Allowances (RDAs) are of great concern as well. This is not only because they are often instrumental in the setting and justification of MPLs and USLs, but also because they are referenced for human health and individual

---

[82] "All Herbs and Supplements." Medline Plus Website. http://www.nlm.nih.gov/medlineplus/druginfo/herb_All.html #V   Accessed April 15, 2010.
[83] Ibid.

intake. In the United States, the RDA is often taken in conjunction with the Estimated Average Requirement (EAR) under the umbrella of the Dietary Reference Intake (DRI) which is set by the Institute of Medicine of the National Academy of Sciences.[84] The RDA is officially defined as "the average dietary intake level that is sufficient to meet the nutrient requirement of nearly all (97 to 98 percent) healthy individuals."[85] The EAR is defined as "the daily intake value that is estimated to meet the requirement . . . in half of the healthy individuals in a . . . group."[86] It goes on to say, "At this level of intake, the other half of a specified group would not have its nutritional needs met."[87] While this book will not deal in depth with this subject, it should be noted that the Institute of Medicine of the National Academy of Sciences has recommended that the national standard of nutritional intake be shifted from the RDA to the EAR.[88] This would effectively slash the DRI by close to half due to the fact that the original referenced values of nutritional intake would be affected likewise.

Another main concern related to RDA's is the fact that they are not adequately set to promote optimal human health. Indeed, RDAs are set at the lowest level for prevention of single-nutrient deficiency diseases. This means that the RDA is not the level at which intake of a particular nutrient is sufficient for good health, but the lowest level that must be maintained in order to prevent a particular deficiency disease. In the case of Vitamin C, for instance, the diseases would be scurvy or rickets. Put plainly, RDA's are the levels of nutritional intake needed to

---

[84] South, James. "Vitamin Safety, RDAs and the Assault on Vitamin Freedom." National Health Federation. March 2004. http://www.thenhf.com/articles_19.htm
[85] Ibid.
[86] Ibid.
[87] Ibid.
[88] Ibid.

barely get by, not remain healthy.[89] As James South points out in his article, "Vitamin Safety, RDAs and the Assault on Vitamin Freedom," the Recommended Dietary Allowances from 1980 plainly stated as much. South quotes them as saying,

> The requirement for a nutrient is the minimum intake that will maintain normal function and health . . . For certain nutrients, the requirements may be assessed as the amount that will just prevent failure of a specific function or the development of specific deficiency signs – an amount that may differ greatly from that required to maintain maximum (i.e. optimum) body stores.[90]

This is a source of confusion for many consumers who believe that RDAs are the levels at which their intake is topped out and adequately achieved. Add to this the fact that RDAs are continually being lowered by the agencies responsible for setting them. In 1989, the National Academy of Sciences revised the RDAs from their already meager levels set in 1980 to even lower levels, some of them by half. Interestingly enough, the National Academy of Sciences exercised some twilight-zone logic similar to Codex Alimentarius when these decisions were made. The assumption made by the agency was that Americans are generally healthy people and, because they generally fail to consume the 1980 RDA levels of nutrients, then a lower standard is adequate for good human health.[91]

Clearly, either lowering the RDAs or creating MPLs is a threat to the natural supplement industry from the perspective of the consumer as well as the manufacturer. Even without acknowledging the ideological and financial reasons behind the push to end access to vitamin and mineral supplementation, the setting of MPLs, especially at

---

[89] Ibid.
[90] Ibid.
[91] Ibid.

low levels, would create a vast increase in the cost of supplements wherever they were sold. Consumers would then be forced to purchase many more times the amount of supplements to achieve the same result as their current dosage. If the MPLs reduce a supplement's levels by half, as many do, then the consumer would need to take two capsules for every one he/she currently takes to achieve an equal amount of nutrition. Translate this into buying two bottles for every one bottle purchased at the current levels. This would not only have a crippling effect on consumers but the industry itself would face similar repercussions as the option of natural supplementation would become unaffordable. Even the supplements themselves would suffer, as each capsule/pill/dose would therefore have to be produced using more filler materials than actual nutrients.

This is actually a concern with another Codex policy that is much less well-known than that of MPLs – minimum levels of nutrients. While many may see this as contradictory to Codex's general position toward natural supplements, it is in fact included within the Codex Guidelines. Section 3.2.1 of the Guidelines states, "The minimum level of each vitamin and/or mineral contained in a vitamin and mineral food supplement per daily portion of consumption as suggested by the manufacturer should be 15% of the recommended daily intake as determined by FAO/WHO."[92] No doubt some, out of ignorance, will assume that this position is positive. In fact the opposite is true. The setting of minimum levels is merely part of a two-pronged attack on vitamin and mineral supplements and levels of nutrition in general. The problem with this position is that it prevents manufacturers from adding trace amounts of vitamins and minerals to supplements that may be desired or needed to aid in the processing of the main nutrient. Instead,

---

[92] "Guidelines for Vitamin and Mineral Food Supplements." Codexalimentarius.net
www.codexalimentarius.net/download/standards/.../cxg_055 e.pdf

filler will have to be added. As Scott Tips writes,

> Besides the obvious moral problem of prohibiting people
> from freely and voluntarily contracting with one another as
> they wish, the practical problem with minimum levels is that
> they foreclose manufacturers from adding something useful
> (such as a vitamin or mineral) in a capsule or tablet instead of
> something worthless, like a filler or excipient. In my view, it
> would be better for a person to get some additional nutritive
> value from a capsule or tablet, than nothing at all.[93]

Keep in mind, the MPLs of vitamin and mineral supplements will be set
so low, according to the risk assessment studies like those of BfR being
conducted, that it will be virtually impossible to include trace amounts
of supplements below the required 15% of the already low levels of the
RDA. They might as well not be included at all, which is the goal of
Codex in the first place.

While the oppressive standards discussed above have largely
been included in the Codex Guidelines for Vitamin and Mineral Food
Supplements, there is one more provision included in the risk
assessment process that even many critics of Codex are unaware of.
This is the goal to not only treat nutrients as toxins, but treat toxins as
nutrients. At first, this is not readily apparent. A closer look at the risk
assessment provided by BfR provides one with the glimmers of what
might one day be a completely Orwellian policy toward vitamins,
minerals, and toxins. The fact that researchers have the audacity to
claim that vital minerals like Iron should not be consumed in
measurements above 0 mg is disturbing enough. However, there is one
more substance added to the findings and, more alarmingly, listed as a
mineral that should be just as frightening. That substance is the very

---

[93] Tips, Scott C. "Codex Gets One Step Closer To Control."
Codex Aliementarius: Global Food Imperialism. Ed. Scott C.
Tips. P.49-50. 2007.

toxic chemical known as fluoride.[94]

This chemical poison is listed only in the "moderately high-risk" level of risk categories.[95] Yet the reality is that fluoride is a very dangerous chemical with serious risks of harm to both health and the environment. In truth, there are actually two different forms of what is called fluoride – calcium fluoride and sodium fluoride. Calcium fluoride appears naturally and is confined, for the most part, to underground water sources and, in some instances, seawater. [96] In this form it is relatively benign but prolonged exposure has been linked to skeletal and dental fluorosis. [97]

However, sodium fluoride, the form of fluoride that is added to most municipal water supplies, food, and drink, is a very dangerous and toxic chemical. It does not occur naturally and is not even one distinct substance. Rather, it is a conglomeration of many different chemicals that is given the name of sodium fluoride and paraded as a health benefit. It is essentially a mix of waste products from the nuclear, aluminum, and fertilizer industries. It is also used for rat poison and pesticides.[98] The results of having water supplies contaminated with

---

[94] " Use of Vitamins in Foods: Toxicological and nutritional-physiological aspects,"Domke, A., Grosklaus R., Niemann B., Przyrembel H., Richter K., Schimdt E., WeiBenborn B., Worner B., Ziegenhagen R., Federal Institute for Risk Assessment, BfR, p. 18-23, 2005.

[95] Ibid.

[96] Fassa, Paul. "How To Detox Fluorides From Your Body," Natural News, July 13, 2009. P.1 http://www.naturalnews.com/026605_fluoride_fluorides_detox.html Accessed May 24, 2010.

[97] Fassa, Paul. "A Fluoride-Free Pineal Gland is More Important than Ever," Natural News, June 2, 2009. http://www.naturalnews.com/026364_fluoride_pineal_gland_sodium.html Accessed May 24, 2010.

[98] Ibid.

fluoride reads like a laundry list of health problems: cancer, genetic DNA damage, obesity, thyroid disruption, reduced IQ, lethargy, chronic fatigue, inability to focus, Alzheimer's disease, accelerated aging, sleep disruption, brain disorders, calcification of the pineal gland, etc. Interestingly enough, sodium fluoride also causes dental fluorosis, a yellowing and hardening of the teeth that causes teeth to break and wear down. This is very ironic considering that the ADA promotes fluoride as an additive that prevents decay and promotes healthy teeth.[99]

The distinction in BfR's results between calcium fluoride and sodium fluoride is not readily made and, as is so often the case, the devil is in the details. Throughout the published study, all forms of fluoride are constantly referred to simply as fluoride with no delineation as to which form is being discussed except by contextualization and observation. Occasionally, a specific form will be mentioned but, for the most part, the umbrella term "fluoride" is sufficient for the purpose of these researchers. This is how the toxin comes to be classified as a mineral and henceforth a nutrient. This is also where the nutrient group methodology comes into play. Sodium fluoride could not, by any stretch of the imagination, be considered to be a mineral or nutrient on its own. However, by using the nutrient group approach, which lumps all forms of the substance tested into one category, it slips under the radar.[100] Indeed, in the section which discusses the sources of fluoride intake BfR states, "Fluoride is taken up from solid foods, drinking water, mineral

---

[99] Ibid.

[100] In truth, even Calcium Fluoride should not be considered a nutrient as there is not enough evidence to show that is vital, or even positively linked, to human life and health. Fassa, Paul. "How To Detox Fluorides From Your Body," Natural News, July 13, 2009. P.1
http://www.naturalnews.com/026605_fluoride_fluorides_detox.html

water, black tea, fluoride-containing toothpaste, dental care products, fluoridised table salt and, eventually, from fluoride-containing medicinal products."[101] There is clearly no distinction here between the different forms of fluoride. For example, the form of fluoride contained in mineral water (unless sodium fluoride was added) is calcium fluoride while the fluoride contained in toothpaste is sodium fluoride. Yet there is no distinction given between the two. While BfR does admit potential danger in the use of fluoride, by using the nutrient group approach, fluoride is still categorized as a nutrient. Thus, the camel now has his foot in the door.

BfR is obviously aware of at least some dangers of fluoride, such as dental and skeletal fluorosis as well as the more serious health problems. The report states, "There are reports of acute fluoride intoxications in people caused by accidents, attempted suicide, or erroneous fluoridation of drinking water. The symptoms are nausea, vomiting, abdominal pain, diarrhea, heavy salivation, cardiac arrest, cramps and coma. Severe hypocalcaemias were observed. An amount of 5-10 g fluoride has been calculated as the 'certainly lethal dose' = CLD for adults."[102] Bad as they are, these conditions are only a few of the adverse effects related to fluoride. It would seem logical then to place very high restrictions on the amounts of fluoride meant for consumption and subsequently a recommendation for no intake. Yet BfR comes to a startling and self-contradicting conclusion.

Even after discussing the dangers of fluoride throughout the study, as well as the fact that it is present in many drinking water

---

[101]Use of Vitamins in Foods: Toxicological and nutritional-physiological aspects." Domke, A., Grosklaus R., Niemann B., Przyrembel H., Richter K., Schimdt E., WeiBenborn B., Worner B., Ziegenhagen R., Federal Institute for Risk Assessment, BfR, p. 230, 2005
[102] Ibid. p. 234

supplies in the world (especially the United States), "medicinal" products, and other sources, the same strict standards of risk assessment and the Global Expectable Average Daily Diet evidently do not apply. If they were, then Americans would probably be in the red in terms of dietary intake of fluoride. BfR admits, "This leaves no scope for a safe maximum dose of fluoride in food supplements. BfR believes that a maximum dose for fluoride of zero in food supplements is the only safe management option."[103] Yet in its final analysis, it determines that the Recommended Daily Intake be established at 3.8/3.1 (m/f) for adults and 3.2/2.9 (m/f) for children.[104] So while limits are set on the amount of fluoride in food supplements, it is still concluded that individuals need a certain amount of fluoride in their diet and fluoride is still considered a nutrient.

This is a very important distinction and some things should be noted. First, the Maximum Permitted Level set for fluoride by BfR's risk assessment deals only with the amount of fluoride to food supplements. It does not deal with the fluoridation of water supplies, the application of fluoride dental treatments, toothpaste, and the utterly ridiculous practice of giving fluoride tablets for "medicinal" purposes. These guidelines would only apply to food supplements that contain fluoride which are unlikely to ever be marketed to anyone seriously knowledgeable and concerned about their health. Certainly, the natural health industry is not beset by requests for fluoride supplements. So it is important to understand what is happening here. There is regulation of fluoride in an area that, for all intents and purposes, it does not exist in. In the areas where fluoride dominates, such as the aforementioned "medicinal" purposes, drinking water, toothpaste, and other dental treatments, there is no regulation by Codex. In fact, not only is there no regulation, the toxin has now been considered a mineral and a nutrient

---

[103] Ibid p. 235
[104] Ibid p. 23

complete with an RDA to encourage its daily intake.

Second, through the flawed process of risk assessment and the Global Expectable Average Daily Diet, BfR is able to set the maximum permitted levels for true nutrients like Iron, Copper, and Manganese at 0 and the Recommended Daily Intake at very low levels for food supplements. BfR is able to do precisely the same thing with fluoride in an area where it has no impact to begin with – thereby lowering the amount of fluoride considered in the GEADD and still allowing fluoride to be considered a nutrient. This because fluoride is not as heavily consumed in food or as a food supplement as it is in its other forms. Therefore, it largely avoids the clutches of the GEADD.

Third, BfR is completely aware of at least some of the many adverse effects of fluoride as well as the environment in which it is created. As quoted above, the BfR report clearly documents that the Institute knows of fluoride intoxication with serious and even fatal side effects. Hence, the creation of the Certainly Lethal Dose (CLD) of 5-10g. Yet animal tests also revealed "a possible carcinogenic effect" [105] and "kidney damage."[106] However, the claim is made that such a reaction does not occur in other species. BfR also claims that the most serious effects are limited to the skeleton and teeth.[107] Although ignoring such conditions as liver and kidney damage, weakened immune system, cancer, symptoms akin to fibromyalgia, lower IQ's, and Alzheimer's disease, BfR is still forced to admit the existence of at least some adverse effects. [108] It is truly hard to believe that such extensive and widely-known research can simply fly under the radar of scientists like

---

[105] Ibid. p. 232
[106] Ibid p. 234
[107] Ibid.
[108] Fassa, Paul. "How To Detox Fluorides From Your Body," Natural News, July 13, 2009. P.1
http://www.naturalnews.com/026605_fluoride_fluorides_detox.html

those conducting the risk assessment experiments. It is also interesting to note that BfR does not mention long-term studies for the adverse effects of fluoride. Rather, the consumption of the chemical at one time. Not only that, but the distinction is not made between calcium and sodium fluoride, once again blurring the lines between the two. Based on the rest of the risk assessment conducted by BfR, it is not hard to believe that only calcium fluoride might have been tested, yet sodium fluoride was still included in the results. While there is no direct evidence to prove that this is the case, there is without a doubt legitimate cause for speculation based on the results of the study BfR has presented.

Furthermore, if there is any doubt as to whether or not BfR combines calcium fluoride and sodium fluoride it is erased when BfR attempts to address the issue of skeletal fluorosis. Here the report states, "Crippling bone fluorosis is mainly observed in tropical areas with a high natural content of fluoride in drinking water or high fluoride exposure from industrial plants."[109] This not only demonstrates the blurring of the lines between calcium and sodium fluoride, but also the prior knowledge by BfR and, subsequently, Codex that one form of fluoride is actually toxic waste. It is important to understand that Codex now recognizes industrial waste as a nutrient.

Lastly, besides the obvious lunacy of labeling a toxic substance as a nutrient, BfR admits that there is no known benefit to consumption of fluoride. This is yet another obvious reason that fluoride cannot be considered a nutrient, even in calcium fluoride form. The study directly admits, "Since fluoride is not essential to man, requirements cannot be

---

[109] Use of Vitamins in Foods: Toxicological and nutritional-physiological aspects,"Domke, A., Grosklaus R., Niemann B., Przyrembel H., Richter K., Schimdt E., WeiBenborn B., Worner B., Ziegenhagen R., Federal Institute for Risk Assessment, BfR, p. 230, 2005

defined. A recommended intake can only be indicated with a view to its favorable impact on dental health. WHO notes that there are no proven clinical symptoms of fluoride deficiency in man and there are no diagnostic parameters which correlate with a fluoride deficiency."[110] Even BfR itself must concede that there is no nutritional benefit to consuming fluoride (even in its' natural form) and there are no known problems associated with lack of fluoride in the diet.[111] Of course, the study refers to the dental health benefits provided by consumption of the chemical but, as mentioned earlier, these so-called benefits are virtually non-existent. In the face of this, BfR and Codex still conduct science that is nothing more than poorly performed magic tricks and continue to ask the rest of us to engage in mental gymnastics and to believe that toxic waste is a nutrient.

The ignorance of the vast majority of Americans toward Codex Alimentarius, including most natural health advocates, is one reason Codex is not a major source of concern. But another, more disturbing reason, is that even those who are aware of the dangers of Codex are convinced that its' decisions will have no impact on the laws of the United States. This will be discussed much more in a later section. With that being said, the United States has seen an increasing interest in the areas of natural healthcare and vitamin and mineral supplements. At the same time, however, the level of activism defending those treatments and industries has been steadily decreasing. This is significant because the amount of attacks against them have been increasing as well. In general, this is because Americans have been lulled into complacency by a false sense of security known as DSHEA.

In 1994, largely due to a public movement to protect dietary supplements and natural alternatives to the pharmaceutical and medical industries, Congress passed the Dietary Supplement Health and

---

[110] Ibid p.229
[111] Ibid. p. 229

Education Act of 1994.[112] A result of widespread public demand and true grass roots organization, DSHEA was the greatest success to date in the battle for health freedom. According to the official summary of the bill by the Food and Drug Administration, "In the findings associated with the DSHEA, Congress stated that there may be a positive relationship between sound dietary practice and good health, and that, although further scientific research is needed, there may be a connection between dietary supplement use, reduced health-care expenses, and disease prevention."[113] Considering the hold that pharmaceutical and medical companies had on Congress even in 1994, this was a bold move. The mass public movement and Congress' fear of losing their reelection bids combined to force a compromise in relation to the freedom of Americans to freely access herbal and nutritional supplements.

One of the best aspects of DSHEA is that it classifies nutrients and herbs as a type of food. [114] Therefore, there are no upper limits set and access is not restricted from the general public. This is perhaps the most important part of DSHEA in its' relation to Codex Alimentarius guidelines. After all, it does stand in direct opposition to the principles of Codex which essentially do not accept that nutrition plays a role in

---

[112] "Dietary Supplement Health and Education Act of 1994." Food and Drug Administration. http://vm.cfsan.fda.gov/~dms/dietsupp.html
[113] Ibid.
[114] Ibid.
See also,
Minton, Barbara. "Codex Threatens Health of Billions." Naturalnews.com. July 30, 2009. http://www.naturalnews.com/026731_CODEX_food_health.html Accessed May 24, 2010.

human health.[115] The law also provides for the availability of "third party materials" that may be used to inform customers of the health related benefits of the supplements for sale. This includes "articles, brochures, book chapters, scientific abstracts," etc.[116] Previously, this was severely restricted. Now, under DSHEA, herbal and supplement retailers may display and sell such material in their establishments. The law also allows various statements to be made on the label of dietary supplement containers although these statements are still severely restricted. Previously only the name (which was also heavily restricted) of the supplement was allowed on the label. However, after DSHEA came into effect, certain claims may be made by the manufacturer about the linkage between a supplement and the reduction of risk of a certain type of disease. DSHEA also provides for the inclusion of "new dietary ingredients, so long as they meet FDA standards."[117]

However, for all the good that DSHEA has done for the natural healthcare community, there are several weaknesses in the law as it stands. First, under this law, the FDA has the authority to seize any supplement that it considers to pose "a significant or unreasonable risk of illness or injury"[118]. But what exactly constitutes a "significant or unreasonable risk of illness or injury" is not defined. The designation of such a circumstance falls to the FDA, FTC, and/or the Secretary of Health and Human Services. The law itself states that a dietary supplement may be considered "adulterated" (and subsequently

---

[115] Walter, Suzan. "Important News From Bonn." Codex Alimentarius: Global Food Imperialism." Ed. Scott C. Tips. FHR. 2007. Pp. 87-88.

[116] FDA.gov, "Dietary Supplement Health and Education Act of 1994." Food and Drug Administration. http://www.fda.gov/RegulatoryInformation/Legislation/Fede ralFoodDrugandCosmeticActFDCAct/SignificantAmendmentst otheFDCAct/ucm148003.htm Accessed May 24, 2010.

[117] Ibid.

[118] Ibid.

removed from the market) when the Secretary of Health and Human Services "declares [the supplement) to pose an imminent hazard to public health or safety."[119] Because there is no definition of what exactly a "significant or unreasonable risk of illness or injury" would be, this phrase can be subject to a wide range of interpretations and potentially allow a perfectly safe supplement to be banned by the FDA for less than benevolent reasons.[120] In this aspect, the FDA already has unreasonable levels of power. However, most health freedom advocates are unaware of this. In the opinion of many, DSHEA is a solid rock that protects all avenues of supplementation and will never be challenged. Clearly, this is not the case. Indeed, one need only look at the FDA banning of vitamin B_{17}[121] and forms of vitamin B_6[122] to realize the danger posed by the control wielded by these agencies.

Second, DSHEA gives the FDA authority to establish Good Manufacturing Practices regulations in the preparation, packing, and holding of dietary supplements.[123] Logically, this gives the FDA the

---

[119] "Dietary Supplement Health and Education Act of 1994." Food and Drug Administration. http://www.fda.gov/RegulatoryInformation/Legislation/FederalFoodDrugandCosmeticActFDCAct/SignificantAmendmentstotheFDCAct/ucm148003.htm

[120] Taylor, Paul Anthony, "The Growing Threats To DSHEA," Page1 http://www4.dr-rath-foundation.org/us/growing_threats.html

[121] "Health Fraud." FDA.gov September 10 , 2001. http://www.fda.gov/NewsEvents/Testimony/ucm115204.htm

[122] Adams, Mike. "FDA Declares Forms of Vitamin B6 a Drug, Effectively Banning Pyridoxamine from Dietary Supplements." Naturalnews.com February 12, 2009. http://www.naturalnews.com/025606_vitamin_B6_pyridoxamine.html

[123] "Dietary Supplement Health and Education Act of 1994," Food and Drug Administration. http://www.fda.gov/RegulatoryInformation/Legislation/Fede

authority to remove any supplement that does not meet these standards.[124] Indeed, the law gives this authority to the Secretary of Health and Human Services directly.[125] Although the law states that these guidelines are to be modeled after regulations in place for the rest of the food industry (at the time of its passing), given the history of the FDA and the FTC, there is ample room for concern that these institutions may introduce standards that are so high that no manufacturer can meet them or so expensive that they will be unable to afford to do so. In fact, in 2003, the FDA proposed a set of rules that would cause these manufacturing processes to be so stringent that they would exceed the standards required of pharmaceutical companies.[126] The implementation of these new rules would cause the production costs to skyrocket, forcing smaller manufacturers to close their doors

ralFoodDrugandCosmeticActFDCAct/SignificantAmendmentstotheFDCAct/ucm148003.htm Accessed May 24, 2010.
[124] Taylor, Paul Anthony, "The Growing Threats To DSHEA," Page1 http://www4.dr-rath-foundation.org/us/growing_threats.html
[125] "Dietary Supplement Health and Education Act of 1994." Food and Drug Administration. http://www.fda.gov/RegulatoryInformation/Legislation/FederalFoodDrugandCosmeticActFDCAct/SignificantAmendmentstotheFDCAct/ucm148003.htm Accessed May 24, 2010.
[126] Taylor, Paul Anthony, "The Growing Threats To DSHEA," Page1 http://www4.dr-rath-foundation.org/us/growing_threats.html
See also,
"Food and Drug Administration, 21 CFR Parts 111 and 112 Current Good Manufacturing Practice in Manufacturing, Packing, or Holding Dietary Ingredients and Dietary Supplements; Proposed Rule." Part 2. March 13, 2003. http://www.fda.gov/OHRMS/DOCKETS/98fr/03-5401.pdf

and the prices to jump through the roof for the remaining products.[127]

Third, a supplement may not make claims regarding the effects it may have in terms of preventing, curing, or treating any disease. One need only read the label of a natural supplement in order to see the effects of this policy. The wording on these products reads thus, "This product is not intended to diagnose, treat, cure, or prevent any disease." This is because of the "Nutritional Support Statements" clause in DSHEA. For instance, claims that a certain supplement cures cancer or relieves the symptoms of osteoporosis are not allowed. Natural dietary supplements are held to the completely biased standards of the FDA (which claims that only a drug has the right to claim to treat, cure, or prevent disease[128]) and the FTC.[129] The claims that can be made must be worded perfectly and only imply a possible link to the supplement in question if the product qualifies to do so. The claim that calcium may be linked to a reduction in risk of osteoporosis might be allowed and claims may also be made describing the particular supplements' effect on the "structure or function" of the body or the "well-being" achieved by consumption of the product.[130] "Structure and function claims are those

---

[127] Taylor, Paul Anthony, "The Growing Threats To DSHEA," Page1 http://www4.dr-rath-foundation.org/us/growing_threats.html
[128] "Claims That Can Be Made For Conventional Foods and Dietary Supplements." FDA.gov September 2003. http://www.fda.gov/Food/LabelingNutrition/LabelClaims/ucm111447.htm
[129] "Dietary Supplement Health and Education Act of 1994." Food and Drug Administration. http://www.fda.gov/RegulatoryInformation/Legislation/FederalFoodDrugandCosmeticActFDCAct/SignificantAmendmentstotheFDCAct/ucm148003.htm Accessed May 24, 2010.
[130] Ibid.

that assert "skeletal system support" or "circulatory system support."[131]

Fourth, while DSHEA grants dietary supplement retailers the right to display "third party" materials in their establishment, the content and location of these materials are strictly limited. Contrary to the First Amendment rights guaranteed in the Constitution, as well as free market principles, they cannot list any supplement by brand name or have any promotional material attached to them. DSHEA guidelines go even further and state that informative materials must be displayed separate from supplements and that they must be displayed with other materials similar to them in order to present a "balanced view."[132] Of course, since the U.S. Government has determined that the FDA and the Department of Health and Human Services are the ultimate authorities in relation to dietary supplements, it follows logically that these organizations have the final say on what a "balanced view" actually is.[133]

Such criticism of DSHEA is not meant to minimize the protection it has afforded to the natural healthcare and dietary supplement industries or to the American citizenry as a whole. After the passage of DSHEA, both of these industries expanded greatly and were able to emerge from the shadows they had been forced to lurk beneath for so long. Individuals were now granted access to an alternative form of healthcare to the modern medical industry that was (and still is) being forced upon them. They were now granted more control of their own

---

[131] "Claims That Can Be Made For Conventional Foods and Dietary Supplements." FDA.gov September 2003. http://www.fda.gov/Food/LabelingNutrition/LabelClaims/ucm111447.htm
[132] "Dietary Supplement Health and Education Act of 1994." Food and Drug Administration. http://www.fda.gov/RegulatoryInformation/Legislation/FederalFoodDrugandCosmeticActFDCAct/SignificantAmendmentstotheFDCAct/ucm148003.htm Accessed May 24, 2010.
[133] Ibid.

lives and health as well as the ability to follow up on their decisions and purchase the appropriate herbs, vitamins, or mineral supplements of their choosing. As a result, millions of Americans have awakened both to the enormous benefits of natural healthcare and the many dangers of modern medical "science."

However, DSHEA clearly does not provide the all-encompassing blanket protection that many think it does. The FDA, FTC, and HHS have more much power than many are aware of. Given the connection between individuals in these agencies and many globalist organizations such as the Bilderberg group as well as the pharmaceutical industry itself, this is a very frightening thought. These agencies have access to all the legal excuses, media spin, and biased "scientific" studies they need to launch a successful attack on natural healthcare as a whole and remove the freedom of choice from the American people. This has already happened several times on a smaller scale. Because of the firm grip that the pharmaceutical industry, international banks, and other globalist functions have on the mainstream media, these attacks were severely underreported and virtually ignored. When they were broadcast, a significant amount of spin, and often outright lies, was employed in order to project the government agencies as benevolent protectors and the treatments and/or practitioners as evil quacks. The only thing truly needed for this to continue and ultimately succeed is the right amount of apathy from the citizenry. Unfortunately, it appears we might finally have reached that point.

Implementation of the Codex machinery has been even more successful in the European Union. In 2002, the EU produced the European Union Food Supplements Directive which is almost identical to the Codex platform for vitamin and mineral supplements.[134] While a

---

[134] Tipps, Scott C. ""Foreword – Codex Alimentarius: Global Food Imperialism – What is Codex?" Ed. Scott C. Tipps. FHR. 2007. P. IV.

grace period of around eight years was allowed for individual states to exercise their dying sovereignty, the Food Supplements Directive (FSD) went into full effect on December 31, 2009 across the EU, making it the country closest to achieving complete Codex compliance.[135] This deadline has given rise to claims that Codex Alimentarius would be implemented on December 31, 2009 the world over, and that, all of a sudden, natural supplements would no longer be available and themselves be replaced by toxic chemicals. The claim that such a situation would occur is not unbelievable. Rather, it is quite probable as one can see through the discussion made thus far. However, that such a situation would occur in such a sudden manner, especially occurring on December 31, 2009 is simply not true. Indeed, time itself has born these statements to be false. Most of the people making these claims did so out of ignorance, and some simply were taken out of context. Regardless of how this rumor was started, it is false and those like it only serve to hinder the fight against Codex and obfuscate its' dangers. No doubt many woke up on January 1, 2010 and dismissed Codex Alimentarius as a silly conspiracy theory with little relevance to their health based upon the fact that the sky did not fall the night before as they had been told it would.[136]

That being said, a major step in the implementation of Codex standards was taken on December 31, 2009 when the EU FSD went into effect. In many aspects, the FSD is almost a carbon copy of the Codex Alimentarius Guidelines for Vitamin and Mineral Food Supplements.

---

[135] Starling, Shane. "Food Supplements Directive: Stay positive (or bans may follow)." Nutraingredients.com January 8, 2010. http://www.nutraingredients.com/Regulation/Food-Supplements-Directive-Stay-positive-or-bans-may-follow

[136] Press Release: National Health Federation. "December 31, 2009 – Where Were You When The Earth Ended?" January 4, 2010. http://www.thenhf.com/press_releases/pr_04_jan_2010.html

Exuding a philosophical and policy similarity, it is mentioned in one of the opening statements of the Directive that "Excessive intake of vitamins and minerals may result in adverse effects and therefore necessitate the setting of maximum safe levels for them in food supplements."[137] From the outset, the FSD expresses the same biased stance towards natural supplements as Codex, even though the adverse effects to taking large amounts of natural supplements are almost completely insignificant, especially when compared to those of pharmaceuticals. Nevertheless, this is the justification used for the ensuing attack on basic god-given rights of European citizens.

Similar to Codex Guidelines, the FSD contains provisions for the establishment of maximum levels of nutrient content for supplements. Paragraph 14 states,

> When maximum levels are set, therefore, account should be taken of the upper safe levels of the vitamins and minerals, as established by scientific risk assessment based on generally acceptable scientific data, and of intakes of those nutrients from the normal diet. Due account should also be taken of reference intake amounts when setting maximum levels.[138]

Not only does the FSD provide for maximum levels for nutrients, it also bases its' determinations, as does Codex, on the flawed methodology known as risk assessment. Also, it will take the Global Average Daily Diet into account. This is what is meant when it states that "intakes of those nutrients from the normal diet" will be given due account.[139] It should

---

[137] Directive 2002/46/EC Of The European Parliament And Of The Council of 10 June 2002 on the approximation of the laws of the member states relating to food supplements. "Codex Alimentarius: Global Food Imperialism." Ed. Scott C. Tips. FHR. 2007. Pp. 237-243
[138] Ibid.
[139] Ibid.

be noted that Article 5 Section 1 completely copies (or vice versa) the Codex Guidelines section 3.2.2. They both state, word for word, "Maximum amounts of vitamins and minerals present in food supplements per daily portion of consumption as recommended by the manufacturer shall be set, taking the following into account: (a) upper safe levels of vitamins and minerals established by scientific risk assessment based on generally accepted scientific data, taking into account, as appropriate, the varying degrees of sensitivity of different consumer groups; (b) intake of vitamins and minerals from other dietary sources."[140] It seems very suspect that a supposedly unrelated "regulatory" agency and a European Union law would contain the exact same language without some kind of common connection between the two. Indeed, as mentioned above, while the rest of the law might not be a literal word-for-word carbon copy of the Guidelines, in principle it is exactly that. It should be a cause for concern or, at the very least, skeptical curiosity, when laws or policies begin to be enacted simultaneously in different countries and/or international governing and administrative bodies.

The FSD also provides for the establishment of minimum levels of nutrients. It states, "To ensure that significant amounts of vitamins and minerals are present in food supplements, minimum amounts per daily portion of consumption as recommended by the manufacturer shall be set, as appropriate."[141] Although, unlike the Codex Guidelines,

---

[140] Ibid.
See Also,
"Guidelines for Vitamin and Mineral Food Supplements."
Codexalimentarius.net
www.codexalimentarius.net/download/standards/.../cxg_055
e.pdf
[141] Directive 2002/46/EC Of The European Parliament And Of The Council of 10 June 2002 on the approximation of the laws of the member states relating to food supplements. "Codex

the Directive is not specific in terms of percentages, it clearly provides for the two-pronged attack of simultaneous maximum and minimum levels of nutrients in food supplements.

The most frightening aspect of the FSD, however, is not the maximum and minimum levels but the Positive and Negative Lists that are created. All the vitamins and minerals allowed in food supplements are included in the FSD Positive List, while those not included are completely banned for use in supplementation. [142] The list itself is quite restrictive, prohibiting the production, sale, and distribution of many different vitamin and mineral substances. As the Directive states,

> Only vitamins and minerals normally found in, and consumed as part of, the diet should be allowed to be present in food supplements although that this does not mean that their presence therein is necessary. Controversy as to the identity of those nutrients that could potentially arise should be avoided. Therefore, it is appropriate to establish a positive list of those vitamins and minerals. [143]

Restricting the inclusion of vitamins and minerals to only those that are part of the diet is bad enough. However, the language of "only vitamins and minerals normally found in, and consumed as part of, the diet," adds an even more limiting scope.[144] This is because such language not only limits the approved substances to those found in food, but to those found in the diet of Europeans specifically. Even then, it is only those substances that are "normally" consumed. Also, the antipathy towards the discovery of new nutrients is clearly expressed in the desire to avoid controversy "as to the identity of those nutrients that could potentially

Alimentarius: Global Food Imperialism." Ed. Scott C. Tips. FHR. 2007. Pp. 237-243
[142] Ibid.
[143] Ibid. p. 237
[144] Ibid.

arise."[145] Not only that, but the Directive quietly gives the Council and the Commission of the EU the authority to remove any substance that it wishes from the Positive List. In Article 4, section 5 of the Directive it states, "Modification to the lists referred to in paragraph 1 [the Positive Lists] shall be adopted in accordance with the procedure referred to in Article 13(2)."[146] Article 13, Section 2 then reads, "When reference is made to this paragraph, Articles 5 and 7 of Decision 1999/468/EC shall apply, having regard to the provisions of Article 8 thereof."[147] When one reads these sections of the cited law, it becomes apparent that the authority to change those substances on the Positive Lists is granted to the Council and the Commission.[148]

Brief Summary

Although December 31, 2009 did not bring immediate worldwide implementation of Codex Alimentarius Guidelines as many claimed, the machinery of Codex did begin to pick up steam with the implementation of the European Union Food Supplements Directive, which is essentially a carbon copy of the Codex Alimentarius Guidelines for Vitamin and Mineral Food Supplements. These Codex Guidelines would use the flawed methodology of risk assessment to establish Upper Safe Levels/Maximum Upper Limits and subsequently Maximum Permitted Levels on the amount of vitamins and minerals in food supplements. This method would essentially cause dietary supplements to become unaffordable and ineffective. The Guidelines would also

---

[145] Ibid.

[146] Ibid. p.239

[147] Ibid. p. 240.

[148] "Council Decision of 28 June 1999 laying down the procedures for the exercise of implementing powers conferred on the Commission (*) (1999/468/EC)" http://www.ena.lu/council_decision_1999_468_ec_laying_do wn_procedures_exercise_implementing_powers_june_1999-02-4941   Accessed April 21, 2010.

create minimum levels for vitamin and mineral supplements which would completely remove some vitamins and minerals and replace them with filler material. While Codex treats natural supplements as toxins, it treats toxins such as fluoride as nutrients. Codex's contractor, BfR, makes no distinction between calcium and sodium fluoride (toxic waste), treats it as a nutrient, and even sets a Recommended Daily Intake level for it. While many believe the DSHEA law of 1994 provides a solid wall of defense for natural supplements, this law can be easily circumvented. The law itself allows the FDA and Department of Health and Human Services a great deal of authority in regulating and banning substances, contrary to popular belief.

Chapter 3

Codex and Food Irradiation

Codex and Food Irradiation

Escaping the rigorous "risk assessment" methods that vitamin and mineral supplements are subjected to, food irradiation is expressly allowed under Codex guidelines. Clearly a threat to public health, irradiated foods are not safe for human consumption and contribute to a host of health problems such as cancer and birth defects. Irradiation also causes genetic damage to cells.[149] One of the reasons for this is the fact that irradiated food is exposed to gamma rays of radioactive material or electron beams causing chemical changes in the food. Essentially, the food becomes mutated by this exposure, a condition which does not occur in nature, and is the cause for many forms of cancer and genetic modification.[150]

Yet Codex pushes irradiation as if it were a great tool of disinfection with no adverse side effects at all. Indeed, prior to the easing of restrictions on food irradiation by Codex, the United States had been irradiating food at an alarming rate. The process began in 1963 when wheat flour became the first food allowed to be irradiated. In 1964, white potatoes were added to the list and the process continued until the present day. As shown below, the Organic Consumers Association documents the timeline from 1963 – 2002. As you can see, after the 2002 inclusions it is almost pointless to detail any other food added to the list as most of the American food supply has

---

[149] Krebs, Al. "WTO Codex To Allow Dangerous Levels of Food Irradiation." Organic Consumers Association. July 10, 2003. http://www.organicconsumers.org/corp/071403_wto_irradiation.cfm Accessed May 24, 2010.

[150] Nausoulas, Andrianna. "Codex Alimentarius and the International Politics of Food Irradiation." Toronto Food Policy Council, July 2003. http://www.publiccitizen.org/documents/codextoronto.pdf Accessed May 24, 2010.

been included. [151]

Foods That Can Be Irradiated In the US[152]	
Year	Food
1963	Wheat flour
1964	White potatoes
1986	Spices, herbs, herb teas, pork, fruits and vegetables
1992	Poultry
1997	Beef
1999	Refrigerated or frozen raw beef, pork, lamb, and poultry
2000	Eggs in the shell, seeds for sprouting (like alfalfa)
2002	Imported fruits and vegetables
2002	Meat purchased by the National School Lunch Program

It should be noted that under current US law, organic food cannot be irradiated. However, that is not the case with Codex standards as there is no categorization of what foods can and cannot be "treated" with radiation. It should also be mentioned that current US law states that all irradiated food must be labeled with the radura symbol and some amount of text stating its' irradiation. However, that labeling only has to be made visible to the "first consumer" and that is generally individuals such as the distributor, not the average grocery store shopper. [153]

---

[151] Fact Sheet: History, Background, and Status of Labeling of Irradiated Foods." Organic Consumers Association. 8/25/2008 http://www.organicconsumers.org/Irrad/LabelingStatus.cfm Accessed on May 13 2010.
[152] Ibid.
[153] Ibid.

Radura Symbol - Signaling the irradiation of food products

However, even these labeling requirements are severely inadequate. While these "first consumers" must, by law, be able to see the words and symbol on some products the law does not require the labeling of many others.[154] It would seem that the FDA, USDA, NRC (National Regulatory Commission), and the DOT (Department of Transportation), if it were truly concerned with the health and welfare of consumers, would require clear and appropriate labeling for any and all foods that have been irradiated. Although, not irradiating at all would be the best policy, at least allowing the real consumer an opportunity to choose seems like a bare minimum in terms of public health and basic fair business practice. However, in contrast to their rhetoric and stated objectives, it is also clear that these regulatory agencies have no real interest in protecting the public from any danger or insuring fair business dealings. Nevertheless, these are some of the labeling requirements for irradiated foods in the US:

---

[154] Ibid.

| A Few Labeling Requirements For Irradiated Food ||
Required labeling for the "consumer"	Not required labeling for "consumer"
Plant foods sold in their whole form (such as a bag of wheat flour, oranges, apples, etc.)	Multiple ingredient products where some, but not all of the individual ingredients were irradiated
Fresh whole fruits and vegetables (must be labeled on the box, the fruit itself, or a display)	Irradiated ingredients in foods prepared or served by restaurants, hotels, hospitals, etc.
Whole meat and poultry in a package (chicken breasts etc.)	Irradiated food prepared by delis or supermarket takeout counters
Unpackaged meat and poultry (meat received from a butcher - meat such as this requires a label on a display)	Spices and herb teas
Irradiated meat and poultry that is part of another packaged food (such as chicken in a pot pie etc.)	Sprouts grown from irradiated seeds
	Ingredients in supplements
	Plant-food ingredients that are processed again (such as apples in apple sauce, or a vegetable/fruit in a salad)

155

As the reader can see, these rules are not only ludicrous; they are full of loopholes for food producers to weave through. These rules are also extremely frightening if you think of how much irradiated food Americans are already consuming with absolutely no idea that we are damaging and changing our DNA. Not to mention the invitation of many different forms of cancer and disease.

The FDA governs most aspects of food irradiation but the USDA, DOT, and NRC regulate some aspects as well. There are some differences in policy, but it should be noted that the latter three agencies only deal with specific aspects of the process. For instance, the USDA deals only with meat/poultry and fresh fruits while the NRC addresses the safety of the facilities used in irradiation. The DOT regulates the transportation of the materials. For the most part, the differences between the policies of these agencies are very slight. Most of the differences exist between the FDA and the USDA but deal only

---

155 Ibid.

with things such as where labels should be posted and what size type and font should be used. For instance, the USDA requirement for multi-ingredient products that contain irradiated meat is that it should be stated to the consumer by the label yet the FDA has no such requirement at all. But before one mistakenly gets the impression that the USDA is somehow more interested in protecting the consumer than the FDA, consider the fact that the USDA even allows claims touting the "beneficial effects" of irradiation.[156] Ironically, vitamin and mineral supplements such as Vitamin C are highly regulated in the claims that can be made about their health benefits but radiation may be touted as safe and beneficial.

To add to the shady language of the labeling requirements already in existence, in 2002 Congress created a loophole that had been the desire of the meat and poultry industry for some time. With the creation of this new escape hatch, companies can now use terms like "electronically pasteurized" instead of "treated with radiation" or "irradiated" by bypassing the FDA and going straight to the Secretary of Health and Human Services to request permission to use the new semantically gifted term. The HHS Secretary has the authority to grant them such permission. Indeed, in 2007, the FDA itself proposed a new rule similar to the congressional loophole. This rule would allow irradiated food to be labeled as "pasteurized" as opposed to "irradiated."[157] The very fact that this rule would even be proposed should worry every American. Clearly, if the FDA were truly concerned about those individuals they are supposed to be protecting from adulterated foods, they would, at the very least, require that companies label their products honestly. This proposal, however, clearly shows the true intent behind FDA policies and regulations.

---

[156] Ibid.
[157] Ibid.

The proposal made by the FDA in April, 2007 is an interesting one indeed. In the opening summary of the text, the FDA states that one of the purposes of the proposal is to make it so that "only those irradiated foods in which the irradiation causes a material change in the food, or a material change in the consequences that may result from the use of the food, bear the radura logo and the term 'irradiation,' or a derivative thereof, in conjunction with explicit language describing the change in the food or its conditions of use."[158] While this may seem like a strengthening of a rule, in reality it is not. This proposal is merely another cover mechanism for the pretense of protecting the consumer with strong regulation, while allowing industry to do just what it wants, i.e. produce high levels of irradiated food to cover up unsanitary manufacturing practices. The FDA acknowledges the fact that irradiation changes the makeup of food when it says in the same proposal "Irradiation has various effects on foods that may cause changes in the characteristics of the food. Such changes may occur in the food's organoleptic, nutritional, or functional properties that would not be noticeable at the point of purchase but could be apparent when consumed or cooked."[159] Of course, the FDA does not go so far as to say that such changes occur at the genetic level causing cancer and a host of other health problems, or even that the changes are dangerous. In fact, they go so far as to say that, out of all the food allowed to be irradiated by the FDA regulations, there have been no changes. The proposal states, "Currently, we are not aware of any changes to the nutritional properties of any food FDA has approved for irradiation."[160] Though not

---

[158] Federal Register Proposed Rule – 72 FR 16291 April 4, 2007: Irradiation in the Production, Processing, and Handling of Food p.1
http://www.fda.gov/Food/LabelingNutrition/FoodLabelingGuidanceRegulatoryInformation/RegulationsFederalRegisterDocuments/ucm077977.htm Accessed May 24, 2010.
[159] Ibid. p. 4
[160] Ibid p.4

a direct contradiction, it seems highly suspect that irradiation is known to cause "changes" in food, so well known that the FDA is forced to admit it, yet it is unaware of any changes to the foods which it allows to be irradiated. This shows that the FDA is proposing a position that would allow it to appear as if it were taking a harder stance with tougher rules, while allowing for the continuation of the approval of irradiated food.

A second rule change, as mentioned earlier, made in the same proposal should also draw much ire. As mentioned above, it allows food producers to discard the "irradiation" label in favor of a more palatable and misleading "pasteurized" designation. As stated in the proposal,

> "FDA is also proposing to allow a firm to petition FDA for use of an alternate term to 'irradiation' (other than "pasteurized"). In addition, FDA is proposing to permit a firm to use the term 'pasteurized in lieu of 'irradiated,' provided it notifies the agency that the irradiation process being used meets the criteria specified for use of the term 'pasteurized' in the Federal Food Drug, and Cosmetic Act and the agency does not object to the notification."[161]

On an interesting side note, the "alternate term to 'irradiation (other than 'pasteurized')" is not clearly defined here.[162] It is possible, because of this clause, to not only allow the term "pasteurized" to be used, but another more evasive unrelated term in its' place. Yet the proposal clearly allows the term "pasteurized" to be used —at least pending the FDA's approval and the harmonization with the criteria of pasteurization. Even though the FDA admits in the proposal that public comments demonstrated labeling irradiated products as anything but irradiated was misleading, they continue on with this policy.[163] As usual,

---

[161] Ibid. p.1
[162] Ibid.
[163] Ibid.

the feelings and opinions of those whom the FDA claims to protect are virtually meaningless.

Yet with all of these loopholes and outright fabrications by our own FDA, Codex goes even further. Using carefully crafted legal loopholes of their own, Codex effectively removes the limit on the dose of irradiation as it has been understood for many years. Previous to the revision of Codex standards in 2003, the limit on the dose of radiation stood at 10kGy. This in itself is a very dangerous amount of radiation as 10kGy is the equivalent to 330 million chest x-rays. [164] Such a large quantity of radiation would obviously be a death wish for anyone who received it, yet it has been rationalized to the public (the very few of them that are actually aware of it) that it is safe to be absorbed into food. Nevertheless, this has been the official Codex guidelines on irradiation limits since they were developed in 1983.[165]

Since Codex classifies irradiation as an additive (not a contaminant), the committee that bears responsibility for it's' regulation is the Codex Committee on Food Additives and Contaminants (CCFAC). In dealing with irradiation, this committee works closely with the International Atomic Energy Agency (IAEA), Joint FAO/WHO Expert Committees on Food Additives (JECFA), and the International Consultative Group on Food Irradiation (ICGFI).[166] All of these organizations are interrelated and have a vested interest in promoting

---

[164] "WTO Codex to Allow Dangerous Levels of Food Irradiation," Organic Consumers Association. July 10, 2003 http://www.organicconsumers.org/corp/071403_wto_irradia tion.cfm Accessed May 24, 2010.
[165] Nausoulas, Andrianna. "Codex Alimentarius and the International Politics of Food Irradiation." Toronto Food Policy Council, July 2003. http://www.publiccitizen.org/documents/codextoronto.pdf Accessed May 24, 2010.
[166] Ibid p.2

the irradiation of food as well as the harmonization of laws and trade between countries for the purpose of globalization. For instance, the IAEA is the leading advocate for the expansion of nuclear technology, which was developed by the UN.[167]The ICGFI another UN facilitated organization created under the FAO and WHO along with the IAEA serves basically as a propaganda arm and direct advocate for food irradiation. The ICGFI has been active in creating fact sheets promoting the "benefits" of irradiation and helping "inform" the public on it's' safety. [168] Also, the JECFA(a globalist agency by its very nature as it is a combination of the FAO and WHO) claims to have "developed principles for the safety assessment of chemicals in food that are consistent with current thinking on risk assessment and take account of recent developments in toxicology and other relevant sciences."[169] Yet with all of these scientific resources, the agency cannot bring itself to acknowledge toxic radiation as anything but an additive. These three organizations are connected to many more globalist international and UN based agencies, but suffice it to say that true independent science, free from political or ideological preconceptions, is not at work here.

It stands to reason then that Codex began "updating" its guidelines for food irradiation several years ago, in 1999. It appears that most of the relaxation of the guidelines and regulations regarding irradiation were spearheaded by individuals in the United States itself. One such man, who was chairman of the Codex Alimentarius Commission at the time of

---

[167] www.IAEA.org
See Also,
http://www.iaea.org/About/index.html   Accessed May 24, 2010.
[168] Tape, N.W. Dr. "International Consultative Group on Food Irradiation: Role, Achievements, and Impacts, 1984-88." http://www.iaea.org/Publications/Magazines/Bulletin/Bull31 1/31105783538.pdf
[169] Joint FAO/WHO Expert Committee on Food Additives. http://www.who.int/ipcs/food/jecfa/en/

the ratification of these new guidelines, is Tom Billy[170], the former administrator of the USDA's Food Safety and Inspection Service.[171] Billy has been credited with playing a major role in the deregulation of the meat and poultry industries during his tenure with the USDA.[172] Incidentally, he was appointed Chair of Codex on June 29, 1999, around the same time that Codex decided to reevaluate their standards on Irradiation. He remained in this position until the revised standards were ratified by the full Codex Commission. Andrianna Natsoulas lays out the timeline of Codex's' Guideline relaxation in her article, "Codex Alimentarius and the International Politics of Food Irradiation,"

---

[170] Beers, Allison. "Billy Re-elected Chairman of Codex." Food Chemical News. July 9, 2001.
http://www.accessmylibrary.com/article-1G1-76444795/billy-re-elected-chairman.html Accessed May 13, 2010.
[171] "Fact Sheet: History, Background, and Status of Labeling of Irradiated Foods" 8/25/2008.
http://www.organicconsumers.org/irrad/labelingstatus.cfm Accessed May 24, 2010.
[172] Ibid.
See Also,
"Pus, Sores, Tumors, & Filth: USDA's Deregulation of the Meat Industry Draws Public Criticism," The Agribusiness Examiner. Issue # 82, July 27, 2000.
http://www.organicconsumers.org/toxic/chixpus.cfm Cited from Organicconsumers.org website. Accessed May 24, 2010.

Timeline of the Ratification of the Proposed Draft Standard for Irradiated Foods[173]	
1999	Codex Commission decides to re-examine the Standard by assigning the project to the CCFAC
1999	Codex Secretariat calls for the Proposed Draft Standard be drawn
2000	The Draft Standard is sent to member nation agencies and international organizations for comments
2001	CCFAC reviewed and modified the Draft Standard
2001	The Codex Executive committee approved the Draft Standard
2001	The Draft Standard is sent back to the designated government agencies and international organizations for comments
2002	There is a delay that lasts for a year due to a new European study on the toxicity of 2-ACB's(2-alkylcycloburamones;chemical byproducts formed in irradiated foods)
2003	The Draft Standard returns once again to CCFAC for committee acceptance
2003	The full Codex Commission ratified the new Codex General Standard for Irradiated Foods

The revised General Standard For Irradiated Food is remarkable because of its crafty use of technical wording to allow much higher, even limitless, amounts of irradiation in food. Prior to the change in 2003, the limits were set at 10 kGy, an amount of radiation that is the equivalent of 330 million chest x-rays, a procedure that is dangerous in and of itself

---

[173]Nausoulas, Andrianna. "Codex Alimentarius and the International Politics of Food Irradiation." Toronto Food Policy Council, July 2003
[174] Nausoulas, Andrianna. "Codex Alimentarius and the International Politics of Food Irradiation." Toronto Food Policy Council, July 2003.
http://www.publiccitizen.org/documents/codextoronto.pdf
Accessed May 24, 2010.

when only done once. [175] However, even the limit set prior to 2003 is not as strict as the current FDA regulations and the regulations of most other nations. Currently, the FDA sets limits on the amount of food irradiation on a case by case basis with some foods allowed to receive more radiation than others.[176] Codex, however, makes no such distinction and levels a blanket endorsement of irradiation regardless of the type of food. [177] Nevertheless, most of the upper limits for radiation set by even the FDA are lower than those set by Codex. Only two categories are allowed the pre-2003 Codex 10kGy maximum. Below is a table containing those food products and their maximum limits on irradiation as determined by the FDA.

---

[175] "WTO Codex to Allow Dangerous Levels of Food Irradiation," Organic Consumers Association. July 10, 2003. http://www.organicconsumers.org/corp/071403_wto_irradia tion.cfm Accessed May 24, 2010.

[176] Morehouse, Kim M., Komolprasert, Vanee. "Irradiation of Food and Packaging: An Overview." Food and Drug Administration. http://www.fda.gov/Food/FoodIngredientsPackaging/Irradiat edFoodPackaging/ucm081050.htm Accessed May 24, 2010.

[177] General Standard For Irradiated Foods Codex Stan 106-1983, REV.1-2003. Codexalimentarius.net. www.codexalimentarius.net/download/standards/16/CXS_1 06e.pdf Accessed May 24, 2010.

Maximum Limits for Irradiation as set by the FDA	
Food Product	Maximum Dose of Irradiation (measured in kGy)
Wheat and Wheat Powder	0.20-0.50
White Potatoes	0.05-0.15
Spices and Dry Vegetables	10.0
Dry or Dehydrated Enzyme Preparations	10.0
Pork carcasses or fresh, non-heated processed cuts	0.30-1.00
Fresh Foods	1.0
Dry or dehydrated aromatic vegetable substances*	30.0
Fresh, Frozen, uncooked pastry	3.0
Refrigerated and Frozen uncooked beef, lamb, goat, and pork	4.5 (refrigerated) 7.0 (frozen)
Fresh shell eggs	3.0

*Used for flavor or aroma; includes turmeric and paprika[178]

The revised version of the Codex standards, however, moves significantly beyond those of the FDA in terms of allowable doses of radiation. This is achieved mainly by including a semantical loophole in the wording of the standards. In the section titled "Absorbed Dose," it reads "The maximum absorbed dose delivered to a food should not exceed 10 kGy, except when necessary to achieve a legitimate technological purpose."[179] While appearing to retain the previous set limit of 10 kGy, the new Codex standards actually weaken if not remove it completely. By adding the latter half of the phrase that states "except when necessary to achieve a legitimate technological purpose," Codex effectively produces a loophole through which irradiation can exceed the limit of 10 kGy. [180]Nowhere in the revised standards is there a definition as to what a "legitimate technological purpose" might be. Therefore, there is the distinct possibility and likelihood that food may be irradiated at virtually any dose for whatever purpose declared to be a legitimate technological usage by the producer or the regulator.

---

[178] "Food Irradiation." University of Minnesota. http://www.cidrap.umn.edu/cidrap/content/fs/irradiation/biofacts/irrad-bkgd.html
[179] Ibid.
[180] Ibid.

Indeed, the Codex standards do not indicate who would even be responsible for determining what a "legitimate technological purpose" might be and makes no mention of the regulatory bodies that might make that decision. This may seem remarkable but the regulatory agencies in the United States such as the FDA, USDA, and FTC have largely already become mere enforcement arms for the corporate/government partnership known as the New World Order. They have all but renounced their original purpose of ensuring the safety of the general public. So while it seems likely that Codex might set the standard for what determines a "legitimate technological purpose" and the international regulatory agencies would enforce them, it seems even more probable that the phrase will be left undefined and that various compromised regulatory agencies would decide the outcome of any disputes that may arise. Nevertheless, the window to unfettered use of irradiation is left wide open.

Yet Codex does not stop there. Another manner in which irradiation levels are allowed to reach limitless amounts is through the process of re-irradiation. Codex generally prohibits the re-irradiation of foods that have low moisture content or those already irradiated in accordance with Codex guidelines. However, this is largely empty language as a loophole similar to the one mentioned above ("except when it is necessary to achieve a legitimate technological purpose") is provided shortly thereafter. Codex goes on to say that food is not to be considered as re-irradiated when:

> (a) the irradiated food is prepared from materials which have been irradiated at low dose levels for purposes other than food safety, e.g. quarantine control, prevention of sprouting of roots and tubers; (b) the food, containing less than 5% of irradiated ingredient, is irradiated; or when (c) the full dose of ionizing radiation required to achieve the desired effect is applied to the food in more than one increment as part of

processing for a specific technological purpose.[181]

According to this statement, food made up of irradiated ingredients can once again be irradiated so long as the irradiated ingredients have been "treated" for "purposes other than food safety."[182] However, it will not be considered re-irradiated. Likewise, a food can be re-irradiated (though not considered irradiated) as long as less than 5% of it's' ingredients are irradiated or if the irradiation process is fulfilled in more than one increment. Keep in mind, these standards are not in addition to one another, they are separate. This means that an irradiation facility does not have to meet all of these standards to re-irradiate food. They only have to meet one. Claiming that re-irradiation was for purposes other than hygiene or safety opens the door for a potentially unlimited amount of radiation into the food supply. So does the process of irradiating food over and over again which, in most circles would be called re-irradiation. However, under the Codex Standards, a facility need only claim that the successive irradiating was part of a single process and the food will not be considered re-irradiated.

While the standards do state that the absorbed dose of radiation should not rise above 10 kGy, there are two escape hatches provided by the language in the statement. The section reads "The cumulative maximum absorbed dose delivered to a food should not exceed 10 kGy as a result of re-irradiation except when it is necessary to achieve a legitimate technological purpose, and should not compromise consumer safety or wholesomeness of the food."[183] First, it should be noted that the amount of radiation in the food is not to exceed 10 kGy

---

[181] General Standard For Irradiated Foods Codex Stan 106-1983, REV.1-2003. Codexalimentarius.net. www.codexalimentarius.net/download/standards/16/CXS_1 06e.pdf Accessed May 24, 2010.
[182] Ibid.
[183] Ibid.

"as a result of re-irradiation," not necessarily the irradiation process as a whole. Second, the same loophole exists here as in the standards for irradiation mentioned earlier as the "except when necessary to achieve a legitimate technological purpose" clause appears in this instance as well. [184]

Brief Summary

Although extremely dangerous to public health, Codex allows and facilitates the irradiation of food to enter the food supply. Pre-2003, Codex Guidelines set the limit of radiation for food at 10kGy, the equivalent of 330 million chest x-rays. Codex Guidelines have since been revised to include loopholes that allow for potentially unlimited amounts of irradiation to occur under the guise of "legitimate technological purposes." Furthermore, the approval of food re-irradiation is similarly included. Along these same lines, the FDA has recently proposed changing the labeling of irradiated food as "irradiated" to "pasteurized" to protect industry from consumer preferences. Indeed, the labeling requirements for irradiated is already quite relaxed. Only the "first consumer" is required to see the label – the "first consumer" being the distributor more often than the actual consumer.

---

[184] Ibid.

Chapter 4

Codex and the Use of Recombinant Bovine Growth Hormone (rBGH)

Codex and the Use of Recombinant Bovine Growth Hormone (rBGH)

In the ongoing battle against the implementation of Codex Alimentarius guidelines, there have been many claims regarding Codex and Monsanto's recombinant bovine growth hormone. Many of these claims have suggested that Codex guidelines will require that all dairy cows and food animals be treated with the hormone.[185] However, there is no evidence for this yet, unfortunately, these claims have found their way into the anti-Codex community as fact. In reality, they are no truer than those that suggested Codex guidelines were going to be implemented on a worldwide scale on December 31, 2009. This chapter should serve as an explanation of the position of Codex Alimentarius regarding recombinant bovine growth hormone as well an introduction to some of the major players in the growth hormone and genetically modified food debate.

Recombinant Bovine Growth Hormone (also known as Recombinant Bovine Somatotropin) is a genetically engineered hormone that is injected into cows for the purpose of increasing milk production.[186] It is derived from bovine somatotropin (bST) which is a hormone that is produced naturally in the cattle by the pituitary gland. This hormone is very important for growth and development as well as other functions of the animals' body. Sometime in the 1930's it was discovered that injecting cattle with bST increased milk production. However, because bST is produced in the animal itself, the only source available was in the pituitary glands of the slaughtered cattle. Genetic

---

[185] Damato, Gregory. "Codex Alimentarius: Population Control Under the Guise of Consumer Protection." September 10, 2008. Naturalnews. http://www.naturalnews.com/024128_CODEX_food_health.html Accessed May 17, 2010.

[186] "Bovine Somatotropin," Iowa State University, p.1 http://www.biotech.iastate.edu/biotech_info_series/Bovine_Somatropin.html

engineering thus came into play. By removing the bovine gene which controls the production of bST and inserting it into a bacterium called Escherichia Coli (E. Coli), scientists and manufacturers are able to reproduce large amounts of bST. This is due to the fact that E. Coli replicates in the human intestinal tract where it is originally found. Essentially, it acts as an industrial unit for the production of bST. This Genetically Modified Organism (GMO) is then injected into the cattle where it replicates causing an increase in milk production. [187] This concept of genetic combination is the foundation for the name "Recombinant" Growth Hormone or Bovine Somatotropin.

As with any GM food, there are very serious health problems associated with the use of rBGH that affect both humans and the animals that are injected with it. Cows who receive the hormone, in addition to the deplorable conditions in which they already find themselves[188], often develop a condition called mastitis, an extremely painful inflammation of the mammary glands. Of the two forms of mastitis (infectious and non-infectious) non-infectious mastitis accounts for only 1% of the cases in existence and is mainly a result of some kind of injury. The other 99% are a result of infections largely due to bacteria produced by the animals' living conditions and the rBGH they receive. There are subsequently four categories of mastitis: peracute, acute, subacute, and subclinical. Of the four, subclinical is the most difficult to diagnose due to the lack of visible physical symptoms. [189] For the most

---

[187] Ibid.

[188] A good documentary regarding the conditions of animals in large manufacturing plants is called "Earthlings."

[189] "Mastitis in Beef Cows – Frequently Asked Questions" Government of Alberta, Ministry of Agriculture and Rural Development.
http://www1.agric.gov.ab.ca/$department/deptdocs.nsf/all/f aq8106

part, it is detected by somatic cell counts.[190] However, the three other
forms of mastitis do render physical symptoms with the peracute form
the most pronounced. In this instance the cow's bag become swollen,
red, hot, and/or sensitive to the touch. This is extremely painful to the
affected animal since she is being continuously milked by automatic
machines and dragging her bag across the floor as she moves in what
little space there is. The animal may also suffer from a fever,
depression, shivering, rapid weight loss, lack of appetite and even
death. Symptoms may be slightly less obvious or pronounced in the
other forms of mastitis, yet they are all part of the same condition
which is becoming more and more prevalent not just in dairy cows but
in beef herds as well.[191] Due to lack of appetite and reduced nutrition as
a result of constant milking (in the case of dairy cows)[192] the amount of
milk produced from the animals affected in this way becomes
significantly smaller. Likewise, beef herds injected with the chemical
tend to be 7% to 12.5% smaller in terms of weight. Ironically, a hormone
injected into animals to make them more productive for dairy and beef
often causes a condition which reduces their output in both categories.
[193] Even in animals who manage to avoid chronic cases of infection, the

---

[190] Section 7.2 "Report of the Canadian Veterinary Medical
Association Expert Panel on rBST." http://www.hc-
sc.gc.ca/dhp-mps/vet/issues-enjeux/rbst-stbr/rep_cvma-
rap_acdv_tc-tm-eng.php
[191] "Mastitis in Beef Cows – Frequently Asked Questions"
Government of Alberta, Ministry of Agriculture and Rural
Development.
http://www1.agric.gov.ab.ca/$department/deptdocs.nsf/all/f
aq8106
[192] "The Issues: Artificial Hormones." Sustainabletable.org
http://www.sustainabletable.org/issues/hormones/
Accessed May 24, 2010.
[193] Ibid.

milk yield as a result of rBGH only increases by 11.3% to 15.6%.[194]

Yet the increased rate of mastitis is not the only injury to the animals as a result of rBGH. The Canadian Veterinary Medical Association Expert Panel conducted a review of the use of rBGH in dairy cows and reported that incidents of lameness increased by as much as 50% in animals treated with the hormone. The report also noted that sterility (or non-pregnancy) as well as culling was significantly increased as well. Twinning, placenta retention, and abortion/fetal loss were also considered and acknowledged as potential side effects of hormone treatment. [195]

Yet the damage does not stop with the animals. The repercussions of using rBGH in dairy and beef cows extend all the way to the humans that consume them. Insulin Growth Factor 1 (IGF-1), another powerful hormone increased in the animals' system by injections of rBGH, lingers in the milk and has been linked to breast, colon, and prostate cancer in humans.[196] IGF-1 is present naturally in

---

[194] "Report of the Canadian Veterinary Medical Association Expert Panel on rBST." Conclusions and Recommendations. Health Canada. November 1998. http://www.hc-sc.gc.ca/dhp-mps/vet/issues-enjeux/rbst-stbr/rep_cvma-rap_acdv_14-eng.php Accessed May 17, 2010.

[195] "Report of the Canadian Veterinary Medical Association Expert Panel on rBST," Health Canada. November, 1998. http://www.hc-sc.gc.ca/dhp-mps/vet/issues-enjeux/rbst-stbr/rep_cvma-rap_acdv_tc-tm-eng.php

[196] "rBGH: How Artificial Hormones Damage the Dairy Industry and Endanger Public Health." Food and Water Watch. http://www.foodandwaterwatch.org/food/report/rbgh-how-artificial-hormones-damage-the-dairy-industry-and-endanger-public-health-2/rbgh-how-artificial-hormones-damage-the-dairy-industry-and-endanger-public-health-1/ Accessed May 24, 2010.

both cows and humans, and is important for mediating cellular response to growth hormones. While the growth hormones themselves are quite different, cow and human IGF-1 are identical to one another.[197] Humans consume their own IGF-1 which is digested in the stomach and, obviously, is harmless. However, the IGF-1 present in cow milk, especially that which comes from animals that were treated with rBGH survives digestion and moves to the intestinal tract. [198] This is due to the fact that the IGF-1 produced in human saliva is free IGF-1 and is digested by the stomach. The IGF-1 in cow milk however, is protected from digestion by the milk protein casein and bypasses the digestive process.[199] There have been many studies have shown a definite link between increased IGF-1 levels and breast, colon, and prostate cancer. Herbert Yu and Thomas Rohan addressed this in their study "Role of the Insulin-like Growth Factor Family in Cancer Development and Progression." In their conclusion they state,

---

[197] Hansen, Michael, Ph.D., Halloran, Jean M., Groth, Edward III, Ph.D., Lefferts, Lisa Y."Potential Public Health Impacts Of The Use of Recombinant Bovine Somatotropin In Dairy Production." ConsumersUnion.org. September 1997. http://www.consumersunion.org/pub/core_food_safety/002 272.html Accessed May 24, 2010.

[198] "rBGH: How Artificial Hormones Damage the Dairy Industry and Endanger Public Health." Food and Water Watch. . http://www.foodandwaterwatch.org/food/report/rbgh-how-artificial-hormones-damage-the-dairy-industry-and-endanger-public-health-2/rbgh-how-artificial-hormones-damage-the-dairy-industry-and-endanger-public-health-1/ Accessed May 24, 2010.

[199] Hansen, Michael Ph.D., Halloran, Jean M., Groth, Edward III, Ph.D., Lefferts, Lisa Y. "Potential Public Health Impacts Of The Use Of Recombinant Bovine Somatropin In Dairy Production." Consumersunion.org. September 1997. http://www.consumersunion.org/pub/core_food_safety/002 272.html Accessed May 24, 2010.

Laboratory experiments demonstrate that IGF's are able to stimulate the growth of a wide variety of cancer cells and to suppress apoptosis. In addition to their direct effects on cancer cells, IGF's also interact synergistically with other mitogenic molecules and counteract antiproliferative molecules that are involved in cancer development and progression. Findings of experimental studies are supported by the observations of epidemiologic studies, which have shown that elevated levels of IGF-1 in the circulation are associated with increased risk for several common cancers.[200]

The National Institute of Health (NIH) conference discussion entitled "Insulin-like Growth Factors and Cancer," which was published in the *Annals of Internal Medicine* in 1995, explains the connection a bit further. Here it is stated:

As could be predicted from the importance of IGF's, their binding proteins, and their receptors in normal cellular growth and development, it has become apparent over the past few years that IGF's are important mitogens in many types of malignancies. Although these conclusions were initially derived from in vitro studies, IGF's may enhance in vivo tumor cell formations, growth, and even metastasis. Insulin-like Growth Factors may reach tumors from the circulation (endocrine) or as a result of local production by the tumor itself (autocrine) or by adjacent stromal tissue (paracrine). Tumors also express many of the IGF-binding proteins, which modulate IGF action, and IGF receptors, which mediate the effects of IGF's on tumors. We highlight

[200] Rohan, Thomas, Yu, Herbert. "Role of the Insulin-like Growth Factor Family in Cancer Development and Progression." Journal of the National Cancer Institute. September 20, 2000. 92 (18). 1472-1489. http://www.ncbi.nlm.nih.gov/pubmed/10995803 Accessed May 24, 2010.

important aspects of IGF's in normal cell growth and their role in certain malignancies.[201]

Essentially, the evidence is becoming clearer and clearer that IGF's (IGF-1, IGF-2, insulin) play an important role in the development and spread of many different forms of cancers.[202]

In relation to breast, colon, and prostate cancer, it is well known that increased levels of estrogen can be a major cause. This is the reason why the improper and overuse of soy products is such a problem at this time and is implicated in the increase in these forms of cancers as well as the physical "feminizing" of young men and the early development of young girls. While neither increased soy nor increased IGF-1 is likely the sole cause of these cancers, they are most definitely a major factor and they apparently work in tandem with one another. Much of the scientific evidence shows that IGF-1 encourages the proliferation of excess estrogen while at the same time encouraging tumor growth. Dr. LeRoith addresses this at the same NIH conference listed above when he says:

> Many cancers, especially those developing in the post-menopausal period, express estrogen and progesterone receptors. . . . . . In addition to classic hormones, several

---

[201] LeRoith, Derek; Baserga, Renato; Helman, Lee; Roberts, Charles T. "Insulin-like Growth Factors and Cancer." Annals of Internal Medicine. January 1, 1995. Vol. 122. No.1. Pp. 54-59. http://www.annals.org/content/122/1/54.full Accessed May 24, 2010.
[202] Hansen, Michael Ph.D., Halloran, Jean M., Groth, Edward III, Ph.D., Lefferts, Lisa Y. "Potential Public Health Impacts Of The Use Of Recombinant Bovine Somatropin In Dairy Production." ConsumersUnion.org. September 1997. http://www.consumersunion.org/pub/core_food_safety/002 272.html Accessed May 24, 2010.

growth factors including transforming growth factors, epidermal growth factors, and IGF's, have been shown to be involved in breast cancer. . . . . . . Estrogen receptor-positive tumors will thus respond to antiestrogens such as tamoxifen, which is widely used clinically. Initially, it was thought to affect cancer cells primarily by blocking the activation of estrogen receptors; it has also been shown, however, to decrease circulating IGF-1 levels in women with breast cancer and may thus prove effective in treating both estrogen receptor-positive and estrogen receptor-negative cancers. Another agent that inhibits the proliferation of breast cancer cells is retinoic acid and its derivatives. . . . . . . The mechanism by which retinoids affect the IGF-induced growth of breast cancer cells seems to involve modulation of local IGF-binding protein production; specifically, retinoic acid may also reduce circulating IGF-1 levels and may thus affect tumor growth in vivo by more than one mechanism. The above data suggest that IGF's are likely to be involved in breast cancer at the level of tumor growth and perhaps at the level of initial development and later metastases. Ongoing studies involve attempts to interfere with the IGF system to develop additional therapeutic regimens.[203]

In effect, Dr. LeRoith is showing that IGF-1 can play a major role in breast cancer due to the fact that breast cancer cells react quite strongly in its' presence. This is also evidenced by the fact that many doctors have recognized this connection and are trying to treat breast cancer through reducing and manipulating IGF levels. But if IGF levels do not cause cancer directly, they still can play a major role in promoting

---

[203] LeRoith, Derek; Baserga, Renato; Helman, Lee; Roberts, Charles T. "Insulin-like Growth Factors and Cancer." Annals of Internal Medicine. January 1, 1995. Vol. 122. No.1. Pp. 54-59. http://www.annals.org/content/122/1/54.full Accessed May 24, 2010.

its' growth through increase in estrogen. This applies to colon and prostate cancer as well.

With respect to colon cancer, for instance, it has been shown that IGF-1 receptors are found throughout the intestines with most of those receptors existing in the colon. In a study published in the British Journal of Cancer, it was found that 5 out of the 8 human colorectal cancer cell lines responded to IGF-1. Indeed, IGF-1 increased growth in the cancerous cells by as much as 3-fold.[204] Furthermore, past studies have offered evidence which may suggest that colon carcinoma tumors produce IGF-1 on their own for the purposes of stimulating their own growth.[205] When taken together, this evidence helps to understand how increased levels of IGF-1 contribute to colon cancer.

However, colon, breast, and prostate cancers are not the only diseases associated with IGF-1. Osteosarcoma, a type of bone cancer, as well as lung cancer has been linked to IGF-1. In the same NIH conference listed above, Dr. Lee Helman states,

Osteosarcoma is the most common bone tumor in children,

---

[204] Lahm, H; Suardet, L; Laurent, PL; Fischer, JR; Ceyhan, A; Givel, JC; Odartchenko, N. "Growth regulation and co-stimulation of human colorectal cancer cell lines by insulin-like growth factor I, II and transforming growth factor." British Journal of Cancer, 65, 341-346. 1992. http://www.ncbi.nlm.nih.gov/pubmed/1558785 Accessed May 24, 2010.

[205] Tricoli, James V; Rall, Leslie B; Karakousis, Constantine P; Herrera, Lemuel; Petrelli, Nicholas J; Bell, Graeme I; Shows, Thomas B. "Enhanced Levels of Insulin-like Growth Factor Messenger RNA in Human Colon Carcinomas and Liposarcomas." Cancer Research 46, 6169-6173, December 1986. http://cancerres.aacrjournals.org/cgi/content/abstract/46/12 Part 1/6169 Accessed May 24, 2010.

usually occurring during the adolescent growth spurt at sites of rapid bone growth. Because IGF-1 was initially described as the factor produced in the liver that directly mediated the effect of growth hormone on skeletal growth, there has been interest in a potential role for IGF-1 in the pathogenesis of osteosarcoma. Support for a role for IGF-1 in osteosarcoma growth comes from data showing that IGF-1 is a potent mitogen for human osteogenic sarcoma cells. Further, several reports have shown that a rat chondrosarcoma (a closely related tumor) and a murine osteosarcoma are growth-inhibited in animals that have had hypophysectomy, presumably through the inhibition of the growth hormone – IGF axis. . . . . . It therefore appears that the growth hormone - IGF-1 axis may play a role in the unregulated proliferation of osteosarcoma tumor cells and that blocking of this axis using somatostatin analogs that reduce the circulating levels of growth hormone and IGF-1 may have therapeutic potential.[206]

IGF-1 is also known to play a role in lung development and for that reason has been implicated as a cause in some forms of lung cancer. Another study published in the British Journal of Cancer in 1992 makes this clear. It says,

> Thus IGF's seem to be important in lung development and are also implicated in growth regulation of lung tumors. Primary lung tumors possess IGF-1 binding sites as shown by autoradiography, with the highest density of receptors in squamous cancers and small cell lung cancer. . . . . Thus there is good evidence that lung cancer cells produce IGF-1 and IGF

---

[206] LeRoith, Derek; Baserga, Renato; Helman, Lee; Roberts, Charles T. "Insulin-like Growth Factors and Cancer." Annals of Internal Medicine. January 1, 1995. Vol. 122. No.1. Pp. 54-59.

BP's, express IGF binding sites and exhibit a mitogenic
response to exogenous IGF-1, suggesting that IGF-1 can
function as an autocrine growth factor for lung cancer. [207]

Indeed, with the evidence cited above, and with no lack of scientific
studies which corroborate the link between IGF-1 and cancer, there is
no logical reason as to why anyone would consume or approve a
product like rBGH in dairy milk.

There is yet one more concern regarding the addition of rBGH
to dairy cows that harkens back to the issue of mastitis. Besides the
immense discomfort caused to the animals, mastitis requires treatment
with antibiotics which has been linked to the development of antibiotic-
resistant bacteria capable of infecting humans.[208] Because the types of
antibiotics used in the animals are often the same kind used in humans
(such as penicillin, ampicillin, and doxycycline[209]), bacteria that become
resistant to these medicines in cows are also resistant to them in
humans if they are transmitted. Indeed, such transmission is quite
possible and likely as these bacteria can be transmitted through the
water and air, through the meat we consume, and by flies. This should
be especially alarming considering the recent concern over antibiotic

---

[207] McCauley, V.M. "Insulin-like growth factors and cancer."
British Journal of Cancer 65, 311-320. 1992.
http://www.ncbi.nlm.nih.gov/pmc/articles/PMC1977607/
Accessed May 24, 2010.
[208] "Recombinant Bovine Growth Hormone: FDA Approval
Should Be Withheld Until the Mastitis Issue Is Resolved." U.S.
GAO, August 6, 1992. http://www.gao.gov/products/PEMD-
92-26 Accessed May 24, 2010.
[209] Hoebben, D. Burvenich, C. Heyneman, R. "Antibiotics
Commonly Used To Treat Mastitis and Respiratory Burst of
Bovine Polymorphonuclear Leukocytes." Journal of Dairy
Science, 81: 403 – 410. 1998.
http://jds.fass.org/cgi/reprint/81/2/403.pdf Accessed May
24, 2010.

resistance voiced even by organizations such as the CDC. [210]

Another concern is that residues of these antibiotics remain in the milk of dairy cows and meat of beef herds.[211] The introduction of antibiotics into a food animals' system for the treatment of a disease such as mastitis is bad enough. However, that is not the only application that they are used for. It is estimated that close to 70% of all antimicrobial use, for any purpose, is given to animals that are not even sick.[212] In these instances, the antibiotics are used as a growth stimulant or as a preventative measure to keep them from becoming ill.[213] This figure does not include antibiotics used to treat mastitis or some other sickness. When one factors in the amount of antibiotics used to treat an

---

[210] "rBGH:How Artificial Hormones Damage the Dairy Industry and And Endanger Public Health." Foodandwaterwatch.org. June, 2009. http://www.foodandwaterwatch.org/food/report/rbgh-how-artificial-hormones-damage-the-dairy-industry-and-endanger-public-health-2/rbgh-how-artificial-hormones-damage-the-dairy-industry-and-endanger-public-health-1/ Accessed May 24, 2010.

[211] Smith, David L., Harris, Anthony D., Johnson, Judith A., Silbergeld, Ellen K., Morris, Glen Jr., "Animal antibiotic use has an early but important impact on the emergence of antibiotic resistance in human commensal bacteria." Proceedings of the National Academy of Sciences, Vol. 99. No. 9, April 30, 2002.

[212] Mellon, Margaret, Benbrook, Charles and Benbrook, Karen. "Hogging It: Estimates of Antimicrobial Abuse in Livestock." Union of Concerned Scientists. January 2001.

[213] "rBGH: How Artificial Hormones Damage the Dairy Industry and Endanger Public Health." Foodandwaterwatch.org. Food and Water Watch. June, 2009. http://www.foodandwaterwatch.org/food/report/rbgh-how-artificial-hormones-damage-the-dairy-industry-and-endanger-public-health-2/rbgh-how-artificial-hormones-damage-the-dairy-industry-and-endanger-public-health-1/ Accessed May 24, 2010.

actual illness, the percentage comes closer to 80%.[214] This is one of the main reasons the Government Accountability Office (GAO) recommended that the FDA withhold approval of rBGH. Yet although growth issues as well as antibiotic resistance are major issues, the possibility of the resulting under-nutrition is rarely talked about. The fact is that even the medical applications of antibiotics have a detrimental effect on the digestive system. These medications do not discriminate against which bacteria they attack and destroy. Therefore, good, helpful bacteria needed for the process of digestion is killed alongside that which is causing the sickness. The digestive system is then not able to break down and absorb the food as well as it once could, thus resulting in under-nutrition and a host of subsequent health problems. It stands to reason then that the addition of antibiotics to our food and milk would increase the amount of health promoting bacteria being destroyed. The unbelievable amount of antibiotics used in food animals can quite possibly be linked to many apparently "unrelated" health problems that are themselves a result of lack of nutrition.

The FDA's position regarding rBGH is one of open denial. In their response to a citizen petition against rBGH, they state "FDA has previously maintained and continues to maintain that levels of IGF-1 in milk, whether or not from rBGH supplemented cows, are not significant when evaluated against levels of IGF-1 endogenously produced and present in humans."[215] As discussed earlier, this statement alone flies in

---

[214] Mellon, Margaret, Benbrook, Charles and Benbrook, Karen. "Hogging It: Estimates of Antimicrobial Abuse in Livestock." Union of Concerned Scientists. January 2001. http://www.ucsusa.org/food_and_agriculture/science_and_i mpacts/impacts_industrial_agriculture/hogging-it-estimates-of.html Accessed May 17, 2010.
[215] "FDA Responds to Citizen Petition on BST." Food and Drug Administration. April 21, 2000.

the face of sound science proving otherwise. But that has never stopped the FDA before and it is not likely to stop it now. For instance, when the question of increased cases of mastitis first arose the FDA refused to acknowledge that rBGH caused an increase in the infection.[216] However, even the GAO couldn't ignore that it was a major contributing factor and suggested that the FDA withhold its' approval of rBGH until the question was resolved.[217] Yet even as late as 1993 the FDA maintained that there was no increase in mastitis due to rBGH.[218] However, as a result of the GAO recommendation, the FDA was forced to revise its' stance. After further review by the FDA Veterinary Medicine Advisory Committee, the FDA had to admit that the rate of mastitis was significantly higher with the treatment of rBGH. Yet the FDA, in the face of all the evidence available to themselves and the public, still refused to admit that there were any health risks to humans from the use of the

---

http://www.fda.gov/AnimalVeterinary/NewsEvents/CVMUpdates/ucm130325.htm Accessed May 24, 2010.

[216] "rBGH:How Artificial Hormones Damage the Dairy Industry and And Endanger Public Health." Foodandwaterwatch.org. June, 2009. http://www.foodandwaterwatch.org/food/report/rbgh-how-artificial-hormones-damage-the-dairy-industry-and-endanger-public-health-2/rbgh-how-artificial-hormones-damage-the-dairy-industry-and-endanger-public-health-1/ Accessed May 24, 2010.

[217] "Recombinant Bovine Growth Hormone: FDA Approval Should Be Withheld Until the Mastitis Issue Is Resolved." U.S. GAO, August 6, 1992. http://www.gao.gov/products/PEMD-92-26 Accessed May 24, 2010.

[218] "rBGH:How Artificial Hormones Damage the Dairy Industry and And Endanger Public Health." Foodandwaterwatch.org. June, 2009. http://www.foodandwaterwatch.org/food/report/rbgh-how-artificial-hormones-damage-the-dairy-industry-and-endanger-public-health-2/rbgh-how-artificial-hormones-damage-the-dairy-industry-and-endanger-public-health-1/ Accessed May 24, 2010.

hormone, IGF-1, or the use of antibiotics stemming from the higher levels of infection and preventive measures. In fact, when responding to a study that demonstrated a possible link between IGF-1 and prostate cancer the FDA, while offering no supporting evidence, simply claims that "Although the mechanism responsible for induction of cancer has not been characterized fully, it is clear that IGF-1 is not the causative agent."[219] Likewise, when addressing the concern over whether or not IGF-1 levels are related to breast cancer the FDA responds that it has found no definitive evidence of any direct link between the two and "Furthermore, FDA has been advised that there is no substantive evidence that IGF-1 causes normal breast cells to become cancerous."[220] This advice was apparently extracted from a letter from Dr. Dennis M. Bier to David Kessler, then Commissioner of the FDA. However, beyond this letter, no evidence is referenced.[221]

Another issue related to the FDA's questionable approval of rBGH is that of the 90-day rat study that has been a central focus of much debate. This 1989 study was conducted by Monsanto itself, the producer of rBGH, and consisted of orally treating rats rBGH and was submitted to the FDA in order to fulfill FDA requirements that all relevant safety information be included in the "sponsor's" application. [222] It should be mentioned that the FDA actually stated that rBGH posed no adverse health risks in 1985 yet it did not complete the official human health study until 1989. The genetically modified hormone was not approved for commercial sale and usage until 1993, however the

---

[219] "Report on the Food and Drug Administration's Review of the Safety of Recombinant Bovine Somatropin." Food and Drug Administration. April 23, 2009. http://www.fda.gov/AnimalVeterinary/SafetyHealth/Product SafetyInformation/ucm130321.htm Accessed May 24, 2010.
[220] Ibid.
[221] Ibid.
[222] Ibid.

FDA allowed for it to be sold and consumed in milk while the "commercial investigation" took place.[223] So the FDA had already claimed that rBGH posed no health risks to humans three years before their official study was concluded. Apparently the agency's mind was made up before the study ever began. Likewise, if the FDA were living up to its' stated goals, it makes no sense to allow a product to be sold and consumed while there is an ongoing investigation into that products' safety. However, the FDA has become so compromised in so many ways that this should come as no surprise.

The FDA effectively kept silent about the red flags popping up in the 90-day rat study mentioned above. After an investigation conducted by Health Canada (the Canadian version of the FDA), it was discovered that the FDA and Monsanto mislead the public on the results of the study. Health Canada determined that the results of the study showed that 20 to 30 percent of the rats in the high dose test group produced antibody responses to rBGH as well as the development of cysts on the thyroid in some of the males. This was the same study made available to the FDA and all the while the agency maintained that there were "no toxicologically significant changes."[224] This was not the view of Health

---

[223] "rBGH:How Artificial Hormones Damage the Dairy Industry and And Endanger Public Health." Foodandwaterwatch.org. June, 2009.
http://www.foodandwaterwatch.org/food/report/rbgh-how-artificial-hormones-damage-the-dairy-industry-and-endanger-public-health-2/rbgh-how-artificial-hormones-damage-the-dairy-industry-and-endanger-public-health-1/ Accessed May 24, 2010.
[224] "Statement of Michael Hansen, Ph.D., Research Associate Consumer Policy Insititue, Consumers Union On FDA's Safety Assessment of Recombinant Bovine Growth Hormone December 15, 1998."
http://www.cosumersunion.org/pub/1998/12/002269print.html

Canada and many others who became aware of this information. The development of thyroid cysts is significant. However, the antibody response to rBGH is even more serious as it suggests that the hormone is being absorbed into the bloodstream. These findings, when first presented to the FDA should have launched a complete review of the effects on human health, particularly on the immune system and carcinogenic effects.[225] Of course, more thorough and unbiased science should have also occurred long before this study but, true to form, it didn't.

Yet even if the science were to show that there were no real correlation between rBGH and antibody response or thyroid cyst development, there are still very real concerns regarding it. As was demonstrated earlier, IGF-1 is one of the main factors in adverse health effects related to rBGH. The FDA continues to reject the idea that IGF-1 survives digestion and is absorbed into the blood stream causing any health problems. Much of this position comes from open denial. For the most part, the agency simply stating that they have reviewed the science and have come to the conclusion that there is no legitimate basis for concern. But it must be pointed out that many of the studies that the FDA uses to back itself up, on the rare occasion that it decides to do so, are studies conducted by the company sponsoring the drug in question. Indeed, there were two studies conducted by Monsanto and Elanco that concluded that IGF-1 does not survive digestion. However, as some scientists have pointed out, there are problems with that assessment. As the scientific team for Consumers' Union state,

> Those studies are not definitive because rats were given free
> IGF-1, without casein or other protective proteins. Thus one
> would not expect the IGF-1 to survive digestion in these
> studies. Even so, a careful review of the Monsanto study

---

[225] Ibid.

suggested that some small amount of the IGF-1 administered in this study survived digestion and affected the rats' growth rate.[226]

Although not for lack of trying, the FDA would be hard pressed to be further from the mark when the agency suggests that rBGH or IGF-1 poses no significant risks of adverse health effects in humans. Indeed, the science says something much different as even free IGF-1, in small amounts, did survive digestion.

When consumers learned that rBGH was being included in their dairy products and subsequently learned of the dangers, there was a backlash of the most effective kind. The public simply began to change where they spent their money and avoided products that contained rBGH. Many companies began to label their products as rBGH free and consequently saw higher consumption than those who used the hormone. This created a snowball effect and even major companies like Hood, Dannon, Yoplait, Kroger, and even Wal-Mart abandoned the use of rBGH milk in most of their dairy products. Logically, the removal of rBGH most likely did not stem from the direction of any moral compass but from the motivation of profit. Consumers refused to buy rBGH so these businesses had little choice but to remove it. [227]

---

[226] Hansen, Michael Ph.D., Halloran, Jean M., Groth, Edward III, Ph.D., Lefferts, Lisa Y. "Potential Public Health Impacts Of The Use Of Recombinant Bovine Somatropin In Dairy Production." September 1997.

[227] "rBGH:How Artificial Hormones Damage the Dairy Industry and And Endanger Public Health." Foodandwaterwatch.org. June, 2009. http://www.foodandwaterwatch.org/food/report/rbgh-how-artificial-hormones-damage-the-dairy-industry-and-endanger-public-health-2/rbgh-how-artificial-hormones-damage-the-dairy-industry-and-endanger-public-health-1/ Accessed May 24, 2010.

As a result, Monsanto did its' best to convince regulatory agencies such as the FDA and the FTC to make it illegal for any dairy to make the claim that its' products were rBGH-free.[228] While these agencies did not fully bend to Monsanto's request, the FDA did devise a policy by which all claims of rBGH-free milk were deemed misleading and, if made, were to be accompanied by a disclaimer that reads "No significant difference has been shown between milk derived from rBST-treated and non rBST-treated cows."[229] Almost immediately after the FDA released the document stating its' new policy, Monsanto filed suit against two dairy farms that had labeled their milk as "rBGH-free." The FDA rushed to the aid of companies like Monsanto and sent warning letters to several other dairies telling them that they were in violation of the Food Drug and Cosmetic Act for misbranding. Monsanto continued to lobby the FDA and FTC arguing that allowing the appearance of any rBGH related labeling on milk was unfairly damaging its' business. [230]

---

[228] Smith, Jeffrey. "You're Appointing Who? Please Obama, Say It's Not So!" July 23, 2009. http://www.huffingtonpost.com/jeffrey-smith/youre-appointing-who-plea_b_243810.html Accessed May 24, 2010.

[229] "Voluntary Labeling of Milk and Milk Products From Cows That Have Not Been Treated With Recombinant Bovine Somatotropin." Federal Register, 59 FR 6279, February 10, 1994. http://www.fda.gov/Food/GuidanceComplianceRegulatoryInformation/GuidanceDocuments/FoodLabelingNutrition/ucm059036.htm Accessed May 24, 2010.

[230] "rBGH:How Artificial Hormones Damage the Dairy Industry and And Endanger Public Health." Foodandwaterwatch.org. June, 2009. http://www.foodandwaterwatch.org/food/report/rbgh-how-artificial-hormones-damage-the-dairy-industry-and-endanger-public-health-2/rbgh-how-artificial-hormones-

When these attempts proved unsuccessful, the companies changed their tactics and moved to the state level. The most widely publicized battleground was in the state of Pennsylvania. Here they found an ally in Dennis Wolff, the state Secretary of Agriculture. Wolff took it upon himself to ban all labeling of dairy products that were free of rBGH such as "hormone-free," "rBGH-free," or "rBST-free." [231] His argument was that since the FDA claimed they could find no difference between non-rBGH treated milk and milk that was treated with the hormone, the marketing of dairy products as "rBGH-free" is false and misleading.[232] Although only implemented at the state level, this would have had nationwide repercussions. Because it would be too confusing and costly for many dairy producers to create separate packaging for only one state, this would effectively remove the non-rBGH label from the all the national and Pennsylvanian brands.[233] After Wolff's behavior became widely known, public outcry forced Pennsylvania Governor Ed

damage-the-dairy-industry-and-endanger-public-health-1/ Accessed May 24, 2010.

[231] Gutierrez, David. "Consumer Outrage May Reverse Pennsylvania's rBGH-Free Dairy Label Censorship Sham." Naturalnews.com.
http://www.naturalnews.com/023575.html Accessed May 24, 2010.

[232] "rBGH:How Artificial Hormones Damage the Dairy Industry and And Endanger Public Health." Foodandwaterwatch.org. June, 2009.
http://www.foodandwaterwatch.org/food/report/rbgh-how-artificial-hormones-damage-the-dairy-industry-and-endanger-public-health-2/rbgh-how-artificial-hormones-damage-the-dairy-industry-and-endanger-public-health-1/ Accessed May 24, 2010.

[233] Smith, Jeffrey. "You're Appointing Who? Please Obama, Say It's Not So!" July 23, 2009.
http://www.huffingtonpost.com/jeffrey-smith/youre-appointing-who-plea_b_243810.html Accessed May 24, 2010.

Rendell to put a halt to the destruction of the 1st Amendment and the right of the consumer to know what he/she is purchasing. Although the initial attack on free speech was halted, Rendell supported the position that any rBGH-free claims must be accompanied by the FDA disclaimer.

Illinois was actually the first state to place a ban on rBGH-free labeling.[234] The ice cream giant Ben & Jerry's, Stoneyfield Farm, and Organic Valley Farms all challenged the law by filing a lawsuit against the Illinois Department of Public Health in a US District Court. However, after a settlement, these companies could only label their products with a statement that says "We oppose rBGH. The family farmers who supply our milk pledge not to treat their cows with rBGH."[235] This statement must also be accompanied by the FDA disclaimer.[236] Also, when the product includes any ingredients other than milk, such as dried milk or milk chocolate, the label must include another statement that says, "Not all suppliers of our other ingredients can promise that the milk they use comes from untreated cows."[237]

On a state level the battle is raging. Pennsylvania and Illinois are not the only states to adopt or at least attempt to adopt draconian and

---

[234] "rBGH:How Artificial Hormones Damage the Dairy Industry and And Endanger Public Health." Foodandwaterwatch.org. June, 2009. http://www.foodandwaterwatch.org/food/report/rbgh-how-artificial-hormones-damage-the-dairy-industry-and-endanger-public-health-2/rbgh-how-artificial-hormones-damage-the-dairy-industry-and-endanger-public-health-1/ Accessed May 24, 2010.

[235] "Settlement Protects Illinois Consumers From Misleading Food Labels," Illinois Department of Health News Release. August 14, 1997. http://www.idph.state.il.us/public/press97/ben.htm

[236] Ibid.

[237] Ibid.

unconstitutional laws protecting giant corporations and damaging public health. Some states have adopted laws based on the FDA's own guidelines which are tyrannical enough. Utah, for example has done just that. However, other states such as Ohio take the guidelines further. The law in Ohio now dictates the size, type, and location of the FDA disclaimer. States like Pennsylvania (mentioned earlier), Missouri, and Indiana have attempted to go even further and ban rBGH labeling altogether.[238] Fortunately, due to public outcry, the legislation in all three states has not passed. Yet the battle is not over. States all over the country are introducing legislation aimed at protecting large agri-business such as Monsanto. Kansas is the most recent state to do so, and it is almost certain that other states will follow.[239]

The approval of rBGH was also another prime example of the revolving door between Monsanto, Big Pharma, and the FDA. The obvious conflict of interest among many of the FDA's employees who

---

[238] "rBGH:How Artificial Hormones Damage the Dairy Industry and And Endanger Public Health." Foodandwaterwatch.org. June, 2009.
http://www.foodandwaterwatch.org/food/report/rbgh-how-artificial-hormones-damage-the-dairy-industry-and-endanger-public-health-2/rbgh-how-artificial-hormones-damage-the-dairy-industry-and-endanger-public-health-1/
See Also,
Rathke, Lisa. "Ben & Jerry's Opposes Monsanto's Move in Several States to Ban rBGH-Free Labels." Associated Press, February 5, 2008. Reprinted by Organic Consumer's Association.
http://www.organicconsumers.org/articles/article_10095.cfm
[239] Morris, Owen. "New Kansas Bill Restricts rBGH Labeling." The Pitch. 3/23/09. Reprinted by Organic Consumers Association.
http://www.organicconsumers.org/articles/article_17366.cfm Accessed May 24, 2010.

were involved in the approval process actually prompted a GAO investigation in 1994. One of the employees, Michael Taylor, began his career in 1976 with the FDA as an attorney. In 1981, he left the agency and took up a position with the law firm King & Spalding where one of his clients was Monsanto.[240] Over his approximately seven years as a lawyer for the corporation, it was found that he had drafted a memo as to the constitutionality of the states' ability to create laws regarding labeling of rBGH. This memo was a part of what was essentially an internal discussion as to whether or not Monsanto could sue states or companies that wished to label their products as free of rBGH.[241] Later, the issue would arise in reality when many businesses decided to do just that. In the end, Taylor was hired was hired by Monsanto through King and Spalding to draft a plan that he would later be integral in implementing as an employee of the FDA. It is also noteworthy that as of July 2009, Taylor was appointed by the Obama administration to the position of senior advisor to the commissioner of the FDA. Riddled with ties to Monsanto, one of the major players in the approval of rBGH is now the American food safety czar.[242]

Margaret Miller was a former employee of Monsanto who, during the course of her employment, was responsible for coordinating animal safety studies regarding rBGH. In 1989 she left her job at Monsanto and went directly to the FDA where she was promoted to the position of director of the toxicology and environmental sciences

---

[240] Ferrara, Jennifer. "Revolving Doors: Monsanto and the Regulators." The Ecologist, Vol. 28, No. 5, September/October 1998.

[241] Smith, Jeffrey. "You're Appointing Who? Please Obama, Say It's Not So!" July 23, 2009. http://www.huffingtonpost.com/jeffrey-smith/youre-appointing-who-plea_b_243810.html Accessed May 24, 2010.

[242] Ibid.

division. This was the division that was directly responsible for the technical review of the safety of rBGH. [243]

Dr. Suzanne Sechen was also investigated by the GAO. Sechen performed a substantial amount of work on rBGH as well as publishing articles on the hormone in outside journals that were based on her research[244] at Cornell University where she performed several rBGH related studies supported by Monsanto's funding. At Cornell, Sechen's faculty advisor was a consultant for Monsanto and much of the research she conducted was a result of an agreement between Monsanto and her advisor.[245] Another example of welfare science, a condition that plagues academia and universities the world over, Sechen received her funding from a large corporation which no doubt would have cut off the money had her conclusions not been to their satisfaction. While at the FDA Sechen was also responsible for evaluating some of the same articles she had published as a Monsanto funded researcher at Cornell.[246]

---

[243] "rBGH:How Artificial Hormones Damage the Dairy Industry and And Endanger Public Health." Foodandwaterwatch.org. June, 2009.
http://www.foodandwaterwatch.org/food/report/rbgh-how-artificial-hormones-damage-the-dairy-industry-and-endanger-public-health-2/rbgh-how-artificial-hormones-damage-the-dairy-industry-and-endanger-public-health-1/

[244] "Ibid.

[245] Ferrara, Jennifer. "Revolving Doors: Monsanto and the Regulators." The Ecologist, Vol. 28, No. 5, September/October 1998.

[246] "rBGH:How Artificial Hormones Damage the Dairy Industry and And Endanger Public Health." Foodandwaterwatch.org. June, 2009.
http://www.foodandwaterwatch.org/food/report/rbgh-how-artificial-hormones-damage-the-dairy-industry-and-endanger-public-health-2/rbgh-how-artificial-hormones-damage-the-dairy-industry-and-endanger-public-health-1/

Yet despite the criminal behavior of regulatory agencies regarding the hormone in the United States as well as the acceptance of so many other dangerous substances, there has been some major success in the battle against rBGH. Most notably, in relation to this book, is the fact that Codex Alimentarius has surprisingly refused to approve the growth hormone for use. Understanding that Codex obviously does not have the consumers' best interest at heart, it is important to understand what might be the causes for it's' rejection of rBGH. Undoubtedly, it was not the overwhelming scientific evidence demonstrating rBGH to be a harmful substance that caused the Commission not to approve it. As it has been already been shown in regards to nutrients, food irradiation, and toxic chemicals, overwhelming scientific evidence tends not to sway Codex in the slightest. Yet aside from science, there were conditions surrounding the rBGH debate that made it virtually impossible to approve the substance and maintain its role as the international food regulating agency of the global government structure.

First, the fact that Canada,[247] the European Union,[248] Australia, New Zealand, and Japan[249] all banned the use of rBGH in dairy products

---

[247] "Health Canada rejects bovine growth hormone in Canada," Health Canada. January 14, 1999. http://www.hc-sc.gc.ca/index-eng.php

[248] "rBGH:How Artificial Hormones Damage the Dairy Industry and And Endanger Public Health." Foodandwaterwatch.org. June, 2009. http://www.foodandwaterwatch.org/food/report/rbgh-how-artificial-hormones-damage-the-dairy-industry-and-endanger-public-health-2/rbgh-how-artificial-hormones-damage-the-dairy-industry-and-endanger-public-health-1/

[249] "Chipotle Mexican Grill is Nation's First Chain to go Entirely rBGH-Free," Chipotle Mexican Grill, November 5,

created a major problem for the Codex Alimentarius Commission. Although Codex could have easily accepted the hormone as safe, then enforced that decision through the WTO, this would have required sanctions on virtually the entire developed world with the exception of the United States. With such a consensus on the lack of safety of rBGH, it is likely that the decision to enforce a decision to approve the hormone through the WTO would provoke an international revolt that would not only have damaged the credibility of Codex, but also its' ability to act as an arm of governance and regulation. Such an open act of favoritism, in the face of sound science, would potentially set off a chain reaction of refusal to accept any of Codex's recommendations.

However, the refusal to accept rBGH in dairy milk did not necessarily come as a result of benevolent governments concerned about the welfare of it's' citizens. It was largely a result of public outcry when rBGH was introduced on a mass scale as well as government regulatory agencies that were slightly less corrupted than the American FDA. As has been mentioned earlier, in the United States consumers initially made a serious stand against the hormone by one of the most effective means of protest ever engaged in – they changed the way they shopped and actively sought out milk that had not been produced using rBGH. Although facing attempts by many corrupt state regulatory agencies to prevent dairies from labeling their milk as rBGH-free, Americans have made the hormone unprofitable enough that Monsanto has actually decided to sell the patented technology to another international corporation, Eli Lilli.[250]

2007. Organic Consumers Association, http://www.organicconsumers.org/articles/article_8847.cfm
[250] "rBGH:How Artificial Hormones Damage the Dairy Industry and And Endanger Public Health." Foodandwaterwatch.org. June, 2009. http://www.foodandwaterwatch.org/food/report/rbgh-how-artificial-hormones-damage-the-dairy-industry-and-

In 1998, the FAO/WHO Joint Expert Committees on Food Additives (JECFA) released its' report which gave rBGH a clean bill of health, claiming no adverse health effects in humans or animals.[251] Another compromised international agency, the JECFA is staffed more by regulatory agency bureaucrats and industry consultants than actual scientists.[252] These individuals are unelected and unaccountable to the people who face the repercussions of their decisions and their obvious conflicts of interest are rarely if ever exposed in the mainstream media. For instance, one of the individuals who played a major role in the attempted approval of rBGH by Codex Alimentarius, Dr. Stephen Sundloff, in addition to his position in the JECFA Committee was also the FDA's Director for Veterinary Medicine. Interestingly enough, Dr. Sundloff was also the chairman of the Codex Committee on Residues of Veterinary Drugs in Foods when the JECFA Committee sent their report to Codex.[253] Not surprisingly, the JECFA report was virtually rubber stamped in the Codex Commission on Residues of Veterinary Drugs in Foods and sent straight to the parent Codex Commission. Although rBGH was on the fast track to becoming approved by Codex, something unexpected occurred when Health Canada issued a "notice of non-compliance," and banned the future sale of rBGH.[254] At the same time, the European Commission[255] had formed two independent committees

---

endanger-public-health-2/rbgh-how-artificial-hormones-damage-the-dairy-industry-and-endanger-public-health-1/

[251] "Monsanto's Genetically Modified Milk Ruled Unsafe By The United Nations," PR Newswire. August 18, 1999. Archived on GENET-News as "1-Hormones: Codex Alimentarius voted in favor for EU ban on rBST." http://www.gene.ch/genet/1999/Aug/msg00054.html

[252] Ibid.

[253] Ibid.

[254] Ibid.

[255] The European Union was known as the European Commission in the transition period to a bloc state.

to study the veterinary and public health effects which both confirmed and expanded the Canadian studies. The European Commission subsequently banned the sale of rBGH as well.[256] Faced with several nations' refusal to accept rBGH, outspoken scientists who balked at the official company line, an rBGH-free advocacy groups, the Codex Alimentarius Commission had little choice but to decline granting approval for rBGH.[257] Indeed, doing so might have pulled the curtain back a little too far, allowing the public to catch a glimpse behind Codex's' cover of domestic laws and regulation.

Although the decision not to approve rBGH is certainly a welcome one and a positive demonstration of the power that the consumer has to affect change, there is plenty of bad news as well. The fact is that all of these small victories could be reversed in the future if consumer vigilance is not maintained. A brief exploration of just some of the existing obstacles in relation to rBGH and Codex Alimentarius is needed highlight this situation.

First, although Codex has not approved rBGH as safe, it should be noted that the organization has not declared it unsafe either. The official stance of Codex is that it will not, at this time, create a draft MRL for rBGH and that the discussion of its approval for safety would be shelved until further scientific study was conducted.[258] But this is

---

[256] "Monsanto's Genetically Modified Milk Ruled Unsafe By The United Nations," PR Newswire. August 18, 1999. Archived on GENET-News as "1-Hormones: Codex Alimentarius voted in favor for EU ban on rBST."
http://www.gene.ch/genet/1999/Aug/msg00054.html
[257] Ibid.
[258] "Report of Codex Alimentarius Commission: 23rd Session, FAO Headquarters, Rome, June 28-July 3, 1999. P. 13-14.
www.codexalimentarius.net/download/report/518/Al99_37e.pdf Accessed May 24, 2010.

problematic in several ways. Although all subsequent meetings of the Codex Alimentarius Commission saw the rBGH MRL discussion shelved and pushed back to the next meeting, the proposition is still on the agenda.[259] This means that, at any time, the question of the safety of the hormone could be revived and, depending upon the current political climate, rBGH could be approved for usage. The only action needed is for one of the Commission member countries' delegates to lobby the commission to address the approval of rBGH and the topic is back on the agenda. This is a far cry from declaring rBGH unsafe and it is even quite different than simply refusing to approve it. In this aspect, Codex is merely waiting out the consumer. As time marches on, the public, especially in the United States, becomes more and more forgetful. As new generations arise and grow, knowing nothing of issues such as rBGH and genetic modification, they live through their lives thinking that these are normal standards. It then becomes the new normal. It should be clear to anyone that time is on the side of those in control, not the general public. As stated in the Codex Alimentarius Commission report from the 23rd session, "it had decided at its 22nd Session to suspend the consideration of the adoption of the MRL's for Bovine Somatotropins (BST) pending the re-evaluation of scientific data by JECFA and the Committee on Residues of Veterinary Drugs in Foods and the examination of the application of the 'other legitimate factors' in relation to BST by the Committee on General Principles."[260] Translated, Codex will wait to reconsider the approval of rBGH until more

---

[259] "Joint FAO/WHO Food Standards Programme: Codex Alimentarius Commission(Thirty-Second Session)" FAO Headquarters, Rome, Italy, June 29 – July 4, 2009. P. 15. www.codexalimentarius.net/download/report/710/al32_26e .pdf Accessed May 24, 2010.
[260] "Report of Codex Alimentarius Commission: 23rd Session, FAO Headquarters, Rome, June 28-July 3, 1999. P. 13-14 www.codexalimentarius.net/download/report/518/Al99_37 e.pdf Accessed May 24, 2010.

regulatory agencies across the world become corrupted further or until the public begins to view the hormone in a more positive light. Obviously, the FDA is already sufficiently corrupted. However, many other countries "food safety" organizations still put on the pretense that they are truly concerned about the condition of the food. That being said, more and more of these agencies are coming around to the thinking of the large corporations and globalist leaders. As will be discussed later, while it did show at least some scientific integrity by refusing to accept rBGH for sale in Canada, it has accepted the use of many other genetically modified foods much to the detriment of consumers, farmers, and the environment. It is safe to say that as corporate agri-business continues to grow and envelope the food industry, their influence will do likewise, eventually reaching every national regulatory agency worldwide.

Nevertheless, a second obstacle for Codex and other national regulatory agencies is the official reason given for many nations' refusal to accept rBGH in dairy milk. Canada's stance is of particular interest because it is viewed, whether correctly or not, as the trailblazer of the move to ban rBGH from commercial use in dairy cows. The official reason given by the Canadian government for the restriction of rBGH is the effects on animal health, not humans. In fact, Health Canada's statement regarding the rejection of rBGH stated, "The committee's review found no significant risk to human safety through ingestion of products from rBST-injected animals. Among its key findings were that rBST poses no carcinogenic risk, that rBST-induced IGF-1 (insulin growth factor) is insignificant when compared with naturally-occurring IGF-1 , that there is little likelihood of increased antibiotic resistance, and only a small potential for allergic reactions."[261] However, in relation to

---

[261] "Health Canada rejects bovine growth hormone in Canada," News Release, January 14, 1999.
http://www.springerlink.com/content/h875812u334m2g01/

animal health, the news release says, "The veterinary experts cited an increased risk of mastitis of up to 25%, of infertility by 18%, and of lameness by up to 50%. These increased risks and overall reduced body condition lead to a 20-25% increased risk of culling from the herd."[262] Nowhere in this study is there the discussion of the dangers of rBGH to humans or of genetic modification which these studies were not equipped to evaluate in the first place. However, it seems rather strange that a substance that would cause so much harm to such a large animal would cause no harm whatsoever to human beings. Of course, there is a reason for this.

Health Canada's studies were conducted by two separate committees formed under its' umbrella direction. One of the committees, led by Dr. Stuart MacLeod, was to deal with the human safety issues regarding the use of rBGH, while the other, led by Dr. Ian Dohoo, was charged with investigating the effects of rBGH on animal welfare. Yet, as the government and corporate watchdog Council of Canadians points out, the human safety committee's has a few obvious conflicts of interest. First, Dr. Stuart MaCleod, the man chosen to spearhead this committee, was forced to reveal under questioning by the Senate Committee that his wife had worked for Searle Canada for 15 years. This is significant because Searle is owned and operated exclusively by Monsanto. Second, Dr. MaCleod himself was Vice President of Clinical Affairs with Innovus. This company specializes in aiding pharmaceutical companies in the process of bringing their products to the marketplace as well as obtaining approval for these products from Health Canada.[263] As quoted by Council of Canadians, Innovus makes the claim that they have "comprehensive internal resources with our network of prominent investigators, academics, and

---

[262] Ibid.
[263] "Safe Milk," The Council of Canadians. 1998.
http://www.canadians.org/archive/documents/safe_milk.pdf

strategic alliances."[264] It appears that Innovus' claims are true indeed.

Dr. MaCleod was not the only compromised scientist on the committee, however. Dr. Rejeanne Gougeon was a nutritionist on the human safety panel.[265] Yet she has been a consultant for Monsanto since 1993 and remained in that capacity until May, 1998. In 1994, she published a paper where she lauded rBGH milk as safe and urged Health Canada to approve the drug. This paper was made possible by a grant from the Canadian Animal Health Institute Biotechnology Information Committee, a lobbying organization partly funded by Monsanto. Gougeon also belonged to the Food Biotechnology Communications Network, another association that receives financing from Monsanto. She has reportedly claimed to never have promoted rBGH outright, but has admitted that she received money to make presentations about the hormone "in a friendly context."[266]

It is certainly interesting to note that of the two committees examining rBGH, the one with so many obvious conflicts of interest and connections to Monsanto found no harmful side effects, while the one without these industry connections came to a completely different conclusion. But such is the nature of modern "science" and it is for this reason that Canada's official position against rBGH is for animal welfare reasons. Certainly, almost any reason to reject the use of rBGH is better than its acceptance. However, the position that rBGH should be banned only because of its' harmful effects on animals and that there are no harmful effects in humans not only flies in the face of known science,

---

[264] Ibid.

[265] Ibid.

[266] Eggertson, Laura. "Expert Worked For Drug Firm: Nutritionist Now Examining Safety Of BST Hormone," The Toronto Star September 21, 1998. http://archives.foodsafety.ksu.edu/fsnet/1998/9-1998/fs-09-21-98-01.txt

but it is a very weak position to take as well. If the mastitis, lameness, or the poor condition related instances in cows can be remedied, covered up, determined to be of no concern, there are no barriers to the use of rBGH in dairy milk. However, a more likely situation is that regulatory agencies and "scientific" investigative committees become further corrupted by the industry giants like Monsanto. It is quite possible that the "science" could change due to new "discoveries" that "prove" rBGH to be safe not only in humans but also in animals. After these developments it would be inevitable that rBGH would be approved for use in Canada or other non-rBGH favoring countries. This would also be a prime opportunity for Codex, under the guise of "new scientific discoveries," to reintroduce the topic of rBGH for discussion and approval.

A third obstacle to the permanent rejection of rBGH is the fact that while many countries have banned its' use, many other countries have done the opposite. In fact, at least twenty countries have accepted it – most notably, the United States, Mexico, Brazil, South Africa, Columbia, Honduras, and Kenya.[267] While this is not only alarming in terms of the number of countries coming to accept Codex's oppressive guidelines, the greatest threat comes from the WTO. As will be discussed later, it is through the WTO that Codex will force the world to come into compliance with its guidelines. For now, suffice it to say that any one of these small third world countries could file a complaint with the WTO against any one of the non-compliant countries for unfair

---

[267] "rBGH:How Artificial Hormones Damage the Dairy Industry and And Endanger Public Health." Foodandwaterwatch.org. June, 2009.
http://www.foodandwaterwatch.org/food/report/rbgh-how-artificial-hormones-damage-the-dairy-industry-and-endanger-public-health-2/rbgh-how-artificial-hormones-damage-the-dairy-industry-and-endanger-public-health-1/

trade practices. If the Codex compliant country wins, which it will, precedent will be set for the rest of the world and every nation on earth will follow suit into accepting the Codex guidelines.

A fourth concern relates to what is largely seen as a victory in the rBGH battle. While it is true that consumers have taken a much stronger stance than Monsanto likely thought they would, even to the point that Monsanto would sell the hormone to Eli Lilly, the sale should be viewed more as a lateral move. Indeed, the idea that Monsanto sold its' product to it's' competitor should not be wholly embraced. While this is not the book to discuss corporations in depth, it is well-known that the owners, board of directors, and stockholders of most major corporations of the world are largely the same individuals who merely weave in and out of these positions, moving between boards and corporations and often holding positions simultaneously. This is a practice that would never be accepted in sound business, but it is accomplished easily in this instance because they are all working toward the same ends. Indeed, Eli Lilly has been embroiled in many legal battles and controversies over the years regarding their own products and business practices. So, with the exception of the reduction of profit for Monsanto, the transition of rBGH from this company to Eli Lilly should not necessarily be viewed as a major victory. At this time, one can only guess as to what Eli Lilly's plans are regarding the future of rBGH. Regardless, it would be safe to say that the maintenance of human and animal safety is not likely to influence that decision. Certainly, Eli Lilli would not have purchased such an expensive product if it didn't think it could bring the company profit in some way.

A fifth obstacle is the very real possibility that the various regulatory agencies and governments around the world become increasingly insensitive to the wishes of the people they claim to serve as well as to the indications of sound science. Such is already the case in the United States where some state regulatory agencies have not allowed dairies to label their products as rBGH-free. In 2008, a poll was taken that showed more than 90% of American consumers supported labeling and wanted to be able to choose between rBGH-treated milk and non-rBGH-treated milk.[268] Yet consumers continue to be ignored. As of 2007, 42.7% of large-scale industrial dairies continued to use the hormone.[269] Although American government agencies' disregard for the public may be accounted for by the fact that Americans in general have become increasingly placid, European governments, especially with the appearance of the European Union, have tended toward the same behavior. Governments, Corporations, International Banks, and Foundations, are becoming more and more open about their plans for society with little resistance from those whom they dominate. So the possibility that regulatory agencies in the EU, Japan, Australia, and Canada might "revisit" the science and come to a new and different conclusion than was drawn when the issue arose is very possible whether or not the consumer likes it. As stated earlier, it would at this point be advantageous for Codex to reintroduce the issue, as public opinion becomes less and less steadfast against rBGH or national regulatory agencies can take the heat and keep the public at bay.

One can see that neither Americans nor anyone else are immune to this process. A similar situation could be seen occurring with rBGH as time marches on. It is unrealistic to believe that the corporations who manufacture the hormone are done with it. Keep in

---

[268] "rBGH:How Artificial Hormones Damage the Dairy Industry and And Endanger Public Health." Foodandwaterwatch.org. June, 2009.
http://www.foodandwaterwatch.org/food/report/rbgh-how-artificial-hormones-damage-the-dairy-industry-and-endanger-public-health-2/rbgh-how-artificial-hormones-damage-the-dairy-industry-and-endanger-public-health-1/
[269] Ibid.

mind, Eli Lilly did purchase rBGH from Monsanto - so it is reasonable to assume that it has some plans for it's' use in the future. It is also an unfortunate reality that the American people are increasingly responsive to propaganda, sophisticated or not. Although television programming is most likely the main source, the dumbing down of the education system, as well as the incessant vaccinations, chemicals like Fluoride in drinking water and other sources of chemical contamination also play a part. Nevertheless, the fact remains that Americans are becoming increasingly susceptible to propaganda and believing whatever they are told by "authorities," "experts," and television overall. With each generation the soft-kill operations launched against the people intensify, so with each passing generation this tendency will likely increase if drastic changes are not made and made soon. So this is where the battle is likely to be waged - the hearts and minds of consumers.

Brief Summary

While many claims in the anti-Codex community have suggested that Codex guidelines mandate the use of Monsanto's rBGH, at least at this time, the evidence does not corroborate this. As its' official position, Codex has not approved rBGH for use. However, Codex has not prohibited its use. Rather, Codex has simply shelved its' discussion of rBGH until further "science" is conducted. The failure to approve Codex came largely because of massive resistance from the public at the national and state levels. It appears that those who control Codex might have realized that they were in danger of extending their reach too far too fast. Coupled with the obvious corruption of regulatory agencies and governments, it is not far-fetched to believe that the "science" may be reviewed in many of the countries now opposed to rBGH usage, declaring it safe, and allowing its use with very little backlash from consumers. Another scenario, to be discussed in more detail later, is that one of the Codex compliant countries files a complaint with the WTO, a process in which the Codex Compliant country automatically wins the suit, thereby forcing the non-compliant country to accept the hormone. Failure to do so could result in crippling fines and sanctions against the offending country – economically breaking the will of consumers.[270]

---

[270] Minton, Barbara. "Billions of People Expected to Die Under Current Codex Alimentarius Guidelines." Natural News. July 21, 2009.
http://www.naturalnews.com/026731_CODEX_food_health.html

Chapter 5

Codex and Genetically Modified Foods

Codex and Genetically Modified Foods

While the debate over rBGH is a passionate one to say the least, the debate over genetically modified (GM) food is even more intense. It is in the midst of this debate that we have seen a battle between national governments as well as between corporations and consumers. As an indication of its' intensity, and that of the parties involved, all of these groups have essentially, for seventeen years, fought each other to a stalemate. That is, until now. As the fight moves forward, the momentum appears to be shifting in favor of corporations and genetic engineering, a situation that is to be expected considering the ever tightening grip that corporations enjoy over governments and regulatory agencies.

The Codex committee that serves as the main battleground for the consideration of GM food is the Codex Committee on Food Labeling. This committee is extremely relevant due to the fact that it can effectively reduce the power of the consumer to virtually nothing if it decides not to force companies or countries to label their GM food, the ability of the consumer to boycott and/or avoid those products is removed. While it is well-known that public sentiment is unimportant to those at the top, governments and corporations tend to pay more attention when votes and sales reflect that sentiment. However, if Codex continues on its' way to allowing unlabelled GM food onto the international market, the repercussions of consumer reaction will be neutralized.

A brief discussion of the history of Codex in terms of GM food is necessary here to understand the direction that the organization is moving towards in regards to it. For most of the seventeen years that Codex member countries have debated the safety of genetic modification of the food supply, the result has been little or no progress for one side or the other.

In 1993, at the behest of the Codex Commission, the CCFL agreed to begin working on the labeling aspect of GM food. Interestingly enough, the CCFL asked the United States, the country that was the most militant in it's' support of genetic modification, to develop a paper that would guide the committee's discussion at the following session. When this session arrived, there was a flurry of opinions tossed around from several different countries. The most sensible position was that all GM foods should be labeled under any circumstances. Yet other countries, especially the pro-Gm ones, argued that labeling should only be required when there is the introduction of health or safety concerns, allergens, or when the food is significantly different from its' traditional counterpart.[271] This is a debate that continues until this day.

The concept of "substantial equivalence" versus "process-based" labeling has also become one of the most hotly contested issues within the Codex GM food labeling debate. Process-based labeling simply means that the driving factor behind the labeling guidelines is the process by which the food is created, grown, or otherwise produced. Therefore, the qualifying factor for labeling GM food would be the process of genetic modification itself, forcing all GM food to be labeled as such. This is essentially the mandatory labeling of all GM food. When this concept was first introduced in 2001, it was supported by such countries as the European Union, India, and Norway. Its' staunchest opponents, of course, were the United States and Canada.[272]

---

[271] MacKenzie, Anne. A. "The Process of Developing Labeling Standards For GM Foods In The Codex Alimentarius." AgBioForum, Vol.3, Number 4, 2000. pp. 203-208. http://www.agbioforum.org/v3n4/v3n4a04-mackenzie.htm Accessed May 24, 2010.

[272] "Canadians Deserve To Know What They Are Eating: Food Safety Must Come Before Trade." Canadian Health Coalition,

Although this method of labeling standards was by far the most sensible if one were concerned about food safety and consumer rights of choice, it has been all but abandoned since the brief discussion at its' introduction. The attention then has necessarily turned to its' competing set of standards known as "substantial equivalence."

"Substantial equivalence" guidelines are by far the most onerous means by which to label GM food outside of the scheme of voluntary labeling (such as what Canada has already pushed for).[273] This set of standards not only provides loopholes through which GM food may enter the food supply, but also opens the door to total acceptance of GM food absolutely free of labeling. The idea behind the substantial equivalence labeling method is that the GM food will be compared to its' conventional counterpart in terms of safety and composition.[274] The food would then only require a label if it was found that there was a substantial difference between the GM product and the natural food or there were an introduction of a common allergen through the process of genetic modification. While at first it may seem that there is a legitimate consideration of safety under these principles, such an impression is far from the truth.

Several problems exist with the concept of substantial equivalence. First, as is often the case with government and bureaucratic initiatives, the semantics of the term "substantial equivalence" leaves the door open to the possible acceptance of

Media Advisory, May 1-4, 2001.
http://www.healthcoalition.ca/codex.html
[273] Ibid.
[274] "Safety aspects of genetically modified foods of plant origin, a joint FAO/WHO consultation on foods derived from biotechnology, Geneva, Switzerland 29 May – 2 June 2000". World Health Organization.
http://www.who.int/foodsafety/publications/biotech/ec_june2000/en/index.html

virtually all GM food. This will be discussed further later in the chapter where the accepted Codex guidelines for testing GM food is mentioned. However, brief mention is required early on in order to understand the dangers of the use of this labeling standard. In order for a food to require labeling, it must do one of two things – introduce a new allergen or be significantly different from it's' "traditional counterpart."[275] The former requirement refers to the introduction of something along the lines of the peanut gene or the introduction of another common allergy to a food, thereby causing a potential allergic reaction to the food after consuming it. However, there are thousands of food allergies besides peanuts. Codex itself admits in its' GM food test protocol that the determination of what may be an allergy is a very difficult procedure. It says "At present, there is no definitive test that can be relied upon to predict allergic response in humans to a newly expressed protein."[276] Although the guidelines go on to say that these potential allergens should be tested on a case by case basis, it is clear that the testing mechanisms being recommended are not necessarily geared for determining the potential allergenicity of newly introduced GM foods. Especially on the scale that is needed to deal with the immense diversity of GM prototypes being introduced and the even greater variety of individual allergies that exists in the population. It should also be noted that while there is some discussion of known allergens, there is no in-depth discussion of the very real possibility of new and previously unknown allergens being introduced due to the process of genetic

---

[275] MacKenzie, Anne. A. "The Process of Developing Labeling Standards For GM Foods In The Codex Alimentarius." AgBioForum, Vol.3, Number 4, 2000. pp. 203-208. http://www.agbioforum.org/v3n4/v3n4a04-mackenzie.htm May 24, 2010.
[276] "Food Derived From Modern Biotechnology." Codex Alimentarius 2nd Edition. P.20 ftp://ftp.fao.org/codex/Publications/Booklets/Biotech/Biotech_2009e.pdf

modification. Indeed, the monitoring of the food once it enters the food chain is only occasionally mentioned throughout the Codex "Foods Derived From Modern Biotechnology" document and those mentions are vague and open-ended.[277] So the question that follows is whether or not all of these potential allergens will be labeled as such or if only the most common ones will be considered. There is no mention of this as there are no actual Codex guidelines for labeling as of yet.

Second, the requirement that a food must be compared and found substantially equivalent to it's' "traditional counterpart" (natural food) is misleading as well. To begin with, one must ask the question of what exactly does "substantial equivalence" mean. Quite obviously, the term does not mean that the GM product must be identical. This is in itself would negate the process of genetic modification. Therefore, differences must necessarily be accepted. However, it is not at all clear just to what level these differences may exist and still be considered equivalent and/or safe. Nowhere is "substantial equivalence" clearly defined. The criterion for what is substantial and what is not is left completely open and subjective. The closest thing there is to a definition is made by Nick Tomlinson of the UK Food Standards Agency in his report, "Joint FAO/WHO Expert Consultation on Foods Derived from Biotechnology" where he references the 1996 expert consultation where substantial equivalence was defined "being established by a demonstration that the characteristics assessed for the genetically modified organism, or the specific food product derived therefrom, are equivalent to the same characteristics of the conventional comparator."[278] Here again the term equivalence is used with the connotation that equivalent does not translate into identical or same.

---

[277] Ibid.

[278] Tomlinson, Nick. "Joint FAO/WHO Expert Consultation on Foods Derived from Biotechnology." 2003. ftp://ftp.fao.org/es/esn/food/Bio-03.pdf Accessed May 24, 2010.

Tomlinson makes this clear when he says "The levels and variation for characteristics in the genetically modified organism must be within the natural range of variation for those characteristics considered in the comparator and be based upon an appropriate analysis of data."[279] By not exactly being descriptive as to how wide a range this "natural range of variation" may be, it is apparent that substantial equivalence does not correlate to identical or even anything that would remotely be considered the "same." Indeed, the very nature of genetic modification precludes this as a possibility to begin with.

The concept of substantial equivalence is unfortunately the theory of labeling requirements adopted by Codex. It is also very similar to the criteria used in the United States and Canada. As to be expected in such pro-GM countries as the United States, the GM labeling requirements are even less restrictive than those of Codex. For the most part, labeling of GM foods in the United States and Canada is completely voluntary. This voluntary labeling scheme based on the concept of substantial equivalence is both a prime example of the weakness of both standards as well as a dark omen as to the direction of Codex guidelines as they continue to be developed.[280]

The FDA does not require GM foods to be labeled unless they meet one of four rather severe criteria. Even then, the labeling refers only to the issue at hand, not the process from which the food was created. The criteria for labeling are as follows:

---

[279] Ibid.

[280] "Guidance For Industry: Voluntary Labeling Indicating Whether Foods Have or Have Not Been Developed Using Biotengineering: Draft Guidance." Food and Drug Administration. January 2001. http://www.fda.gov/Food/GuidanceComplianceRegulatoryInformation/GuidanceDocuments/FoodLabelingNutrition/ucm059098.htm

1.) If a bioengineered food is significantly different from its traditional counterpart such that the common or usual name no longer adequately describes the new food.

2.) If an issue exists for the food or a constituent of the food regarding how the food is used or consequences of its use, a statement must be made on the label to describe the issue.

3.) If a bioengineered food has a significantly different nutritional property, its label must reflect the difference.

4.) If a new food includes an allergen that consumers would not expect to be present based on the name of the food, the presence of that allergen must be disclosed on the label.[281]

So, as these recommendations suggest, a GM food must only be labeled when it is so different from its "conventional counterpart" that it cannot even be considered the same food, is the cause of reactions or consequences that the natural version of it would not have caused, has a "significant" difference in nutritional composition, or if it introduces an allergen that would not otherwise have been present. It should be noted, like the Codex guidelines for substantial equivalence mentioned earlier, that "significant" difference in nutritional composition is not clearly defined. So what some may consider to be truly significant might not even be considered worth any concern by the FDA and certainly not by the manufacturing company. Also, as mentioned earlier, there is no discussion of whether or not the inclusion of allergens to a food includes those less common allergies or just the most popular such as peanuts. Yet even meeting these criteria does not necessarily draw the label of "genetically modified" - merely the potential side effects of consuming these foods.[282]

Only when one of these four criteria has been met must companies label their products in a manner that may suggest genetic modification and, even then, only in a subtle manner. In all other

---

[281] Ibid.
[282] Ibid.

instances however, the labeling is completely voluntary. Just as disconcerting as voluntary labeling is the fact that the alleged "safety testing" is not even conducted by the FDA or any other regulatory agency, but by the food producers themselves. The FDA merely takes for granted the truth of whatever is provided them by industry if anything is provided to them at all.[283] As stated in the federal register as far back as 1992, the FDA says, "FDA has traditionally encouraged producers of new food ingredients to consult with FDA when there is a question about an ingredient's regulatory status, and firms routinely do so, even though such consultation is not legally required."[284] It is certainly concerning to know that, at best, firms are encouraged to consult with the FDA but are not required to do so. Interestingly enough, this is not the position taken in regards to proven safe and effective natural and herbal supplements.

Adding to absurdity of the voluntary labeling policy held by the FDA, the regulatory agency works on the premise that GM foods are safe to begin with and that there is no difference between GM food and natural food.[285] In the 1992 FDA Federal Register, the agency makes the claim, "In most cases, the substances expected to become components of food as a result of genetic modification of a plant will be the same as or substantially similar to substances commonly found in food, such as proteins, fats and oils, and carbohydrates."[286] Notice the similar terminology of "substantially similar" as compared with the "substantial equivalence" of Codex. This adds even more credibility to the idea that

---

[283] "Statement of Food Policy – Foods Derived From New Plant Varieties," FDA Federal Register Vol. 57. 1992. http://www.fda.gov/Food/GuidanceComplianceRegulatoryInformation/GuidanceDocuments/Biotechnology/ucm096095.htm Accessed May 24, 2010.
[284] Ibid.
[285] Ibid.
[286] Ibid.

the Codex model of GM food regulation is based on that by the pro-GM FDA. Not only that, although the difference between the wording might seem unimportant to some, the term "similar" is even more open-ended than the Codex "equivalent." But how did the FDA come to these conclusions? The agency admits that there is no premarket testing by the FDA itself; merely relying on industry to voluntarily consult with the FDA only when the industry feels there might be a problem with the product. [287] Yet the agency still maintains, through basic assumption, that GM foods are not different from the natural versions. In the same Federal Register it says,

> Under this policy, foods, such as fruits, vegetables, grains, and their byproducts, derived from plant varieties developed by the new methods of genetic modification are regulated within the existing framework of the act, FDA's implementing regulations, and current practice, utilizing an approach identical in principle to that applied to foods developed by traditional plant breeding. The regulatory status of a food, irrespective of the method by which it is developed, is dependent upon objective characteristics of the food and the intended use of the food (or its components). The method by which food is produced or developed may in some cases help to understand the safety or nutritional characteristics of the finished food. However, the key factors in reviewing safety concerns should be the characteristics of the food product, rather than the fact that the new methods are used. [288]

The FDA here is claiming that the process of genetic modification, even though it has not evaluated it thoroughly, is not only safe but, for the most part, irrelevant to the question of food safety. Of course, this merely manufacturing conclusions out of thin air. The FDA asserts the safety of GM food because there is "substantial equivalence" between

---

[287] Ibid. p. 5.
[288] Ibid p. 4.

the two. However, there is "substantial equivalence" only because the FDA claims that this is the case. There is a massive lack of evidence to support any of these claims.

The FDA also claims that genetic engineering is no different from "traditional plant breeding," an argument that is often made within the pro-GM community. Such is the belief (or argument) that traditional means of plant breeding such as grafting and cross-pollination are essentially the same as removal and insertion of DNA from one life form to another. As will be discussed later, this is absolutely not the case. This argument would be akin to claiming that breeding of humans of different ethnic backgrounds is the same as breeding between humans and horses. In addition, the question of how the FDA would know this, since it has not conducted any scientific experiments regarding this claim, arises again. Yet it continues to blend the two very different methods together by defining genetic engineering as the "alteration of the genotype of a plant using any technique, new or traditional."[289] Thus, the FDA puts the insertion of a pig gene into a tomato into the same category as natural birth, since genes change and develop with each generation. If there were any doubt as to whether or not this is the FDA's position their claim that "Most, if not all, cultivated food crops have been genetically modified," should remove it. [290] This claim is only true if one accepts the FDA's definition of natural reproduction as genetic engineering.

Jumping back to the early 1990's, around the time the FDA was announcing its' own policy toward GM food, the debate in Codex was heating up as well. Most of the arguments were taken up by the CCFL and, for the most part, pitted the United States and Canada against the European Union, India, and Norway. In 1996, because little could be agreed upon, the CCFL asked for guidance from the CAC on how labeling

---

[289] Ibid.
[290] Ibid.

guidelines might be developed and in 1997 the CAC produced a document for that purpose. These recommendations were that foods not "equivalent" to natural foods in nutritional value, intended use, or composition should be labeled. Yet this was not accepted into Codex guidelines as Australia, New Zealand, Peru, and Brazil joined with Canada and the United States in opposing these recommendations. Definitions of terms also became an issue at this meeting.[291]

At the 27th CCFL session in 1999, it was decided that the Proposed Draft Recommendations for GM food labeling be reconsidered and rewritten. For this purpose, Codex created the Ad Hoc Working Group. Their stated mission was to more fully define "biotechnology-derived foods" and to revise the options considered for labeling between process-based and substantial equivalence methods. The Working Group also agreed to consider establishing a maximum level of GM ingredients in a food as well as a minimum level for accidental inclusion of GM ingredients or food within a food. As mentioned earlier, substantial equivalence has emerged as the most favored method of labeling within Codex. Indeed, it is easily understood why this is the case when one takes a closer look at the Working Group developed to evaluate and rewrite labeling recommendations. While certain instances may seem harmless when viewed separately, when taken together they reveal a rather obvious attempt to stack the odds in favor of pro-GM sentiment by the CCFL. First, Canada, perhaps the most pro-Gm Codex member country besides the United States, was selected to chair the Group as well as coordinate the Group's direction. Also, a smaller Drafting Group was created under the Working Group to "hold the pen." It was this group that would do much of the actual work in

---

[291] MacKenzie, Anne. A. "The Process of Developing Labeling Standards For GM Foods In The Codex Alimentarius." AgBioForum, Vol.3, Number 4, 2000. pp. 203-208. http://www.agbioforum.org/v3n4/v3n4a04-mackenzie.htm May 24, 2010.

terms of hammering out the Recommendations document. However, five of the six countries represented in the Drafting Group were pro-GM countries.[292] Clearly, it would be difficult for a non-favorable view of GM food to win out in a situation such as this.

In 2000 an attempt was made by the CCFL to direct the Working Group to streamline the two different methods of labeling (process-based and substantial equivalence) into a Codex Guideline as well as other key issues involving GM food labeling. A document of this nature was subsequently produced by the United States. Yet despite the packing of the Drafting and Working Groups, the CCFL was still unable to approve the guidelines that the groups produced. However, the Committee was able to approve the use of three definitions related to GM food.[293] They are as follows:

1.) Food and food ingredients obtained through certain techniques of genetic modification/genetic engineering – food and food ingredients composed of or containing genetically modified/engineered organisms obtained through modern biotechnology, or food and food ingredients produced from, but not containing genetically modified/engineered organisms obtained through modern biotechnology.

---

[292] Ibid.
Please Note:
While it is true that the European Union had two representatives on the panel, it also true that the EU speaks with one voice. Even if one were to argue that this would give them extra representation, pro-GM nations still outnumber anti-GM nations.
[293] MacKenzie, Anne. A. "The Process of Developing Labeling Standards For GM Foods In The Codex Alimentarius." AgBioForum, Vol.3, Number 4, 2000. pp. 203-208. http://www.agbioforum.org/v3n4/v3n4a04-mackenzie.htm May 24, 2010.

2.) Genetically modified/engineered organism – an organism in which the genetic material has been changed through modern biotechnology in a way that does not occur naturally by multiplication and/or natural recombination.

3.) Modern Biotechnology – the application of:

a. In vitro nucleic acid techniques, including recombinant deoxyribonucleic acid (DNA) and the direct injection of nucleic acid into cells or organelles

b. Fusion of cells beyond the taxonomic family, that overcome natural physiological, reproductive, or recombination barriers and that are not techniques used in traditional breeding and selection.[294]

When one looks at the definitions agreed upon at the 29th session of Codex, it can be seen that there is a move toward using the term "modern biotechnology" in place of "genetic engineering/modification." This is largely an attempt to use semantics in an effort to reduce, through ignorance, the apprehension of the public to the consumption of GMO's.

However, in the face of such controversy, in 2003 Codex did produce and approve a set of Guidelines for the assessment of the safety of GM food. Entitled "Codex Principles and Guidelines On Foods Derived From Biotechnology," the Guidelines do not deal with labeling concerns at all, but with the standards for the science used to assess these foods for safety.

Codex Principles and Guidelines On Foods Derived From Biotechnology

The "Codex Principles and Guidelines On Foods Derived From Biotechnology" is made up of four sections, two of which deal with GM plants while the other sections deal with GM organisms in general and

---

[294] Ibid.

GM animals respectively. Similar to the "Guidelines for Vitamins and Mineral Supplements," these guidelines are not only unscientific but carefully crafted to allow the approval of dangerous GM foods. The game, in essence, is clearly rigged.

When looking at the first section of the guidelines one is able to see a very real correlation to those designated for vitamins and minerals. Using a form of risk analysis to determine the safety of GM food, Codex seeks to explain the reason for its' choice of methodology. It states "While risk analysis has been used over a long period of time to address chemical hazards (e.g. residues of pesticides, contaminants, food additives and processing aids), and it is being increasingly used to address microbiological hazards and nutritional factors, the principles were not elaborated specifically for whole foods."[295] This is an interesting statement considering the fact that risk analysis was indeed considered adequate for the safety examination of vitamins, minerals, and nutritional supplements. However, for whole foods, GM foods in particular, Codex has decided that risk analysis is not appropriate. The very next section of the Introduction admits that while risk analysis can in fact be applied to foods (including GM food) "in general terms", "it is recognized that this approach must be modified when applied to a whole food rather than to a discrete hazard that may be present in food."[296] One can gain an understanding of how the process is adapted to suit the needs of Codex by reading through the guidelines as a whole. This will be demonstrated during the course of the discussion of GMO's. However, suffice it to say that this modification is generally the removal of all standards and qualifications that might illuminate the vast amount

---

[295] "Foods Derived From Modern Biotechnology," 2nd edition. Codex Alimentarius. P.1
ftp://ftp.fao.org/docrep/fao/011/a1554e/a1554e00.pdf
Accessed May 24, 2010.
[296] Ibid.

of safety concerns present in GM foods.[297]

Another disturbing statement made in the introduction casts
even more doubt upon the scientific validity of Codex's guidelines. The
Guidelines state, "Where appropriate, the results of a risk assessment
undertaken by other regulatory authorities may be used to assist in the
risk analysis and avoid duplication of work."[298] While on it's' face, this
statement appears only to be a call for labor efficiency, at its' best it
assumes the objectivity of the regulatory authorities doing the testing.
However, what is most concerning about this policy is that risk
assessment "conclusions" reached by regulatory agencies such as the
FDA and Health Canada may be accepted in place of an independent
examination. Truthfully, the likelihood of a legitimately independent
assessment made possible by Codex is almost nonexistent. However, in
the case of GMO's, the odds are even less so for the FDA and Health
Canada, two agencies that have been largely bought and paid for by
Monsanto and other large agri-business corporations. Indeed, as far as
GM foods go, the FDA assessments have largely been completed since
the agency claims that there is no difference between genetic
modification and traditional plant breeding.[299] This agency has also
made it clear that safety testing is to be conducted by the manufacturer
of the product rather than the agency itself, relying solely on the
company's scientific and moral standards. In effect, as mentioned
earlier, the science determining the safety of GM foods comes straight
from the manufacturer itself.[300] With this in mind, one can clearly see

---

[297] Ibid.

[298] Ibid.

[299] "Statement of Food Policy – Foods Derived From New
Plant Varieties," FDA Federal Register Vol. 57. 1992.
http://www.fda.gov/Food/GuidanceComplianceRegulatoryInf
ormation/GuidanceDocuments/Biotechnology/ucm096095.ht
m Accessed May 24, 2010.

[300] Ibid.

that the same line of ascension exists in Codex Alimentarius. If Codex is willing to accept the safety assessments of regulatory agencies without independent testing of its' own and regulatory agencies are willing to accept the safety assessments of corporations without independent testing of their own, then Codex is willing to accept the safety assessments of corporations without independent safety testing of their own. Indeed, this syllogism adequately reflects the reality of the relationship between Codex, corporations, and the future of GM foods.

Another issue of great concern is the definition of conventional counterpart. Because Codex uses the concept of substantial equivalence[301], this seemingly requires that the GM product be compared to its' natural counterpart. However, the definition of conventional counterpart, according to Codex, is "a related organism/variety, its components and/or products for which there is experience of establishing safety based on common use as food."[302] This definition poses a potential problem because it does not make clear (in the body of the text) that the conventional counterpart must be the natural version of the food. In a footnote, the statement is made that "It is recognized that, for the foreseeable future, foods derived from modern biotechnology will not be used as conventional counterparts."[303] The phrase, "for the foreseeable future" raises its' own difficulties, because it provides a potential loophole. "Foreseeable future" does not set a timeline for the current policy to run out, but it does leave open the possibility of allowing a change in the current practice. Allowing GM products to be compared to other GM products for substantial equivalence is an enormous blow to the environment,

---

[301] "Foods Derived From Modern Biotechnology," 2nd edition. Codex Alimentarius. P. 9
ftp://ftp.fao.org/docrep/fao/011/a1554e/a1554e00.pdf
Accessed May 24, 2010.
[302] Ibid. p.2
[303] Ibid.

human health, and consumer choice. Such an action would completely undercut the already weak and ridiculous method of substantial equivalence and would turn the entire nature of our food supply upside down. One would be comparing a dangerous product to another dangerous product but labeling it safe because it was substantially equivalent to the first dangerous product. Like the situation involving vitamins and minerals, this is the Twilight Zone reality produced by Codex once it gains power of the food supply.

Unfortunately, this potential concern is now an imminent one because Monsanto has in fact submitted an application for a GM corn called LY038. In its' submission for approval, Monsanto provided the regulators' assessing the product with information comparing LY038 with another GM corn product called LY038 (-), another GM corn product.[304] True to form, in many of the pro-GM countries such as New Zealand, Australia, Japan, Canada, the Philippines, and South Korea, the LY038 corn was approved based upon the method of using a GM corn as a conventional counterpart.[305] The United States, being the most open to GM food, and only requiring voluntary submission, has also approved LY038 for cultivation.[306] Thankfully, the Monsanto agenda stalled in the European Union and, in 2009, Monsanto withdrew its application for

---

[304] "New Attack on GM Food Safety Testing Standards," Centre for Integrated Research in Biosafety, University of Canterbury. February 2007.
http://www.sustainabilitynz.org/docs/Backgrounder_NewAttackonGMFoodSafetyStandards.pdf Accessed May 24, 2010.
[305] "Monsanto pulls GM corn amid serious food safety concerns," GM Free CYMRU.
http://gmfreecymru.org/Press_Notice9Nov2009.htm
[306] "Transgenic high-lysine corn LY038 withdrawn after EU raises safety questions," The Bioscience Resource Project, Nov. 10, 2009.
http://www.bioscienceresource.org/news/article.php?id=43 Accessed May 24, 2010.

the product in Europe.[307] This is largely due to a small group of relatively independent scientists from the Centre for Integrated Research in Biosafety (INBI) out of New Zealand who brought out many risks evident from a close reading of the Monsanto application dossiers. As a result of their work, the European Food Safety Authority (EFSA) requested for additional research and safety data. That was all that was needed in order to cause Monsanto to withdraw its application for LY038 use in Europe.[308] Monsanto claimed that the reason for the removal of its submission purely economical and that "although our preference would have been to complete the EU approval of LY038, conducting further studies, as requested [by the EFSA GMO Panel], can no longer be justified, in view of the additional costs involved and the reduced commercial interest in this product."[309] However, those who are aware of Monsanto's track record have a different take. In a statement made to Biosafety Information Centre, Prof. Jack Heinemann, who led the INBI research team, summed up the situation succinctly.

> I personally don't believe that the withdrawal of LY038 from commercialization was a budget blow-out. Monsanto estimated that the street-value of LY038 was going to be US $1 billion/year. People are still feeding corn to cows, chickens and pigs and corn is still being converted to biofuel in the US. The price of corn is at historical highs and is not expected to decrease. Do we really believe that a market of $1 billion/year is too small for Monsanto? I don't. . . . . . The

---

[307] "Europe balks at GE corn in NZ," Stuff.co.nz, Feb. 11, 2009. http://www.stuff.co.nz/national/3020246/Europe-balks-at-GE-corn-in-NZ

[308] "Monsanto pulls GM corn amid serious food safety concerns," GM Free CYMRU. http://gmfreecymru.org/Press_Notice9Nov2009.htm

[309] "What has happened to high lysine corn?" Biosafety Information Centre. http://www.biosafety-info.net/bioart.php?bid=583&ac=st

> major issue raise by EFSA was Monsanto's use of another GM
> product as a control in all its safety studies. This violates both
> international food safety testing guidelines and European
> rules. INBI was the first in the world to point this out. FSANZ
> [Food Standards Australia New Zealand] ignored it. EFSA
> didn't. Monsanto pulled the product. We estimate that
> upwards of US $1 billion had already been invested and if it
> were just a matter of demonstrating that a safe product was
> safe, then a few tidy up scientific studies would have cost
> nothing in comparison.[310]

The obvious reason that the application was pulled, at least according to
this researcher and, seemingly, Prof. Heinemann, is that Monsanto's
LY038 was absolutely unsafe for consumption and that it would never
have stood up to any scientific testing of its' safety. It is also likely that
the company's own research data would have proven its danger since it
would not even submit the requested material to EFSA. In conjunction
with this, Monsanto may have been afraid that exposure of this fact
would have crippled its progress with the countries that did approve
LY038. However, while it did not succeed with the EU (this time), the
precedent has been set for using a GM product as a conventional
counterpart. This will undoubtedly affect Codex guidelines in the future,
especially considering the fact that so many and such major players
have accepted these standards of testing.

Returning to the Codex document itself, it should be noted that
the risks associated with GMO's are dealt with in a rather curious
manner. Indeed, the monitoring and management of risks from GM
food after their approval is mentioned rather blandly in the introductory
section of the Guidelines. It says,

> "Post market-monitoring may be undertaken for the purpose

---

[310] Ibid.

of:

A.) Verifying conclusions about the absence or the possible occurrence, impact and significance of potential consumer health effects; and

B.) Monitoring changes in nutrient intake levels, associated with the introduction of foods likely to alter nutritional status significantly, to determine their human health impact. [311]

It should be noted that these are issues which should be resolved in a scientific setting prior to market. Yet Codex is obviously content to allow the public to act as lab rats in the real world rather than force these side effects to be addressed in an actual lab. Absolute disregard for the global population is evident here. As will be discussed later, when one understands the ultimate purpose of Codex Alimentarius, it becomes clear as to why policies like this emanate from the organization. Such is the case when Codex mentions the management of risks finding their way into the market and the need for post-market tracing for the purpose of recall.[312] It is important to note that tracing food materials is a difficult task, especially if those products have already found their way into the environment and have begun to reproduce.

Although already mentioned here, the second chapter of Codex's' "Foods Derived From Modern Biotechnology" makes what should be considered a revelatory admission. It says,

> The Codex principles of risk analysis, particularly those for risk assessment, are primarily intended to apply to discrete

---

[311] "Foods Derived From Modern Biotechnology," 2nd edition. Codex Alimentarius. P. 4
ftp://ftp.fao.org/docrep/fao/011/a1554e/a1554e00.pdf
Accessed May 24, 2010.
[312] Ibid. p.4

chemical entities, such as food additives and pesticide
residues, or a specific chemical or microbial contaminant that
have identifiable hazards and risks; they are not intended to
apply to whole foods as such.[313]

Essentially, this is an admission that risk assessment methodology is absolutely incapable and inappropriate when dealing with the safety of a whole food. As Codex makes clear, the principles for risk assessment were never intended to address anything other than chemicals and additives. However, one should remember that risk assessment is just the method used to determine the safety of vitamins, nutrients, and minerals by Codex Alimentarius in order to label them unsafe at unreasonably low levels. But Codex continues with even further admission that the testing the testing methods used are not nearly as intense as one might think. The document reads,

> Traditionally, new varieties of food plants have not been
> systematically subjected to extensive chemical, toxicological
> or nutritional evaluation prior to marketing, with the
> exception of foods for specific groups, such as infants, where
> the food may constitute a substantial portion of the diet.
> Thus, new varieties of corn, soybean, potatoes and other
> common food plants are evaluated by breeders for
> agronomic and phenotypic characteristics, but generally,
> foods derived from such new plant varieties are not subjected
> to the rigorous and extensive food safety testing procedures,
> including studies in animals, that are typical of chemicals,
> such as food additives or pesticide residues, that may be
> present in food.[314]

Simply put, Codex is admitting, albeit cleverly, that the testing method

---

[313] Ibid P. 7
[314] Ibid. p.8

for whole foods is inadequate, and that the testing itself is not nearly as extensive as it would for evaluating a known toxin like a chemical, pesticide, or apparently, vitamins and minerals. As related to the earlier chapter on vitamins and minerals, Codex considers genetically modified foods that have been engineered to produce a deadly chemical or pesticide to be a whole food, but vitamin C is considered a toxin. Yet Codex does not stop here with the prefacing of their intended deceit and the admission of flawed and manipulated science. It says,

> Animal studies cannot be readily applied to testing the risks associated with whole foods, which are complex mixtures of compounds, often characterized by a wide variation in composition and nutritional value. Owing to their bulk and effect on satiety, they can usually only be fed to animals at low multiples of the amounts that might be present in the human diet. In addition, a key factor to consider in conducting animal studies on foods is the nutritional value and balance of the diets used; this is in order to avoid the induction of adverse effects that are not related directly to the material itself. Detecting any potential adverse effects and relating these conclusively to an individual characteristic of the food can, therefore, be extremely difficult. If the characterization of the food indicates that the available data are insufficient for a thorough safety assessment, properly designed animal studies could be requested on the whole foods. Another consideration in deciding the need for animal studies is whether it is appropriate to subject experimental animals to such a study if it is unlikely to give rise to meaningful information.[315]

But there are several problems with this statement. First, let it be made clear that the author of this book does not support the use of animals

---

[315] Ibid. p.9

for laboratory testing for any reason. However, this issue is not the focus of the book and it will be repeatedly referred to in its proper context in terms of scientific debate. That being said, what Codex has admitted to in this statement, albeit subtly, is that test subjects will actually be fed significantly less of the GM food in question than exists in the standard human diet. Nowhere does Codex mention that the amount fed to the test subjects can be adjusted per *capita* but simply that the amount fed to them will be "at low multiples of the amounts that might be present in the human diet."[316] Furthermore, Codex attempts to convince the reader that because of differences in nutritional values and diet balance in the animals being tested it is extremely difficult to determine if there are any adverse effects resulting from the material being tested or another material/condition. Hence, Codex would have the reader believe that this problem could not be solved by the addition of a control group. In the end, the overall conclusion of Codex, is that testing GM foods is largely unproductive and that, for the most part, should only be conducted in very special circumstances. Mere post-market tracking is looked upon as the most favorable route. This, however, leaves the consumer as the test subject and corrective action can only be taken after it is too late for hundreds, thousands, or even millions of people.

Codex furthers this claim with an admission of it's' acceptance of "substantial equivalence" as a testing standard. Because of the problems associated with using risk assessment to address dangers in whole foods (but evidently not nutrients and vitamins), Codex claims it must rely on substantial equivalence to address intended and unintended changes in the food. Hence, Codex officially accepts the concept. [317] In subsequent sections, Codex claims that even weak standards like substantial equivalence may not be required. The

---

[316] Ibid. p.9
[317] Ibid. p.9

guidelines state, "For the reasons described in Section 3, conventional toxicology studies may not be considered necessary where the substance or a closely related substance has, taking into account its function and exposure, been consumed safely in food."[318] However, there is no discussion of exactly how it will be determined that these substances have been consumed safely in food to begin with. Considering the fact that toxic substances like fluoride and rBGH have been consumed "safely" in food for many years, it is certainly frightening to think that even more substances may be created and added to the food supply under the guise of a history of safe consumption. Nevertheless, this process (or lack thereof) is not only unscientific, it is very dangerous.

Although Codex clearly maintains a double standard in regards to GM food versus vitamins and nutrients, there are some similarities in the risk assessment procedure applied to them. One of the few instances in which Codex applies the same standards for GM food as for dietary supplements is the area of nutritional properties of the food. In fact, this procedure is in direct correlation to the Guidelines for Vitamin and Mineral Food Supplements and works in tandem with them in order to create a lower acceptable level of nutrients in the food itself. In relation to this situation, it is important to pay close attention to several statements made within the guidelines. For instance,

> Information about the known patterns of use and consumption of a food, and its derivatives should be used to estimate the likely intake of the food derived from the recombinant-DNA plant. The expected intake of the food should be used to assess the nutritional implications of the altered nutrient profile both at customary and maximal levels of consumption. Basing the estimate on the highest likely

---

[318] Ibid. p. 14

> consumption provides assurance that the potential for any
> undesirable nutritional effects will be detected. [319]

While this language is carefully crafted to appear benign and concerned only with the welfare of different cultures consuming the GM food, what is actually being presented is the idea of a Global Expectable Average Daily Diet for purposes of creating an Upper Limit not on GM food, but on the nutrients existing within the food itself while, at the same time, allowing genetically engineered food to be virtually unregulated. As mentioned in the chapter dealing with vitamin and mineral supplements, the Global Average Daily Diet is simply taking the "average" level of consumption of a food or nutrient across the world and using that level as a base level standard for what will be considered the average intake of the product by all populations. The highest or lowest levels are usually chosen based on the needs of the scientist, particularly in situations like these where researchers have ulterior motives. Remember the case of vitamin and mineral food supplements where the highest level of intake was used instead of the real average. This was because third world countries were not included properly in the average. Like the GADD for vitamins and nutrients, the highest level of consumption will be used to examine GM food. However, using the highest level of consumption, in this case, will have an entirely different effect than it did upon vitamins and minerals.

Using the highest level of consumption estimation in concert with the concept of substantial equivalence, Codex creates an environment where it would be difficult for GM food not to be approved. Consider this hypothetical scenario: We might imagine that potatoes have a higher consumption rate in North America and Europe than in other regions of the world. So researchers would determine, based on the rate of potato consumption of Europe and North America,

---

[319] Ibid. p.17

the Global Expectable Average Daily Diet. This average consumption rate would be applied worldwide regardless of other cultures' consumption of potatoes. Likewise, using the concept of substantial equivalence, GM potatoes would be approved with an Upper Limit of the highest rate of consumption worldwide.

There are two dangers to this methodology. First, the damage to the food supply does not end with the introduction of GM foods. The Maximum Permitted Levels for vitamin and minerals developed by Codex will remain in place. So, because the risk assessment for GM food based on substantial equivalence will inevitably determine the GM food itself to be safe, the problem then becomes the nutritional value within the food. The nutrition then becomes the enemy and must be removed. While this might seem both improbable and impossible, in fact it is neither. The seeming improbability of a Codex declaration of nutrients as toxins has already been realized and the genetic manipulation of the nutritional properties of food is not an impossibility at all. While the cover story for the introduction of GM food often involves the alleged wish to bring about the end of malnutrition by increasing nutritional properties of the food genetically (a blatant contradiction if one accepts that nutrients should be treated as toxins), the ability to decrease nutrition through genetic modification is just as realistic. We then have a situation where nutritionally deficient GM food is not only allowed, but required due to the dangerous amount of vitamins and minerals that exist in the natural food. Codex even admits later on in the Guidelines that nutrients will be focused on rather than the dangers of the GM food. It says,

> To assess the safety of a food derived from a recombinant-DNA plant modified for a nutritional or health benefit, the estimated intake of the nutrient or related substance in the population(s) is compared with the nutritional or toxicological reference values, such as upper levels of intake, acceptable

daily intakes (ADIs) for that nutrient or related substance.[320]

The question then is not the safety of the GM food, but of the amount of vitamins and nutrients included in it. Continuing through the Guidelines, such a statement is cleverly made. It says, "Rather than trying to identify every hazard associated with a particular food, the intention of a safety assessment of food derived from recombinant-DNA is the identification of new or altered hazards relative to the conventional counterpart."[321] Not only is this an extremely limiting set of standards for assessing the safety of the product, what is actually meant by "hazard", although not explicitly stated, is nutrients. This is made even clearer in the next paragraph which states, "Upper levels of intake for many nutrients that have been set out by some national, regional and international bodies may be considered, as appropriate. The basis for their derivation should also be considered in order to assess the public health implications of exceeding these levels."[322] Clearly, nutrients are the focus of much of the risk assessment methods applied to GM food. This may initially cause some GM food products to be rejected by Codex due to the higher level of nutritional properties being produced. That is, until the food is modified once again to have a lower nutritional value. When seen in this light, it becomes obvious that many of the Codex Guidelines are intertwined with one another. However, none are more important than those related to vitamins, minerals, and nutrients.

A second problem with the Codex methodology, which will be examined later, is the fact that, regardless of its' decisions and procedures, Codex is still exercising control over the food supply and the choice that every human being has a right to make. It is a very real

---

[320] Ibid. p.27
[321] Ibid. p.25
[322] Ibid.

possibility that if Codex Alimentarius is not stopped, we will live in a much smaller world, where starvation, sickness, and hunger are rampant and where we must be our multinational corporate masters for a bite of the toxic mass that we will have no choice but to eat.

Returning to the Codex Guidelines themselves, the organization leaves itself yet another loophole by claiming that, in a situation where even the unbelievably weak substantial equivalence method cannot allow the approval of a GM food, that the food used as a conventional counterpart may be changed in order to suit the GM product being evaluated. It says,

> When the modification results in a food product, such as vegetable oil, with a composition that is significantly different from its conventional counterpart, it may be appropriate to use additional conventional foods or food components (i.e. foods or food components whose nutritional composition is closer to that of the food derived from recombinant-DNA plant) as appropriate comparators to assess the nutritional impact of the food.[323]

In this statement Codex is openly admitting that it will simply change the "scientific" process that we are supposed to put our faith in, in order to accommodate the GM substance being tested. If the conventional counterpart is not substantially equivalent, change the conventional counterpart to one that is.

Another concern addressed by the Codex Guidelines has to deal with antibiotic resistance created through the process of genetic engineering. Yet the agency makes several misleading and unsettling statements in this regard as well. While Codex does state that methods

---

[323] Ibid. p.17

should be used that do not result in antibiotic resistance, it qualifies that claim by stating that these methods should be used "where such technologies are available and demonstrated to be safe."[324] This is certainly no mandate. It is merely a suggestion that will most likely be completely ignored by industry. The Guidelines then go on to say that "Gene transfer from plants and their food products to gut micro-organisms or human cells is considered a rare possibility because of the many complex and unlikely events that would need to occur consecutively."[325] This statement stands in direct contradiction to the science which will be discussed later. Indeed, the series of events that would have to transpire in order for the transfer of modified genes from a plant to human DNA or cells are neither unlikely nor rare. In a footnote to this statement, Codex makes the claim "In cases where there are high levels of naturally occurring bacteria that are resistant to the antibiotic, the likelihood of such bacteria transferring the resistance to other bacteria will be orders of magnitude higher than the likelihood of transfer between ingested foods and bacteria."[326] Yet while this may in fact be true the statement is still misleading. The issue being discussed in the footnoted statement is the likelihood of DNA transfer from GM plants to humans. Furthermore, if such events were so unlikely, why would it be important not to use antibiotic resistant gene technology in the future?

Another concern presented in the section dealing with GM plants is the question of potential allergens being brought within the food products as well as the introduction of entirely new allergens that have never before existed in nature. While Codex claims that "all newly expressed proteins" as well as "a protein new to the food supply" should be tested for safety, there is legitimate questions as to whether

---

[324] Ibid. p.18
[325] Ibid. p.18
[326] Ibid.

or not Codex has the ability or the desire to test for such possibilities. [327]

First, while it is quite possible to know what foods occurring naturally are allergenic it is much more difficult to come to these conclusions about new substances or proteins. This is partly due to the fact that naturally occurring materials have so many millions of years of history and use which, in itself, tends to naturally weed out the allergenic foods from the non-allergenic ones in a populations' diet. GM products do not have this history. Indeed, the idea that over time a population tends to form its' own guidelines through natural process adds to the ease in which scientific inquiry may form knowledge of the food properties in relation to the population itself. Again, this is not the case with GM food. Therefore, another problem with the Codex Guidelines is made manifest. Because Codex works on a global scale, the potential allergens are listed globally and may not take into consideration (in future labeling) the geographic concerns of individual populations. When one considers the fact that allergens differ across geographic boundaries, with some foods being allergenic in one culture but not in others, he/she is confronted with the task that, in order to introduce a new substance into the food supply with new proteins, all of these populations must be tested separately. The tests of course should also be conducted over a longer period of time to investigate prolonged exposure as well. However, Codex makes no mention of this problem and likewise, mentions no remedy for it. Are we really supposed to believe that, hidden deep within the Guidelines, Codex plans to organize representative samples of every culture across the globe for every new protein added to the food supply? This is not likely even if one believed the organization was working truly working for food safety.

Secondly, Codex itself admits tremendous flaws in it's' ability to test for new allergens. It says quite plainly that "there is no definitive

---

[327] Ibid. p. 27

test that can be relied upon to predict allergic response in humans to a newly expressed protein."[328] Because of this lack of a standardized and easily deciphered test, it goes on to say "A critical issue for testing will be the availability of human sera from sufficient numbers of individuals."[329] This, however, is a major problem due to the fact that, in order to test for just one allergy, a minimum of eight sera is required for a major allergy, and a minimum of twenty-four sera for a minor allergy.[330] This is a rather large amount of material for testing purposes. It should be noted that this is the required sera for just one test subject. This test would have to be repeated hundreds and perhaps even thousands of times per geographic region or culture. It would then have to be replicated hundreds or thousands of times more on a global scale to account for these regions and cultures. Even Codex admits, albeit in a footnote, that "It is recognized that these quantities of sera may not be available for testing purposes."[331] With this in mind, it is clear that testing for allergens in GM products would prove extremely difficult to organize and conduct, even if Codex were truly committed to its' professed goal of food safety.

Up to this point, all of the problems with the Codex Guidelines mentioned are regarding the section focusing on GM plants. There are, accordingly, two more sections - one dealing with GM Micro-Organisms and the other dealing with GM animals. While it may seem at first that this book focuses more attention on the first section (GM plants), the fact is that all three sections are very similar in their language and directives, with only a few changes in the wording made to apply to the new topic. In many of these sections the language is word for word, copied and pasted to reiterate the same purpose as the first section.

---

[328] Ibid. P.20
[329] Ibid.
[330] Ibid.
[331] Ibid. p.22

Therefore, I will not repeat my criticisms of the second and third sections that have appeared in my criticism of the first section. Suffice it to say that all the problems existing in the GM Plant section exist in the GM Micro-Organism and GM Animal sections as well, namely those of questionable scientific practices, the ignoring of relevant data, and so on. This claim is easily verifiable by reading the Guidelines document cited in the footnotes.

With that said, some attention should be paid to the section entitled, "Guideline For The Conduct Of Food Safety Assessment Of Foods Produced Using Recombinant-DNA Micro-Organisms." This section deals mainly with bacteria, yeasts, and certain types of fungi in their uses in food production. While making many of the same admissions present in the GM plant Guidelines, one of the most startling statements made regarding GM micro-organisms is the admission that they can in fact survive digestion. Codex says, "In some processed foods, they [GM micro-organisms] can survive processing and ingestion and can compete and, in some cases, be retained in the intestinal environment for significant periods of time."[332] While this statement is not revolutionary, it is quite surprising to see it uttered by Codex Alimentarius, an organization that seems to go to great lengths to approve GM products. Nevertheless, as will be discussed later, the fact that these micro-organisms can survive digestion is extremely important to the GMO safety debate. So are the questions of rDNA retention in the intestinal tract, the potential for changing the intestinal flora of those consuming the GM product, and the subsequent effects on the immune system. These are all concerns that Codex tacitly admits the existence of, simply by acknowledging the need to test them.[333] Yet the tendency of GM micro-organisms to survive digestion and begin to change the makeup of the human intestines is mentioned later, in a footnote,

---

[332] Ibid. p.39
[333] Ibid. p.42

where it is stated quite openly,

> Permanent life-long colonization by ingested micro-organisms
> is rare. Some orally administered micro-organisms have been
> recovered in feces or in the colonic mucosa weeks after
> feeding ceased. Whether the genetically modified micro-
> organism is established in the gastrointestinal tract or not,
> the possibility remains that it might influence the microflora
> or the mammalian host.[334]

It should be noted that the idea that "life-long colonization by ingested micro-organisms is rare"[335] is highly contested by many independent scientists.[336] Yet, even if one were to assume the truth of Codex's statement, the fact that it is rare means that it is still possible. More importantly is that the statement admits, that even without long-term residence in the intestinal tract, there is still the distinct possibility that it will still significantly affect the intestinal flora and likewise the host itself.

Similar, more obviously biased concerns exist in the subsection dealing with the information that should be provided on each of the DNA modifications or micro-organisms. This information is, for the most part, very basic. It contains such data as which genes are added, the number of insertion sites, etc. However, two sources of information to be included cause some concern. The first is the inclusion of the "identification of any open reading frames within inserted DNA or created by the modifications to contiguous DNA in the chromosome or in a plasmid, including those that could result in fusion proteins."[337] The

---

[334] Ibid. p.48
[335] Ibid.
[336] Smith, Jeffrey. "Seeds Of Deception." YES Books, 2003.
[337] "Foods Derived From Modern Biotechnology," 2nd edition. Codex Alimentarius. P. 44.

second is the "particular reference to any sequences known to encode, or to influence the expression of, potentially harmful functions."[338] Yet both of these expressions (fusion proteins and genes that express harmful functions) are considered potentially dangerous even under the weak Codex standards. These expressions refer to the ability of some proteins to fuse with other proteins of the same and other species, mutating the DNA of the species, or forcing it to produce potentially adverse affects. Neither of these characteristics should be present in food, yet Codex mandates only that they be reported, not removed, as a result of the testing. This appears to be a continual thread of Codex's Guidelines. They continue saying that additional information should be provided

> to demonstrate whether the arrangement of the modified genetic material has been conserved or whether significant rearrangements have occurred after the introduction to the cell and propagation of the recombinant strain to the extent needed for its use(s) in food production, including those that may occur during its storage according to current techniques;[339]

as well as

> to demonstrate whether deliberate modifications made to the amino acid sequence of the expressed protein result in changes in its post-translational modification or affect sites critical for its structure or function;[340]

---

ftp://ftp.fao.org/docrep/fao/011/a1554e/a1554e00.pdf
Accessed May 24, 2010.
[338] Ibid. p.45
[339] Ibid. p.45
[340] Ibid. p.45

While reporting information related to the instances above might seem like a good idea (and certainly few would argue that it isn't), simple reporting is not enough. Indeed, these issues, as well as the others mentioned in this section of the Guidelines, related directly to the question of the stability of genetically modified organisms. This is mentioned briefly in this section of the Guidelines, most notably in a footnote where it says,

> Microbial genes are more fluid than those of higher eukaryotes; that is, the organisms grow faster, adapt to changing environments, and are more prone to change. Chromosomal rearrangements are common. The general genetic plasticity of micro-organisms may affect recombinant DNA in micro-organisms and must be considered in evaluating the stability of recombinant DNA micro-organisms.[341]

This will be addressed later as well, when the dangers of GM foods are discussed. However, suffice it to say that these GM organisms are often dangerously unstable. Many of them carry genes that overproduce a certain characteristic, cannot be turned off, or simply begin to change even after it has been bonded to the new strain of DNA.

Yet with all of these admissions by Codex as to the dangers that GM micro-organisms pose to those who consume it as well as the fact that GM DNA is often unpredictable, the Codex Guidelines recommendations for testing suggests that these micro-organisms should be assessed based upon tests conducted on the conventional counterpart, not the micro-organism itself. If tests conclude that the questionable micro-organisms are removed or rendered non-toxic in their individual and natural states, then "viability and residence of

---

[341] Ibid.

micro-organisms in the alimentary system need no examination."[342] Embodying the impracticality and unscientific methodology of substantial equivalence in this context, Codex does not take into account the various potential dangers that it mentioned just a few short paragraphs previous.

Even on the question of antibiotic resistance, Codex takes the position of ignoring sound science in terms of its allowance of antibiotic resistant genes to be used as recipient organisms. It says,

> In general, traditional strains of micro-organisms developed for food processing uses have not been assessed for antibiotic resistance. Many micro-organisms used in food production possess intrinsic resistance to specific antibiotics. Such properties need not exclude such strains from consideration as recipients in constructing recombinant-DNA micro-organisms. [343]

Although Codex does suggest that transmissible antibiotic resistant genetic strains should not be used, it clearly states that they should not be removed from consideration for use. This does little to ease the concerns related to antibiotic resistance in general. This is because, as mentioned earlier, any gene that is inserted into another organism via genetic modification is inherently unstable. Not only that, but this process creates the potential to destabilize any other gene as well. So the possibility still exists even when not using what is considered a "transmissible" gene. Codex, of course, does not address this issue. It merely suggests that these antibiotic resistant genes not be removed from consideration as potential transfers and recipients.

---

[342] Ibid p.49
[343] Ibid. p.49

The final mention of Codex's treatment of GM micro-organisms revolves around some of the testing methods used to determine the potential of allergenicity – Sequence Homology and Pepsin Resistance testing. With the exception of the specific serum tests mentioned earlier (the more reliable form of testing when adequately provided for), these are the only two methods mentioned for determining potential micro-organism allergens. The problem with both of these methods is that they are insufficiently geared to the task. By Codex's own admission, Sequence Homology only assesses "the extent to which a newly expressed protein is similar in structure to a known allergen," not whether the protein actually is an allergen.[344] But even this limited testing ability is challenged by the fact that the test can only be conducted by using sequences of allergens that are already known and available in scientific literature and public databases.[345] The document also says, "There are also limitations in the ability of such comparisons to detect non-contiguous epitopes capable of binding themselves specifically with IgE antibodies."[346] Therefore, the Pepsin Resistance test is just as problematic as Sequence Homology because, as Codex admits, "a lack of resistance to pepsin does not exclude that the newly expressed protein can be a relevant allergen."[347] Because several food allergens have demonstrated a resistance to pepsin digestion, it was conceived that this method of testing would be useful for determining potential food allergens. However, this is obviously not the case as the correlation between pepsin resistance and allergenicity has not been fully investigated in its own right.[348] There is also the potential for Codex to use the some to ignore the many, i.e. actually using pepsin resistance

[344] Ibid. p.53
[345] Ibid. p.54
[346] Ibid. p.54
[347] Ibid. p.54
[348] Ibid.

testing to claim that if a substance has no pepsin resistance, then it is not a potential allergen.

The "Guideline For The Conduct Of Food Safety Assessment Of Foods Derived From Recombinant-DNA Animals," is as interesting for the concerns that it does not address as for the ones that it does. Largely a copied and pasted version of the two sections before it, the GM animal Guidelines does not address some very key issues such as:

1.) Animal welfare
2.) Ethical, moral and socio-economic aspects
3.) Environmental risks related to the environmental release of recombinant-DNA animals used in food production
4.) The safety of recombinant-DNA animals used as feed, or the safety of animals fed with feed derived from recombinant-DNA animals, plants and micro-organisms.[349]

As can be easily seen, these issues are extremely important in their own right. Just the moral issues, in addition to the hazards of potential GM animals being released into the environment, are enough to fill volumes. However, because Codex chooses not to deal with them in its Guidelines, they will be dealt with (in part) in a later section of this book.[350] That being said, because Codex treats GM animals essentially the same as GM plants, there is very little difference in the guidelines. This shows a lack of scientific zeal as animals are fundamentally different than plants. Yet one area where Codex does address a different aspect of the GM safety question is related to veterinary drug residues. It says,

Some recombinant-DNA animals may exhibit traits that may

---

[349] Ibid. p.57
[350] Animal welfare and moral issues will not be dealt with at all in the scope of this book.

result in the potential for altered accumulation or distribution of xenobiotics (e.g. veterinary drug residues, metals), which may affect food safety. Similarly, the potential for altered colonization by and shedding of human pathogens or new symbiosis with toxin-producing organisms in the recombinant-DNA animal could have an effect on food safety.[351]

With its' implicit admission of the instability of modified genes, Codex now also admits that these genes, when changed in animals, could affect the distribution and retention of veterinary drugs and other substances which would necessarily change the content of the food product derived from that animal. As Codex states, this same situation could also apply to human pathogens as well as veterinary drugs.

Continuing the discussion of Codex's history, it appears that 2007-2008 was a very beneficial year for GMO food producers. Not only were the pro-GM testing Guidelines approved by Codex, but many countries, such as the European Union who had been opposed to the introduction of GM food up to this point, began changing their position to that which was slightly more open to GMO. For instance, in 2008, Codex Alimentarius approved Guidelines that would allow low levels of GM products that have not been approved by the countries' regulatory agencies inside products imported into the country. This would include products like grain, corn, and oats. Codex claims that this set of standards merely recognizes the fact that GM products will inadvertently mix with non-GM products during processing and transportation and that it means to provide guidance in this unavoidable situation.[352] However, this presupposes that GM

---

[351] Ibid. p.71
[352] "Codex Alimentarius Commission: New Standards, old concerns," July 14, 2008.
http://www.freshplaza.com/print.asp?id=25392

contamination of food shipments is unavoidable when in fact just the opposite is the case. If GM products were not used to begin with, the entire issue would not need to be addressed in the first place. Also, if countries that did not approve of GM products would simply refuse to import them if they were contaminated with one single GM organism, then the fact that the majority of people do not want GM food would be driven home. This would be a great move for both the exporting and importing countries in that GM would be made economically unfeasible as well as forcing the importing country to produce their own food. It may come as a surprise to many that these Guidelines were approved with the consent of the European Union, the very state that has voiced much dissent to GM products in the past. This is a clear signal that the European Union, now that is has become even more integrated than when the GM debate first appeared, is preparing to accept GM food on the level of the United States in the future.

While these Guidelines only apply to GM contamination of imported food, the European Union's own guidelines have become much more relaxed in relation to GM food production within its' borders.It is here that the various European countries are experiencing the tyranny of being a member of a European superstate that undermines their national sovereignty. In March 2010, against the objections of countries such as Italy and Austria, the European Union's European Commission approved an antibiotic resistant genetically modified potato.[353] These countries who, before joining the EU, would have had complete authority to block the importation and production of GM material now must defer to the EU court and commission system that are clearly undemocratic and unconcerned with the safety of the

---

[353] Hickman, Martin; Roberts, Genevieve. "Fury as EU approves GM potato." The Independent. March 4, 2010. http://www.independent.co.uk/environment/green-living/fury-as-eu-approves-gm-potato-1915833.html

European people. This is the same situation that occurred in 1998 when the European Union approved the MON810 strain of GM maize developed by Monsanto against the protest of several EU states. Subsequently, several member nations banned the cultivation of the maize which now pits them against the European Commission in an ongoing battle for national sovereignty.[354] However, sovereignty is not likely to win out. In 2007, the European Court of Justice overturned Austria's' ban on cultivation of GMO's even though Austria has the broad support of it's' people and other nations. The court also ruled that individual countries had no right to deny farmers the ability to grow GM crops that the EU had previously approved. This ruling has effectively removed Austria's total cultivation ban. While many other Austrian regulations are in place that will make it a little more difficult for GMO production than in other countries, the European Commission and Courts will likely continue to chip away at them little by little.[355]

India has also relaxed its opposition to GM foods as evidenced, also in 2007, by the fact that the Indian Ministry of Environment and Forests announced that organisms that are not living (living being defined as an organism capable of replication) will now be exempt from the existing approval processes. This effectively allows all "non-living organisms" into India without any testing at all. This would apply to a wide range of products such as those containing GM corn or soy.[356]

---

[354]"EU food authorities say genetically modified maize is safe." AFP. June 30, 2009. http://www.france24.com/en/20090630-eu-food-authorities-say-genetically-modified-maize-safe- Accessed May 24, 2010.

[355] "Further 'Rubberstamp' GMO Approvals In The Pipeline In Europe." Bridges Trade BioRes October 5, 2007. Vol. 7 No. 17. http://ictsd.org/i/news/biores/60002/ Accessed May 24, 2010.

[356] "India Fast-Tracks Imports Of Non-Living GM Material." Bridges Trade BioRes October 5, 2007. Vol. 7 No. 17.

It should also be mentioned that as of January 2009, the FDA has announced that labeling of GM food animals is not required at the consumer level. While GM animals are required to be labeled while alive, when the animals reaches the food stage the labeling requirements disappear. GM animals are only required to be labeled at the food stage when this seen to be a substantial difference in the food product.[357] However, it should be remembered that, because the FDA works on an even more relaxed version of substantial equivalence than Codex, it is already assumed that these foods will not be significantly different from a conventional counterpart. Thus, we have unfettered access of GM animal food products to the food supply with no way for the consumer to determine whether or not the product he/she is eating has been genetically modified.

The Dangers of Genetic Modification

The dangers of genetic modification can be divided into two categories: human health and environment. In the limited amount of independent study given to GM products, alarms have been raised on almost every front. Damage to adjacent DNA, various health problems, and almost infinite environmental pollution are just some of the known adverse effects of genetic modification.

In terms of human health, among the known side effects are

---

http://ictsd.org/i/news/biores/59999/ Accessed May 24, 2010.

[357] Reinberg, Steven. "FDA Issues Final Regulations for Geneticially Engineered Animals." US News And World Report. January 15, 2009. http://health.usnews.com/health-news/managing-your-healthcare/policy/articles/2009/01/15/fda-issues-final-regulations-for-genetically.html Accessed May 24, 2010.

cancer, obesity, and increased allergies. But that is only the most widely known. Countless other dangers most likely exist, but are currently unknown due to lack of testing. One of the studies that illustrate the danger of GMOs most efficiently was one conducted by Arpad Pusztai in the late 1990's. Pusztai was a leading scientist in his field of experimental biology and was well distinguished in terms of his credentials. In 1995, he, along with colleagues from the Rowett Institute, Scottish Crop Research Institute, and University of Durham School of Biology, were awarded £1.6 million by the Scottish Agriculture, Environment, and Fisheries Department for the purpose of creating a model testing procedure for genetically modified foods. At the time, there had been no published scientific research on the safety of GMO. This experiment began genetically modifying a potato to produce a lectin, a pesticide which occurs in nature that some plants produce to ward off insects. This pesticide is safe for humans to eat as well as rats. This is evidenced by a study that Pusztai himself published years earlier in which he fed the lectin to rats at 800 times the amount that his current GM potatoes were programmed to produce and there was no apparent damage to the rats at this level. However, Pusztai found several surprises. First, and contrary to the FDA and Codex's claims of inherent substantial equivalence, the GM potatoes were in fact very different from their parent organisms. Some GM potatoes contained less protein than the parent lines, with one line containing 20% less. Second, even the GM potatoes, grown from the same parent lines in the same conditions, differed significantly from each other in composition and nutritional value. This fact alone shows that GMO's are unstable because, otherwise, the nutritional value would not vary.[358]

Yet this was not the most surprising discovery Pusztai made. It should be kept in mind that Pusztai's study was not the all-too-common

---

[358] Smith, Jeffrey. "Seeds of Deception." YES Books, 2003. Pp.11-12

industry funded whitewash. His was meticulously organized and thoroughly conducted. He fed the lab rats GM potatoes, natural potatoes, and natural potatoes spiked with the same amount of the same lectin being produced by the GM potatoes. The potato preparation was varied between raw, boiled, and baked potatoes and even varied the amounts in their diets. Protein content of the rats' diet was varied and the tests were conducted over both 10 day and 110 day periods. Pusztai found several things. First, the rats that were fed the GM potatoes had damaged immune systems. Their white blood cells also responded much more slowly which left them more easily susceptible to disease. Not only that, but the organs related to the immune system were damaged as well. These rats also had smaller, less developed brains, livers, and testicles. Some had enlarged intestines, pancreas, and other tissues as well as liver atrophy. Lastly, significant structural changes of cells in the intestines, as well as their abundance, signaled the amplified potential for cancer. [359]

In this study, only the rats that were fed the GM potatoes experience the negative side effects. While at first glance, many might blame the lectin for the adverse effects. One must keep in mind that rats had been fed 800 times the amount of lectin than was present in the GM potatoes with no recognizable harmful side effects in previous studies. Also, the rats fed the natural potatoes spiked with the lectin did not experience these problems either - only the rats fed the GM potatoes. Clearly, this shows that it was not the lectins causing such health problems but the process of genetic engineering itself.[360] In 2007, a Russian study was partially released that confirmed the cancer links to GM food. Conducted by the Institute of Nutrition of the Russian Academy of Medical Sciences almost eight years before in 1998, rats were again fed GM potatoes and the results were very similar. Those

---

[359] Ibid. p.12
[360] Ibid. pp.12-13

that were fed the GM potatoes developed serious organ and tissue damage. These results were apparent even after those who conducted the story violated normal scientific practice and took results only from the rats that survived. This is highly significant because half of the rats in the study died.[361] Like the Pusztai study, these results were suppressed for some time and only through the legal system were they even partially revealed.[362]

One may also remember the discussion of rBGH, another genetically modified substance, in the previous chapter and its' connection to increased cancer. This will not be revisited in the current chapter but it should be noted that rBGH is also a genetically modified product with strong links to the illness as well.

Another factor involved in genetic engineering related to increased rates of cancer is that of the CaMV promoter. Cells naturally protect their DNA from foreign invasive genes through an elaborate defense system. This system normally prevents the invading genes from entering cell and grasping on to the DNA. However, there are some organisms that can successfully defeat the defenses of the cell. These organisms are usually viruses, some of which can cause cancer. This is important because, in the process of genetic engineering, it is one of these carcinogenic viruses, Cauliflower Mosaic Virus (CaMV), that is used as the promoter. Essentially, the promoter acts as an on/off switch

---

[361] Brown, Colin. "Suppressed report shows cancer link to GM potatoes." The Independent. February 17, 2007. http://www.independent.co.uk/life-style/health-and-families/health-news/suppressed-report-shows-cancer-link-to-gm-potatoes-436673.html May 24, 2010.
[362] Ibid.
See Also,
Smith, Jeffrey. "Seeds of Deception." YES Books, 2003. Pp. 5-44.

for the gene. This CaMV promoter is designed to overcome the defenses of the cell, take over the mechanics of the genes, and copy itself. Not only does it invade and take over the gene, but it also acts independently of the gene that it has dominated and can force it to turn on at its command. This, however, forces the gene to remain turned on 24/7, potentially draining some systems while at the same time rapidly increasing others. Accordingly, the CaMV promoter not only turns on the gene it is attached to, but often turns on the native genes as well. It may turn on genes that are located some distance away from it in the DNA sequence or even those located on other DNA strands completely. There is no way that these genes can be turned off or adjusted once they are inserted nor is there any way to tell exactly what these genes will do when they reach the DNA.[363] As Jeffrey Smith stated in his book "Seeds of Deception," "Turning genes on or off is another form of Russian roulette."[364]

The major worry relating CaMV promoters to cancer is cell proliferation and the waking of sleeping viruses within the GM organism or the consumer. Arpad Pusztai noticed the cell proliferation caused by GM potatoes in his rat studies when he discovered the thickening of the intestines. It was suggested then that this improper cell growth may have a correlation to the onset of cancer. Stanley Ewen, a leading tissue disease expert in Scotland reaffirms this idea.[365] As quoted by Jeffrey Smith, he says that the CaMV promoter "could affect stomach and colonic lining by causing a growth factor effect with the unproven possibility of hastening cancer formation in those organs."[366] While Ewen refers to the unproven possibility of cancer, it is scientifically well-

---

[363] Smith, Jeffrey. "Seeds of Deception." YES Books, 2003. Pp.62-64
[364] Ibid.
[365] Ibid. P. 65.
[366] Ibid. p. 65

documented that cell proliferation is linked to increases in cancer.[367] In a paper written for The Institute of Science in Society entitled "Cauliflower Mosaic Viral Promoter – A Recipe for Disaster?" scientists Ho, Ryan, and Cummins state, "...because the CaMV promoter is promiscuous in function (see above), it has the possibility of promoting inappropriate over-expression of genes in all species to which it happens to be transferred. One consequence of such inappropriate over-expression of genes may be cancer."[368] This is one possible reason for the significant increase in the cancer rate.

The waking of sleeping viruses provides an equally disturbing circumstance. It has already largely been established that the insertion of genetically modified viruses into plant DNA can create new viruses that are themselves highly virulent. [369] This is extremely dangerous in its own right due to the potential for the release of these viruses into the environment and the ultimate consumption of them by humans and/or animals. Contrary to what the GMO industry would have the public believe, the transfer of modified genes from one species to another is quite common. In fact, it occurs so regularly that it has even been given a name – "horizontal gene transfer." Indeed, studies conducted in the late 1980's confirmed that the GM DNA does in fact survive digestion. Not only that, it is found in the blood, intestinal wall, liver, and spleen, intact and alive, as well as in feces and the digestive system. It has also been found to linger in these areas for more than five days. In 2002, a study was conducted on human volunteers. Each of these volunteers had their large intestines removed and wore colostomy bags. The study results revealed that a large portion of the GM DNA survived digestion

---

[367] See rBGH chapter.

[368] Ho, Mae-Wan; Ryan, Angela; Cummins, Joe; "Cauliflower Mosaic Viral Promoter-A Recipe for Disaster?" Institute of Science in Society. http://www.i-sis.org.uk/camvrecdis.php

[369] Smith, Jeffrey. "Seeds of Deception." YES Books, 2003. P. 64

and passed all the way through the small intestine. Furthermore, three of the seven participants experienced horizontal gene transfer. Some of the human digestive bacteria in these three individuals contained the herbicide-resistant gene used in GM soybeans.[370]

The fact that horizontal gene transfer can occur as well as the knowledge that insertion of plant or insect virus genes into crops can cause highly virulent new viruses is very concerning because it demonstrates that the same result can be produced in humans. As Jeffrey Smith suggests, "Suppose, for example, that the CaMV promoter from a GM corn kernel wanders off inside the stomach of a human and gets reattached to the DNA of a dormant virus. Instead of promoting an insecticide gene as was intended, it may now be switching on a virus."[371] The insecticide gene is dangerous enough, but a dormant virus, potentially one that has never before existed, is much more frightening. Ho, Ryan, and Cummins confirm this suspicion. They say,

> Horizontal transfer of the CaMV promoter not only contributes to the known instability of transgenic lines, but has the potential to reactivate dormant viruses or creating new viruses in all species to which it is transferred, particularly in view of the modularity and interchangeability of promoter elements. In this regard, the close relationship of CaMV to hepadnaviruses such as the human hepatitis B is especially relevant.[372]

Here we see another possibility for the increase of disease, specifically cancer, which we are witnessing across the world. Coupled with the

---

[370] Ibid. pp. 59-60
[371] Ibid. pp. 64-65.
[372] Ho, Mae-Wan; Ryan, Angela; Cummins, Joe; "Cauliflower Mosaic Viral Promoter-A Recipe for Disaster?" Institute of Science in Society. http://www.i-sis.org.uk/camvrecdis.php

potential for antibiotic resistant bacteria explained in the previous section, we are witnessing what could potentially be an unprecedented public health crisis.

As mentioned earlier in the chapter, the inherent instability of GMO's play a major role in their danger. For all the knowledge that scientists have about GMO's, they simply have no way to accurately predict exactly how these organisms will act once created. This, in and of itself, creates many more dangers than would even be present in a GM food that produces a dangerous toxin. One contributing factor is that, for many years, scientists claimed to be sure that each gene only produced one protein but, as it turns out, this is not the case. One gene can actually produce many different proteins. This immensely reduces the chance that one will be able to predict the correct protein or trait that will occur in the modified organism. [373]

Spliceosomes are known to play an important role in the instability of GMO's. Nicknamed "Code Scramblers" by Jeffrey Smith because of their job function, they are a group of molecules involved with the creation of proteins by DNA. Essentially, in order to create a protein, DNA directs RNA to form and assemble amino acids (which form proteins). In some cases, however, the spliceosomes arrive before the RNA can finish its' task, break up the RNA, rearrange, and reassemble it. This causes the RNA to have an entirely new set of instructions for protein creation resulting, quite logically, in an entirely new protein. As stated earlier, the resulting protein can be one of thousands of different variations of proteins. Also, contrary to what it may seem, this "code scrambling" action is not at random. The spliceoseomes do not attach to just any RNA, but rather to those whom they were already looking for, usually those with introns attached.

---

[373] Smith, Jeffrey. "Seeds of Deception." YES Books, 2003. P. 52-75.

There is very real concern that these spliceosomes could grasp on to modified RNA, thinking that there is a match between it and the RNA it was intended to scramble, and begin to create new proteins. Not only are there too many possibilities to predict what protein might be created, there is also the possibility that the protein will be one that has never been seen before. There is no historical basis by which to postulate in this regard. The new protein could be toxic, allergenic, or even a new disease. Generally, in the process of genetic modification, these new proteins are not tested for. Indeed, in cases where the RNA is not usually scrambled, such as bacteria genes, engineers go the extra mile to make sure that scrambling is a possibility (though not for this stated purpose). For the most part, in plant and animal DNA, it is the RNA with introns attached that gets scrambled. When using bacteria genes, however, the scientists assume that the genes will not be scrambled so they actually attach introns. This not only pumps up the production of proteins, but it also enables "code scrambling." This in an area where it would not have normally even occurred before. If the DNA and RNA respond to the introns, it would logically follow that the spliceosomes might also respond, then resulting in previously unknown proteins that, in some cases, could be turned on at their full capacity. · The pro-GMO camp, of course, ignores this possibility.[374]

Another concern, of which less is known, is the effect of "hitchhiker" molecules on the protein and "chaperone" proteins that come into contact with the newly created protein. The hitchhiker molecules are simply those that are added onto the protein such as sugars, phosphates, sulfates, or lipids. These hitchhikers vary throughout different areas of the body and, depending on the area in which they are found, may change the protein in different ways if they attach themselves. The question in regards to GMO's is whether or not the newly created protein (such as the Bt gene in Bt corn) will pick up a

[374] Ibid. p. 52-55.

hitchhiker molecule that will result in changes to that protein and thus the overall organism.

The "chaperone" proteins are a bit different. In order for a protein to function properly, it must be organized in precisely the right way structurally. When the protein is not arranged in the sequence needed for a particular trait, the protein is inactive. However, sometimes these proteins come into contact with a protein referred to as a "chaperone," that unfolds them making them active. The question, like that of the hitchhiker molecule, is whether or not a foreign protein, inactive at the time of meeting, will be activated by the chaperone protein.[375]

Even the initial process of inserting foreign genes into natural host DNA creates the potential for instability as well. Jeffrey Smith describes the process of inserting the DNA as follows,

> We have used the word "insert" when describing the "placement" of foreign genes into a host DNA. That's more than polite. One common method used to "insert" genes is to blast them into the DNA with a 22-caliber gene gun. Scientists first coat thousands of tiny shards of gold or tungsten with the foreign gene. Then they point it at a dish containing thousands of unsuspecting cells. Then they fire, hoping that at least some of the foreign genes will end up in the right place in at least some of the DNA. This, by the way, is what the biotech industry refers to as their highly precise method of gene transfer.[376]

As one might suspect, this method can result in damage to the native genes and potentially the inserted ones as well. These genes may be

---

[375] Ibid. p. 55-57.
[376] Ibid. p.57.

damaged in ways that are unidentifiable thereby prohibiting the knowledge of how they will react when they fuse. As quoted on the website belonging to Mothers for Natural Law, Senior Lecturer in Molecular Pathology in London, UK, Dr. Michael Antoniou says about this method, "This procedure results in disruption of the genetic blueprint of the organism with totally unpredictable consequences."[377] This process opens the possibility of foreign genes being inserted in the wrong way, several copies of the gene scattered throughout the genetic makeup, or even inserted inside other genes. Compound this with the fact that some genes, as a result of genetic modification, can turn on or off unexpectedly as well as the potential for the production of new toxins or the amplification of existing ones and it can be seen just how unstable GMO's actually are. "Insertion mutation," another example of instability, a term used to describe a change in the host's DNA. This reaction has been linked to leukemia in children when produced as a result of human gene therapy. The causation of such a disease is known as "insertion carcinogenesis."[378]

When one discusses the randomized positioning of inserted foreign genes into DNA it is also important to mention "position effects." This is essentially where the inserted gene ends up in the DNA strand. Because DNA, contrary to its' surface appearance, is very precise, the location of the foreign gene is very important. In some locations the gene may produce its' protein at reduced levels while at other locations it may not produce the protein at all. A common position effect is gene silencing. This occurs when either the foreign gene or the natural gene in it's' vicinity gets shut off completely and is

[377] "What Do Scientists Say About the Dangers of Genetic Engineering?" Mothers for Natural Law. http://www.safe-food.org/-issue/scientists.html
[378] Smith, Jeffrey. "Seeds of Deception." YES Books, 2003. P. 57-58.

no longer able to produce its protein. This often happens when the foreign gene lands in the middle of the natural gene. However, this is not a prerequisite scenario as the silencing is highly unpredictable.[379] In his book, "Seeds of Deception," Jeffrey Smith mentions an experiment in which this scenario did occur and resulted in the death of the mouse embryos being tested. Along these lines, another major concern is that a natural gene that was responsible for suppressing a toxin, might be turned off, allowing the toxin to actually increase. [380]

Another aspect of genetic modification that bears some discussion is that of promoter genes. Promoter genes pose another risk in addition to cancer viruses. Like the factors mentioned above, they also contribute greatly to the instability of GMO products. Because of the precision of DNA, wherein genes work hand in hand with each other to achieve their own particular task, the insertion of foreign genes quite simply throws the entire system into disarray. In their natural state, while some genes work continuously, others hang back until they are needed, and others do not "do" anything (at least from what we can see). Science does not completely understand this process. However, what is known is that, once foreign genes are inserted into the natural DNA, the cells have no idea what to do with the new material. This can result in massive confusion of the DNA as well as widely varied instability. The cell DNA does not know whether to turn the gene on or off, switch on only when needed, or any other function that genes normally have. This is the main reason promoter genes are used in GM products. These promoters are made up of genetic material with instructions to turn on the gene. They are then sent in with the foreign genes permanently in the "on" mode, usually set to the highest intensity possible. In addition to the potential for awaking dormant viruses, these promoters often turn on the natural genes in their

---

[379] Ibid. P. 47-77.
[380] Ibid. pp. 60-61.

vicinity. There is no real way to turn off, adjust, or predict these genes.[381]

Other factors that contribute to GMO instability are genetic disposition and gene stacking. Genetic disposition comes into play any time the foreign genes are inserted into the natural DNA. This is because the gene expression levels vary greatly, even when added to DNA from the same plant species, depending upon the disposition of the natural genes. Gene stacking, the process by which organisms are engineered with more than one gene, is another issue. It can be accomplished intentionally or accidentally by cross pollination. Obviously, increasing the amount of foreign genes to the DNA of the organism adds even more possibilities for variation. Yet it appears that this process also tends to increase the potency of pesticides genetically engineered into the organism. One can only guess what effects this may have on the consumer or the environment.[382]

Allergies provide another major concern related to genetic modification. Essentially, there are three ways in which allergies could be produced from the process of genetic engineering. First, the modification could increase the level of an already naturally occurring allergen with the modified food. Second, the allergenic property could be transferred from one organism to the other. Third, the process of genetic engineering could result in entirely unknown allergens never before seen in the human food supply due to the process itself.[383]

An example of the first scenario can be found in the case of the introduction of GM soy in the UK. In 1999, it was discovered by York Laboratory that soy allergies in the UK had increased by 50 percent. This

---

[381] Ibid. pp.62-64
[382] Ibid. pp. 67-68.
[383] Ibid. p. 69.

pushed soy into the top ten allergies list for the first time where it was listed alongside other foods and food products that have a long history of producing allergies. Many of the people reacted with serious symptoms such as irritable bowel syndrome, digestion problems, skin rashes, eczema, and other chronic illnesses. These reactions were traced to antibodies present in the blood as a result of the soy. Another interesting discovery was that the increase in soy allergies in the UK directly corresponded to the entrance of GM soy into the food supply on a widespread basis. While there are many different reasons why GM soy might be more allergenic than natural soy (some reasons have already been discussed), Trypsin inhibitor which is found in natural soy and has been identified as an allergen, is present at about 27 percent higher amounts in some GM varieties of soy than in natural soy. Soy has been known to cause allergies for some time even in its' natural state but the level of allergenicity has never reached the levels that it exists at today. It should be noted that, in the U.S., GM soy is used in most of the processed foods consumed on an ever increasing basis. GM soy is mixed with natural soy in these cases, therefore it is almost impossible to avoid the GM products unless one eats wholly organic foods. Even then, the chances that one may consume GM foods inadvertently are fairly high.[384]

The second manner in which allergens may be introduced by GM foods is the transfer of allergenic properties of one organism to the other. As a brief example, soy can once again be used. Around 1995, Pioneer Hi-Bred wanted to genetically engineer a soybean that would be more suitable for animal feed in terms of protein. For this purpose, a gene from the Brazil nut was chosen. When tested, it was first believed that nothing of importance would turn up, since only one protein of the nut was used and it was assumed by many scientists that one must isolate the particular protein of the nut that causes allergies if the final

---

[384] Ibid. p. 160-161.

product were to cause them. However, what they found was that the finished soybean did, in fact, cause allergic reactions in people with allergies to Brazil nuts.[385] As Smith points out in his book, an article in the Washington Post states, "In trying to build a better soybean, the company had made a potentially deadly one." [386] Not only that, but as the article rightly points out, the danger is even more real "because people with allergies to nuts wouldn't think to avoid soy."[387] As a result of this discovery, FDA toxicologist Louis Pribyl critiqued the FDA's policy of allergy testing requirements. The FDA provides a list of allergens (shellfish, fish, milk, eggs, nuts, wheat, and legumes) and specifies that, if any manufacturer uses a gene from one of these food products, the company should consult with the FDA about risks of allergies. While these items make up close to 90 percent of all known food allergies, the other ten percent are not listed. The FDA's obviously unscientific and political bias towards genetic modification aside, these consults are largely voluntary and the information provided to the agency does not have to be provided in full. This is partly why Pribyl criticized the policy. He rightly points out that very few allergens have indentified at the gene or protein level, therefore, at this point at least, it is virtually impossible to be sure if GM products are free of transferred allergens.[388]

The possibility of the introduction of entirely new allergens to the human food supply has been mentioned several times already. For that reason, the science of how new allergens can be created will not be rehashed. However, it exists as a very real possibility for the both the present as well as the future. Because allergy testing is largely not

[385] Ibid. pp. 161-163.
[386] Weiss, Rick. "Biotech Food Raises a Crop of Questions." Washington Post. August 15, 1999.
http://www.organicconsumers.org/ge/biotechfood.cfm
[387] Ibid.
[388] Smith, Jeffrey. "Seeds of Deception." YES Books, 2003. Pp. 161-163.

conducted in regards to GM foods, whether in initial laboratory testing situations or in the context of public health, we do not know to what extent these potentially new allergens will or already have invaded the food supply. It is even unclear as to how many individuals suffer from food allergies as diagnosed by a doctor, let alone undiagnosed altogether. Indeed, allergies are on the rise for reasons that are, as of yet, unknown.[389] Considering the opposition and propaganda from industry, the regulatory agencies, and welfare scientists, this knowledge is likely to remain hidden and distorted for some time. For now, we are forced to rely on those persecuted, underfunded, but decent scientists who have the courage to speak the truth.

The other major concern with GM foods is the impact they have on the environment. The introduction of only one product to the environment, intentionally or by accident, may have devastating effects that can never be reversed. Micro-organisms, plants, and animals produced by genetic modification have the potential to not only contaminate natural species, but also dominate and destroy them. A perfect example of this ticking time bomb is the Aqua Bounty Salmon developed by Aqua Bounty Farms. These salmon were genetically engineered with a growth hormone to increase their size and growth rate. These particular salmon can grow up to seven times bigger than their natural counterparts. However, there are several problems that arise. In testing, the survival rate of the modified salmon was significantly reduced even to the point of extinction in tanks containing modified fish. Not only did the GM fish out compete the natural fish for food, they attacked them and, in many cases, resorted to cannibalism. The fish that did survive were the most aggressive modified fish. It was in the natural salmon-only tanks were the only ones that experienced

---

[389] Ibid. pp. 161-181.

normal growth and development. [390] The question then arises as to the effect that the release of the engineered fish would have on the environment.

Unfortunately, the environmental impact would be devastating. The worst case scenario, often referred to as the "Trojan gene" hypothesis, is that the Aqua Bounty fish outcompete the natural salmon for food, resources, and mates and lead to the extinction of the entire wild salmon species. [391] Although this is only a hypothesis, it is one that is quite plausible and possible. Indeed, the impacts may not even end with the extinction of wild salmon but have ripple effects throughout the environment. For instance, beyond the moral issue of eradicating a species, we are unaware of the consequences of removing the salmon themselves from the ocean. One can only wonder what kind of effects would have on other species both animal and plant. The salmon's natural predators would naturally be affected if the salmon were to become extinct and, even if the GM salmon remained, their abnormal size and aggression would likely affect the predators as well. These are ripple effect likely to be felt all throughout the ecosystem and no one truly knows just how far they will permeate out.

Yet these concerns are not potential disasters so much as imminent ones. Hundreds of thousands of Atlantic salmon have escaped fish farms in the Northwest when floating pens were damaged or nets

---

[390] "GM Salmon Muscle In on Wild Fish When Food Is Scarce." Scientific American. June 8, 2004. http://www.scientificamerican.com/article.cfm?id=gm-salmon-muscle-in-on-wi Accessed May 24, 2010.
[391] "Gene Altered Giant Salmon Cannibals." Mercola.com. June 23, 2004. http://articles.mercola.com/sites/articles/archive/2004/06/23/gene-altered-salmon.aspx

ripped apart by inclimate weather or sea lions.[392] Because of this fact, many have suggested that it is not a question of if GM fish are released into the environment but when. Not only is there a risk of unintentional release, but there is a possibility that some farms could release infected and diseased fish into the environment to avoid paying for their disposal in a landfill as regulations require. This is a fairly common occurrence with fish farms and the farmers are rarely penalized for the incursion. For the most part, the claim is made that the nets ripped accidentally and the matter is overlooked.[393] The response to these concerns by companies like Aqua Bounty is that these GM fish will be made sterile and thus incapable of reproducing in the natural environment if they do escape. Yet this is a weak, if not deceptive, argument at best. While companies would have the public believe, through inference, that there is some method for testing each and every one of the millions and millions of fish being produced in their farms to ensure their infertility, realistically there isn't. Not only is this virtually impossible, it is not cost effective in any way. The price tag for these fish and the means to produce them would then become so high that no one would be able to afford them in the first place, removing the incentive to produce them. In addition, as we have seen earlier, the process of genetic modification is nowhere near an exact science. So, if millions of fish were engineered, one could only imagine the range of variability in the finished products. In many fish, the sterility gene simply would not function at all. Because of the techniques being used in the genetic modification process as well as the lack of knowledge in many areas regarding it, we are simply

[392] Doughton, Sandi. "Research fuels fear of gene-altered fish." The Seattle Times. June 08, 2004. http://seattletimes.nwsource.com/html/localnews/20019507 89_genefish08m
[393] "Genetically Modified Fish: A Disaster Waiting To Happen." www.mercola.com. February 01, 2003. http://articles.mercola.com/sites/articles/archive/2003/02/0 1/gm-fish.aspx

guaranteed that some of these fish will be able to breed and reproduce. Thus we have an enormous ticking time bomb that the general public is not even aware exists.

The fact that a drastic change in the natural state of one species can reverberate to another species is widely known. Not only is this well known in the world of science, it is basic common sense among those who choose to use it. This can also be seen in the case of the effect that GM Bt producing corn plants had on the Monarch butterfly. The Bt pesticide the corn was engineered to produce, one might remember, was intended to kill the European corn borer. While this should be controversial in its' own right, the GM corn had an additional effect. In tests being conducted by researchers at Cornell University, it was noticed that the caterpillars being observed were acting much more sluggish than usual. At the end of the experiment, they had attached themselves to the plant they were placed on, turned black, and began to rot. The result was that 44% of them died. This is because they were placed on a milkweed plant that had been dusted, not with the Bt pesticide, but with the pollen from the Bt corn. Fortunately, this made national news and began to awaken some members of the public to the dangers of GMO's. As expected a heavily funded pro-industry debunking campaign was launched to devalue the science as well as the scientists. However, although not heavily publicized, a comment by Arnold Foudin of the USDA was quite telling. In an interview the assistant director of scientific services said, "We knew things like monarchs and other butterflies would be susceptible. That's part of the general background noise."[394] This statement clearly shows that there was foreknowledge of

---

[394] Yoon, Carol Kaesuk. "News Analysis; What's Next for Biotech Crops? Questions." New York Times. December 19, 2000. http://nytimes.com/2000/12/19/science/news-analysis-what-s-next-for-biotech-crops-questions-.htm?pagewanted=1&pagewanted=print

the effects that GMO's (at least this particular one) would have on the environment. It also shows, at the very least, complacency in the attempt to cover these dangers up.

Almost every GM product created has the potential to infiltrate the ecosystem and continue to contaminate it for eternity. Such can be seen in one of the most widely known GM food scandals involving Starlink corn, a GM strain of corn that produced the Bt pesticide. However, the Bt pesticide produced by Starlink, Cry9C, is different even from other GM strains that produce Bt.[395] This version of the toxin is more resistant to heat and gastric juices. This resistance gives the body more time to overreact to the toxin, hence an allergic reaction. Its molecular weight is also consistent with a substance that can trigger allergic reactions.[396] Many of those who unknowingly ingested food materials made with the Starlink corn experienced symptoms ranging from very mild allergic reactions, diarrhea, abdominal pain, and skin rashes, to serious life threatening issues such and reactions similar to an anaphylactic response. This was a phenomenon that occurred all across the country with individuals who consumed the Cry9C Starlink corn. While the corn was never supposed to be consumed by humans, and even the EPA (because it oversees GM crops that produce their own pesticide) did not approve it for human consumption, it nevertheless found its way into the human food supply. True to form, the FDA, however, was not so diligent as it did not express concern about Starlink.[397] As quoted by Jeffrey Smith, a letter written by the FDA to

---

[395] Smith, Jeffrey. "Seeds of Deception." YES Books, 2003. P.166.

[396] Kaufman, Marc. "Biotech Corn Is The Test Case For Industry: Engineered Food's Future Hinges on Allergy Study." Washington Post. March 19, 2001. http://www.gmfoodnews.com/wp190301.txt

[397] Smith, Jeffrey. "Seeds of Deception." YES Books, 2003. P. 165-167.

AgrEvo the FDA stated,

> Based on the safety and nutritional assessment you have conducted, it is our understanding that AgrEvo has concluded that corn grain and forage derived from the new variety are not materially different in composition, safety, or other relevant parameters from corn grain or forage currently on the market, and that they do not raise issues that would require premarket review or approval by the FDA.[398]

It should be noted that, as the above quotation indicates, that the FDA completely relies on studies and assessments done by the industry. This is standard procedure for all GM products. Although the EPA restricted Starlink corn from being consumed by humans, it did allow it to be used for animal feed with the stipulations that it would be segregated from other types of corn when grown. However, it appears these guidelines were only as good as the paper they were written on. In many cases, farmers and grain elevators simply were not aware of the guidelines for the GM corn due to the fact that the special instructions were readily distributed. Many farmers even claimed that they were misled by the labels on the corn which stated, "You are licensed upon purchase of this product only to produce forage or grain for food, feed or grain processing."[399] Their claim of deception seems to circle around the fact that this statement is similar to that on other labels of corn previously purchased. The manufacturers obviously dispute this, yet the farmers maintain their claims.[400] Whatever the case, the end result was that Starlink was mixed with grain in silos all across the country, eventually contaminating 22% of the corn tested by the USDA. Almost every

---

[398] Ibid. P. 167

[399] Ryberg, William. "Growers of biotech corn say they weren't warned." Des Moines Register. August 20, 2000. http://www.gmfoodnews.com/dm251000.txt

[400] Ibid.

product made of corn was contaminated. Yet the tragedy did not end with the discovery of the contamination.[401] In an attempt to lobby the EPA to legalize Starlink corn presence in the food supply, Aventis admitted that the contamination could never be retracted. Because of cross-pollination and other reasons, Starlink will be present in the food supply forever.[402] This is but one example of how GMO's can contaminate the natural environment and the disastrous results that can persist for eternity. It is estimated that, as of July 2007, 91% of soy, 88% of cotton, 80-85% of canola, 85% of corn, and over half of Hawaiian papayas are genetically modified. When one takes into account how many different foods use at least of one these ingredients, the amount of genetically modified food we eat every day is staggering. A brief listing of some other sources of GMO's is provided below.

Brief Listing of common GMO's in the Food Supply	
Milk	Any milk produced using rBGH
Food Additives	Ascorbic acid/ascorbate (Vitamin C), cellulose, citric acid, cobalimin (vitamin B12), cyclodextrin, cystein, dextrin, dextrose, diacetyl, fructose, glucose, glutamate, glutamic acid, gluten, glycerides (mono and di-), glycerol, glycerine, glycine, hemicelluloses, hydrogenated starch hydrolates, hydroloyzed vegetable protein or starch, inositol, invert sugar, inverse syrup (inversol or colorose), lactic acid, lactoflavin, lecithin, leucine, lysine, maltose, maltitol, maltodextrin, mannitol, methylcellulose, milo starch, modified food starch, monooleate, monosodium glutamate (MSG), oleic acid, pheylalanine, phytic acid, riboflavin (Vitamin B2), sorbitol, stearic acid, threonine, tocopherol (Vitamin E), trehalose, xantham gum, zein

[401] Smith, Jeffrey. "Seeds of Deception." YES Books, 2003 Pp. 165-167.
[402] Ibid P.170.

Animal Products	Meat, eggs, dairy products, etc, from GM animals or from animals that have been fed GM material, honey and/or bee pollen that has sources of GM pollen
Ingredients from soybeans	Soy four, soy protein, soy isolates, soy isoflavones, soy lecithin, vegetable proteins, textured vegetable protein (TVP), tofu, tamari, tempeh, soy protein supplements
Ingredients from corn	Corn flour, corn gluten, corn masa, corn starch, corn syrup, cornmeal, high-fructose corn syrup
Oils/Margarine	Any vegetable oil, vegetable fat, or margarine made with soy, corn, cottonseed, or canola
Flavorings etc.	Enzymes, flavorings, processing agents, sweeteners and rennet. Especially aspartame (Nutrasweet®)
Tobacco	Quest®

[403] *(continued from previous page)*

While this is only a brief listing of sources of GMO's contaminating the food supply, it would almost be more accurate to claim that that every food item has the potential for contamination. Certainly this is true for crops. The above list, as well as the ones below, are only those most common sources for GMO's. As once can see, even the lists for the most common sources is extensive.

Brief Listing of common sources of GMO contamination of Food and Non-Food Items	
Food Items	Infant formula, salad dressing, bread, cereal, hamburgers, hotdogs, margarine, mayonnaise, crackers, cookies, chocolate, candy, fried food, chips, veggie burgers, meat substitutes, ice cream, frozen yogurt, tofu, tamari, soy sauce, soy cheese, tomato sauce, protein powder, baking powder, powdered/confectioner's sugar, confectioner's glaze, alcohol, vanilla, powdered sugar, peanut butter, enriched

---

[403] "Genetically Modified Ingredients Overview." Seedsofdeception.com
http://www.seedsofdeception.com/Public/BuyingNon-GMO/index.cfm.

	flour, vanilla extract, pasta, malt, white vinegar
Non-Food Items	Cosmetics, soaps, detergents, shampoo, bubble bath

[404]

Brief Summary

The Codex Committee on Food Labeling (CCFL) is the committee taking charge of most of the work regarding Genetically Modified Organisms (GMOs). The CCFL does not deal with labeling so much as the standards for the safety testing of GM food. Unfortunately, these standards are much less than satisfactory and similar to those of the FDA. What Codex does say about labeling reveals that it accepts the concept of "substantial equivalence" rather than process-based labeling. Codex uses the process of risk assessment for the testing of GM food, a process that it admits is inadequate and incapable of testing whole foods. Interestingly enough, Codex does not mention this when it performs the same methodology on vitamin and mineral food supplements. Nevertheless, it uses this process to intentionally establish high tolerances and the appearance of safety. Throughout its' publicly available documents, Codex frequently admits that it can, will, and does change the scientific procedures based on the desired outcome. All of this is highly dangerous because of the inherent dangers of GMOs in terms of human health and environmental destruction.

---

[404] Ibid.

Chapter 6
Codex and Persistent Organic Pollutants

Codex and Persistent Organic Pollutants

As is quite typical of Codex guidelines and regulations, dangerous pesticides and persistent organic pollutants (POPs) largely escape the application of rigorous standards that vitamins and minerals receive. While it may be common knowledge to many, there are those who are unaware of the extent to which pesticide residues exist in the average unit of food. The fact is that virtually any and all pesticides used in food production eventually ends up in the food itself, even in the animals that consume that food as feed. Logically, these pesticides end up in the systems of those that consume these plants and animals. Even at this stage of scientific capabilities, the full extent to which these pesticides are damaging to humans is not fully known. However, for many of these chemicals there is clear research is linking them to adverse health effects, while for others the status is less clear, largely due to lack of compiled data. At the very least, it is safe to say that these pesticides are not healthy. Due to the large amount of pesticides in existence, the detailed testing of all these individual substances has not been conducted as of yet. The scientific research that does exist, however, is clear that pesticides do cause adverse effects in humans.

For the purpose of this discussion we will distinguish between two types of pesticides: general pesticides and persistent organic pollutants (POPs). General pesticides are essentially any pesticides not considered a POP by the Stockholm Convention.[405] As the Stockholm Convention, as well as most national governments, banned the use of POPs, general pesticides are the most widely used throughout the world. Many of these substances have been linked to neurological problems, cancer, and parkinson's disease.

---

[405] These designations are only made in the context of this book and should not be taken as designations used for discussion outside of it.

Chlorpyrifos, a general pesticide, serves as a perfect example of the harmful effects of such chemicals. For years, it was one of the most widely used insecticides in both the United States and the world. Millions of pounds of the chemical were used in houses, schools, daycares, and public housing facilities exposing the occupants, children in particular, to the toxin. The insecticide is a known neurotoxin and cause of developmental disorders which is the main reason that the EPA, after years of exposure, finally announced it was ready to ban the chemical. Before it was banned, however, Dow Chemical Co. "voluntarily" removed the product from home market. Yet although chlorpyrifos was removed from home market, the agricultural uses continued with the tacit approval of the EPA. An interesting side note, one should remember that insecticide use in agricultural products is regulated by the EPA. So the approval of chlorpyrifos as an agricultural pesticide is in direct contradiction to its' own stated policy.[406] This is because the EPA "acknowledged the special susceptibility and sensitivity of children to developmental and neurological effects from exposure to chlorpyrifos," on its' own website.[407] If this is the case, then the ingestion of the chemical should also be viewed as dangerous. If simply being in the same house as chlorypifos can be harmful, then certainly its' ingestion would be even more dangerous. Even if one were to claim that the proximity to the chemical were the main cause of the adverse effects associated with it, certainly they would not argue that touching or inhaling would be more dangerous than ingestion. Yet this is apparently the position taken by the EPA because, elsewhere on their own website, they claim that children are at no risk from eating chlorypifos treated food crops. Not only that, but they back up their

---

[406] Schneider, Andrew. "Harmful pesticides found everyday food products." Seattle Post Intelligencer. January 30, 2008. http://www.seattlepi.com/local/349263_pesticide30.html
[407] Ibid.

statements with no evidence and there is no real agreement among the EPA as to how much of the chemical is too much.[408] This is merely one example of how the EPA is compromised when it comes to its regulatory duties and how agencies, when bedfellows with corporations, can speak publicly out of both sides of their mouth with no real consequence.

Chlorypifos is but one example. Many scientists have studied the effects of pesticides on human health and come to the conclusion that exposure to them results in adverse effects. Parkinson's disease is one of the most widely known risks associated with pesticide use. One such study was published in the Archives of Neurology and detailed a link between contact (not even ingestion) with pesticides and an increase in Parkinson's disease. The study found that there was an increased risk for the disease in jobs related to construction and extraction, legal, and religious occupations. The study also found that ever having worked in these fields as well as business and finance, transportation, or material moving was associated with a subtype of Parkinson's' characterized by gait disturbances and postural instability. Some surprises of this study were that agricultural, education, and health care workers did not see an overall increase in risk for Parkinson's. However, only eight types of pesticides were studied in this regard so, logically, the amount of exposure to these particular chemicals would vary depending on the individual's lifestyle and occupation.[409] In relation to this, the authors state, "Other pesticide exposures such as hobby gardening, residential exposure, wearing treated garments or dietary intake were not assessed. Because these exposures may affect many more subjects, future attention is

---

[408] Ibid.
[409] Baker, S.L. "On-the-job pesticide exposure is linked to Parkinson's disease." Naturalnews.com October 9, 2009. http://www.naturalnews.com/027202_Parkinsons_pesticides_disease.html

warranted."[410] However, the overall conclusion was that "The association of disease risk with pesticides support a toxicant-induced cause of parkinsonism."[411] The reader should keep in mind that this study only dealt with a small number of pesticides and one disease. Considering the enormous amount of pesticides being used, the numerous different types of adverse effects that are possible, and long-term intake effects, these findings are only a very small part of the tip of the iceberg of pesticide dangers. Indeed, the knowledge that pesticides can cause Parkinson's disease is already well known even without the aforementioned research. For years, researchers have regularly created Parkinson's in lab animals by injecting them with pesticide chemicals. In fact, many of the diseases created in lab animals for research are created by injecting them with common pesticides and chemicals. This is quite interesting considering the claim made by many medical "professionals" who claim that the cause of Parkinson's is unknown.[412] Evidently, the cause is only unknown when confronted with the damage to the profits of the pharmaceutical and chemical industry giants.

Pesticides have been linked to cancer as well. A study published in "Blood," the journal of the American Society of Hematology, found that exposure to certain pesticides doubled an individual's risk of

[410] Ibid.
[411] Tanner, CM, Ross GW, Jewell SA, Hauser RA, Jankovic J., Factor SA, Bressman S. Deligtisch A., Marras C, Lyons KE,Bhudhikanok GS, Roucoux DF, Meng C., Abbott RD, Langston JW. "Occupation and risk of parkinsonism: a multicenter case-control study." Archives of Neurology. September 2009. 66(9): 1106-13. http://www.ncbi.nlm.nih.gov/pubmed/19752299 (link to abstract)
[412] Evans, Kim. "Pesticides Cause Parkinson's Disease." Naturalnews.com September 25, 2009. http://www.naturalnews.com/027098_pesticides_disease_Parkinsons.html

developing Monoclonal Gammopathy of Undetermined Significance (MGUS) compared to individuals in the general population.[413] MGUS is a "pre-cancerous condition that can lead to multiple layer myeloma which is a painful cancer of the plasma cells the bone marrow."[414] When one is diagnosed with MGUS, the patient requires life-long monitoring because it is a condition that virtually every multiple layer myeloma patient experiences prior to developing the myeloma.[415]

In a study conducted as part of the Agricultural Health Study and published in the American Journal of Epidemiology, a potential link between pesticides and prostate cancer was reported. In particular Methyl Bromide, a gas used to kill pests in the soil and fumigate grain bins and storage areas, was associated with increased risk of the disease by approximately two to four times as much as those who were not exposed to the pesticide. This is not surprising considering the fact that the National Institute for Occupational Safety and Health acknowledges Methyl Bromide as a potential occupational carcinogen.[416] A link between other pesticides such as chlorpyrifos, coumaphos, fonofos, phorate, permethrin, and butylate, was also established for men who had a family history of prostate cancer. One interesting note regarding this study is that the individuals examined by scientists were compared to the incidence rates of the two states in which the subjects lived. That is, they were compared to the average occurrence of prostate cancer

---

[413] "Individuals Who Apply Pesticides Are Found to Have Double the Risk of Blood Disorder." American Society of Hematology." June 12, 2009.
http://www.hematology.org/news/2009/4171.aspx
[414] Ibid.
[415] Ibid.
[416] "Agricultural Pesticide Use May Be Associated With Increased Risk of Prostate Cancer." National Cancer Institute. May 1, 2003.
http://www.cancer.gov/newscenter/pressreleases/agricultur ehealthstudy

for that area.[417] However, since more in-depth analysis had not been conducted at the time, we have no way of knowing just how many cases of prostate cancer in the average occurrences were caused by pesticide exposure themselves. This could have been caused by pesticide residues in food or proximity to these particular chemicals.

Children, of course, are at particular risk for the adverse effects of pesticides because of their development systems. So it is not entirely surprising that a link between childhood cancers and pesticides has been discovered as well. Researchers from Georgetown University Lombardi Comprehensive Cancer Centre completed a study involving 41 pairs of children with Acute Lymphoblastic Leukemia (ALL) and their mothers who were tested and compared with 41 pairs of healthy children and their mothers. The study found that children with ALL, a cancer that commonly develops between and seven years, had a higher ratio of household pesticides in their urine than the healthy children, indicating a possible link between the chemical and the cancer.[418]

The link between pesticides and childhood brain cancers are slightly more established. In a study published in Environmental Health Perspectives in 2009, researchers confirmed a link between pesticide exposure and increase in astrocytomas (brain cancers).[419] The study confirmed previous research that has suggested a link between industrial and household use of pesticides and herbicides with

---

[417] Ibid.

[418] "Household pesticide link to cancer." The Ecologist. July 30, 2009.
http://www.theecologist.org/news/news_round_up/294917/household_pesticide_link_to_cancer.html

[419] Lazaris, Lous. "Residential Pesticides Linked to Childhood Brain Cancer." April 29, 2009.
http://www.naturalnews.com/z026155_brain_pesticides_exposure.html

childhood brain cancer.[420] Not only that, but there is the distinct potential that the parents use or exposure to pesticides may affect the child even before birth. As the study claims,

> Parental exposures may act before the child's conception, during gestation, or after birth to increase the risk of cancer. Before conception, exposures may cause mutations or epi-genetic alterations in gene expression, such as genomic imprinting or DNA methylation, in the sperm or egg. Exposure after conception (i.e. during the pregnancy or after birth) may cause somatic cell mutations or alterations in hormonal or immunological function that affect cancer risk.[421]

This merely reaffirms the knowledge that humans have had for millennia, i.e. that what the parents ingest into their bodies can and probably will affect the child they produce. Pesticides are no different in this respect. As discussed earlier, pesticides also pose a cancer risk for adults, particularly those who work with these chemicals. A study published in Occupational and Environmental Medicine in June 2007 found that agricultural workers who had the highest exposure to pesticides were 2 times more likely to develop brain cancer as those whose occupations did not bring them into contact with these chemicals. It was also found that those who used pesticides on their

---

[420] Hamlin, Heather. "Pesticides blamed for some childhood brain cancers." Enviromental Health News. April 7, 2009. http://www.environmentalhealthnews.org/ehs/newscience/pesticides-linked-to-child-brain-cancer

[421] Shim, Youn K., Mlynarek, Steven P., van Wijngaarden, Edwin., "Parental Exposures to Pesticides and Childhood Brain Cancer: U.S. Atlantic Coast Childhood Brain Cancer Study." Enviromental Health Perspectives. Vol. 117 Number 6. June 2009. http://www.ncbi.nlm.nih.gov/pmc/articles/pmc2702394/pdf/ehp-117-1002.pdf

house plants were at an elevated risk for brain cancer.[422] Recent research has also suggested that pesticides and industrial chemicals are linked to testicular cancer, genital abnormalities, low amounts and potency of semen, and other male reproductive conditions.[423] Indeed, the connection between these substances and cancer is widely known. As the researchers mention in the Environmental Health Perspectives study, the EPA itself classifies chlordane, heptachlor, tetrachlorvinphos, carbaryl, and propoxur as probable or likely carcinogens to humans and lindane, dichlorvos, phosmet, and permethrin as suggestive or possible carcinogens.[424] While it is not known exactly how these chemicals cause cancer, it is known that many pesticides exude hormone-mimicking, mutagenic, and/or immune-hampering qualities and these properties have been linked to cancer in their own right.[425]

Neurological and developmental problems are also associated with pesticide exposure. This is not surprising considering the fact that many insecticides kill their targets by attacking their nervous systems. As with other concerns, children are at highest risk, including those still in the womb. Although more research has been conducted on the effects of some these chemicals on animals and humans, researchers suggest that these effects are quite similar. As a study published in the

[422] "Heavy Pesticide exposure linked to brain cancer." Reuters. June 12, 2007. http://www.reuters.com/article/idUSTON27410120070612
[423] Guitierrez, David. "Chemicals Pass Through Breast Milk to Cause Testicular Cancer." www.naturalnews.com February 9, 2010. http://www.naturalnews.com/z028124_brst_milk_testicular_cancer.html
[424] Ibid.
[425] Gutierrez, David. "Pesticides Cause Childhood Brain Cancers." www.naturalnews.com September 29, 2009. http://www.naturalnews.com/z027121_pesticides_cancer_brain_cancer.html

Canadian Medical Association Journal states,

> Neuordevelopmental, hematological, immunologic, and
> reproductive effects have been found in animals at levels of
> exposure that overlap the range of exposures and body
> burdens found in humans. The health effects of POPs in
> humans is unclear, although available epidemiological
> evidence suggest they are similar to those in animals,
> affecting neurodevelopment, and thyroid, estrogen, and
> immune function. The developing brain and immune system
> may be most vulnerable.[426]

While toxicity of pesticides in humans may not have been studied ad naseum, it is safe to say that it is well established. In a more recent study published in Frontiers In Bioscience, it was stated more directly. The authors state,

> Most pesticides are not highly selective, and are also toxic to
> nontarget species, including humans. A number of pesticides
> can cause neurotoxicity. Insecticides, which kill insects by
> targeting their nervous system, have neurotoxic effect in
> mammals as well. . . . . . Insecticides interfere with chemical
> neurotransmission or ion channels, and usually cause
> reversible neurotoxic effects, that could nevertheless be
> lethal. Some herbicides and fungicides have also been shown
> to possess neurotoxic properties. The effects of pesticides on
> the nervous system may be involved in their acute toxicity, as
> in case of most insecticides, or may contribute to chronic

---

[426] Abelsohn, Alan., Gibson, Brian L., Sanborn, Margaret D., Weir, Erica. "Identifying and managing adverse environmental health effects:5. Persistant Organic Pollutants." Canadian Medical Association Journal. June 11, 2002. 166 (12). http://www.cmaj.ca/cgi/content/full/166/12/1549 Accessed May 24, 2010.

neurodegenerative disorders, most notably Parkinson's disease.[427]

In past research there have also been connections drawn between Persistant Organic Pollutants and diabetes. In a cohort study published in 2006, serum concentrations of POPs (Persistent Organic Pollutants) were examined in accordance with diabetes prevalence. What the scientists found was "striking dose-response relations between serum concentrations of six selected POPs and the prevalence of diabetes."[428] Although, admittedly, there are several limitations to this particular study, clearly this is a subject that needs to be further investigated.

The term Persistent Organic Pollutant applies to specific types of pesticides and chemicals. These substances have been used mostly in pest control, "disease control," agriculture, and other different industries. The EPA distinguishes between two different types of POPs in terms of their production – intentional and unintentional. Intentionally produced POPs are those which are produced for the purpose of being used in manufacturing, agriculture, pest/disease control, or other industrial uses. To put it quite simply, intentionally produced POPs are those that are produced intentionally.

---

[427] Costa, LG., Giodano, G., Guizzetti, M., Vitalone, A., "Neurotoxicity of pesticides: a brief review." Frontiers of Bioscience. January 1, 2008. 13. Pp. 1240-1249. http://www.ncbi.nlm.nih.gov/pubmed/17981626 Accessed May 24, 2010.

[428] Lee, Duk-Hee., Lee, In-Kyu. Song, Kyungeun. Steffes, Michael. Toscano, William. Baker, Beth A., Jacobs, David R. Jr., "A Strong Dose-Response Relation Between Serum Concentrations of Persistent Organic Pollutants and Diabetes." Diabetes Care. Vol. 29. Number 7. July 2006. American Diabetes Association. http://care.diabetesjournals.org/content/29/7/1638.abstract Accessed May 24, 2010.

Unintentionally produced POPs are those that are essentially byproducts of industrial processes or combustion (like the incineration of waste) etc.[429] The chemical in question has to meet fairly stringent requirements in order to obtain the status of POP, however. The label "organic" means the chemicals must be carbon-based (organic) substances. According the website of the Stockholm Convention on Persistent Organic Pollutants, they must also meet the following requirements.

> They possess a particular combination of physical and chemical properties such that, once released into the environment, they:
> - Remain intact for exceptionally long periods of time (many years)
> - Become widely distributed throughout the environment as a result of natural processes involving soil, water and, most notably, air;
> - Accumulate in the fatty tissue of living organisms including humans, and are found at higher concentrations at higher levels in the food chain; and
> - Are toxic to both humans and animals. [430]

Initially, the Stockholm Convention, the United Nations treaty that requires nations to cease or reduce the production, application, and release of POPs, distinguished 12 substances as those that should be eliminated. This treaty places the POPs into 3 different categories: pesticides, industrial chemicals, and by-products. The following chart

---

[429] "Persistant Organic Pollutants: A Global Issue, A Global Response." Environmental Protection Agency. December 17, 2009. http://www.epa.gov/international/toxics/pop.htm
[430] "What are POPs?" Stockholm Convention on persistant organic pollutants. Accessed March 23, 2010. http://chm.pops.int/Convention/ThePOPs/tabid/673/language/en-US/Default.aspx

illustrates these POPs in their respective categories.

Initial 12 Persistent Organic Pollutants Targeted by the Stockholm Convention		
Pesticides	Industrial Chemicals	By-products
Aldrin	Hexachlorobenzene	Hexachlorobenzene
Chlordane	Polychlorinated biphenyls (PCBs)	Polychlorinated dibenzo-p-dioxins
Dichlorodiphenyl trichloroethane (DDT)		Polychlorinated Dibenzofurans
Dieldrin		PCBs
Endrin		
Heptachlor		
Hexachlorobenzene		
Mirex		
Toxaphene		

431

In May 2009, the Conference of the Parties to the Stockholm Convention agreed to add 9 new chemicals to the list of POPs.[432] They are as follows:

9 New Persistent Organic Pollutants Added in 2009		
Pesticides	Industrial Chemicals	By-Products
Chlordecone	Hexabromobiphenyl	Alpha Hexachlorocyclohexane
Alpha Hexachlorocyclohexane	Hexabromodiphenyl ether, Heptabromodiphenyl ether	Beta Hexachlorocyclohexane
Beta Hexachlorocyclohexane		Pentachlorobenzene
Lindane	Pentachlorobenzene	
Pentachlorobenzene	Pefluorooctane Sulfonic Acid, its salts, and Perfluorooctane Sulfonyl Fluoride	
	Tetrabromodiphenyl ether, Pentabromodiphenyl ether	

433

[431] "What are POPs?" Stockholm Convention on persistant organic pollutants. http://chm.pops.int/Convention/ThePOPs/tabid/673/language/en-US/Default.aspx Accessed March 23, 2010.

[432] Ibid.

[433] Ibid.

The major difference between general pesticides and POPs is not necessarily in their level of danger but the fact that they meet the guidelines listed above and that they remain intact for long periods of time, become widely distributed, and accumulate in fatty tissue. The accumulation of POPs in fatty tissue is at the heart of the problem with these chemicals. POPs can pose an even more serious threat to predators at the top of the food chain than those at the bottom. This is due to the process known as biomagnification, where POPs accumulate in the fatty tissue of organisms and become more and more concentrated as they move from one organism to the other. As they work their way through the food chain, becoming more and more contaminated as they move along, those organisms at the very top of the food chain will be ingesting the largest amounts of the chemicals. It is for this reason that even small releases of POPs can be disastrous, especially for localized ecosystems that dine on local game/fish. An example cited on the EPA's website reflects on a study conducted by the Arctic Monitoring and Assessment Programme, where it was found that caribou in the Northwest Territories of Canada had as much as 10 times the amounts of PCBs as the lichen that they ate. Not only that, but the wolves that dined on the caribou contained 60 times the amount of PCBs as the lichen.[434]

The adverse effects of POPs on wildlife are very similar to those on humans. Studies conducted on wildlife communities showed "reproductive, developmental, endocrine, immunologic, and carcinogenic effects."[435] Other studies have shown further connections

---

[434] "Persistant Organic Pollutants: A Global Issue, A Global Response." Environmental Protection Agency. December 17, 2009. http://www.epa.gov/international/toxics/pop.htm
[435] Abelsohn, Alan., Gibson, Brian L., Sanborn, Margaret D., Weir, Erica. "Identifying and managing adverse environmental health effects:5. Persistant Organic Pollutants." Canadian Medical Association Journal. June 11,

between thyroid and estrogen disorders.[436] Marine animals warrant a particular concern due to the fact that POPs have low water solubility and therefore bond easily with particulate matter in sediment. This gives them the ability to lay dormant for a long time in the water supply, becoming active again when disturbed years later. Not only this, but the fact that POPs do not have to be directly applied to an area or species to be present or have an effect on these organisms creates a pollution problem that knows no boundaries. The discovery of POPs in the Alaskan Arctic, thousands of miles away from any known source, is a prime example of this. It is well-known that POP compounds can attach themselves, not only to aquatic sediment material, but also to airborne particles. Along with the ability of most POPs to exist as gases, this allows them to have increased ability to travel long distances and potentially pollute the entire globe. Some of these chemicals are able to evaporate from land and water sources into the air, and return to the earth in rain, snow, and mist. Add to this the transportability of the POPs by airborne and aquatic means, as well as by the very human and animal organisms being contaminated by them, and one can easily see the problem posed here.[437] However, it should be noted that although only 21 of these substances are listed as POPs, the potential for any of the thousands more combinations of chemicals to do the same is very real.

In 2001, The Stockholm Convention on Persistent Organic Pollutants was adopted with the stated goals of eliminating or reducing the production and use of POPs. The Stockholm Convention entered into force in 2004 and is overseen by the United Nations Environment Program. The Conference of the Parties of the Stockholm Convention

---

2002. 166 (12).
http://www.cmaj.ca/cgi/content/full/166/12/1549 Accessed May 24, 2010.
[436] Ibid.
[437] Ibid.

(COP) manages the POPs Convention with each of the members of the Stockholm Convention being the members of the COP. The function of the members of the Convention is to implement the obligations of the treaty at the national level. Although 50 countries have ratified the treaty, the U.S. is not one of these countries. However, the U.S. has largely begun to implement the treaty on a national level. This has been accomplished through a series of national laws and other international agreements. Since 1972, the United States and Canada have signed several agreements involving the removal of POPs from the Great Lakes such as the Great Lakes Water Quality Agreement and the Great Lakes Binational Toxics Strategy. The U.S. is also party to the Rotterdam Convention on the Prior Informed Consent Procedure for Certain Hazardous Chemicals and Pesticides in International Trade with 71 other countries and the European Union. On a national level, the U.S. has passed four major laws that involve the ban or restriction of POPs. The Federal Insecticide, Fungicide, and Rodenticide Act (FIFRA), the Toxic Substances Control Act (TSCA), the Clean Air Act (CAA), and the Clean Water Act (CWA). The table below will provide a brief synopsis of the 12 main POPs and their status in the United States in terms of how they are regulated by law.[438]

12 Major POPs and their U.S. Regulation		
POP	Description	U.S. Law
Aldrin and Dieldrin	Insecticide on corn and cotton; termite control	FIFRA No registrations in U.S.; Most uses canceled in 1969 All uses canceled by 1987 All tolerances on food crops revoked in 1986 No production, import, or export allowed.
Chlordane	Insecticide on various crops including vegetables, small grains, potatoes, sugarcane, sugar beets, fruits, nuts, citrus, and cotton. Home and garden	FIFRA No registrations in U.S. All tolerances on food crops revoked in 1986.

---

[438] Ibid.

	pests. Termite control.	CAA Regulated as a hazardous air pollutant. No production, import, or export allowed.
DDT	Insecticide on agricultural crops, especially cotton. Insects that carry malaria and typhus.	FIFRA No registrations in U.S. Most uses canceled in 1972 All used canceled in 1989 Tolerances on food crops revoked in 1986. CAA DDE (a metabolite of DDT) regulated as a hazardous air pollutant. CWA Considered a priority toxic pollutant. No production, import, or export allowed.
Endrin	Insecticide on crops such as cotton and grain. Rodent control.	FIFRA No U.S. registrations. Most uses canceled in 1979 All uses canceled by 1984. CWA Priority toxic pollutant. No production, import, or export allowed.
Mirex	Insecticide for fire ants, termites, and mealy bugs. Used as a fire retardant in plastics, rubber, and electrical products.	FIFRA No U.S. registrations. All uses canceled in 1977. No production, import, or export allowed.
Heptachlor	Insecticide for soil insects and termites. Used against some crop pests and insects that carry malaria	FIFRA Most used canceled by 1978 All pesticide tolerances on food crops revoked in 1989. No production, import, or export allowed.
Hexachlorobenzene	Fungicide used for seed treatment. An industrial chemical used in the production of fireworks, ammunition, synthetic rubber, and other products. Unintentionally produced during combustion and the manufacture of certain chemicals. An impurity in	FIFRA No U.S. registrations All uses canceled by 1985. CAA Regulated as a hazardous air pollutant CWA

	certain other pesticides.	1.) Priority toxic pollutant No production, import, or export allowed. Approved for manufacture and use for chemical intermediate (allowed under the Convention).
PCBs	Various industrial functions such as electrical transformers and capacitors, heat exchange fluids, paint additives, carbonless copy paper, and plastics. Unintentionally produced during combustion.	TSCA Manufacture and new use prohibited in 1978. CAA Regulated as a hazardous air pollutant CWA Priority toxic pollutant.
Toxaphene	Insecticide used to control pests on crops and livestock. Used to kill unwanted fish in lakes.	FIFRA No U.S. registrations. Most uses canceled in 1982. All uses canceled by 1990. All tolerances on food crops revoked in 1993. CAA Regulated as a hazardous air pollutant. No production, import, or export allowed.
Dioxins and Furans	Unintentionally produced during most forms of combustion involving the burning of medical and municipal waste, household waste, and industrial processes. Found as "trace contaminants" in certain herbicides, wood preservatives, and PCB mixtures.	CAA Regulated as hazardous air pollutants. CWA Dioxin in the form of 2, 3, 7, 8-TCDD is a priority toxic pollutant.

439

While the above chart details various levels of restrictions placed on POPs by U.S. regulatory agencies, the main function of this discussion is on the issue of POP residues in food. Indeed, it is this subject that Codex exerts its authority over.

---

439 Ibid.

We now arrive at one of the more baffling instances of the Codex Alimentarius global guideline machine. While it is well-known that pesticides are becoming increasingly permissible and accepted all across the world, it is quite predictable that Codex would allow a vast majority of them to exist as residues in food. Yet POPs, which are banned or restricted by not only national laws but international agreements as well, are also allowed to reside in food. It is not at all surprising that Codex would disregard national laws. This is common practice. Yet to fly in the face of international agreements is quite another matter. Especially agreements formulated by the very organizations that played such a vital role in the creation of Codex. But this is in fact the case. We are witnessing an ordinary mode of function of the process of incrementalism – in this situation, the incremental creation and establishment of a one world government. Many instances of tyranny begin with benefits in the beginning. In this case, the benefit of signing treaties under the auspices of the United Nations produced some relevant and positive results – the banning and restriction of POPs. However, as the nations move further and further along and the UN begins to show its' true colors, the relevance of these treaties will be diminished and the new global bodies such as Codex Alimentarius will begin to change the very few agreements that have done any good in the world.

An example of this can be seen clearly within the Codex Committee on Pesticide Residues in comparison with U.S. law. As expressed in the chart provided above, the United States has eliminated the registration of most POPs for use inside the country and has revoked tolerances for many of these substances in food. Codex, however, has done exactly the opposite. In the face of both national law and international agreements to the contrary, the Codex Committee on Pesticide Residues (CCPR) and subsequently the Codex Alimentarius

Commission permits seven of the original twelve POPs to exist as residues in food. Even though these substances have been banned virtually the world over, the fact that Codex allows them to exist in food suggests to many that the door is open to reversing this position once Codex is firmly in place as a regulatory standard.[440]

While the upper limits set on the residues of non-POP pesticides are labeled as Maximum Residue Limits (MRL), the labeling is slightly different for POP residues. For these chemicals, the designation is Extraneous Maximum Residue Limits. However, this distinction is merely semantical as the supposedly "extraneous" MRLs are not very different from the common MRLs used for non-POP pesticides. Indeed, the limits imposed upon POPs in food are barely distinguishable from those set for any other pesticide residue. The values are expressed as mg/kg (ppm) and reflect the same level of concern as any other chemical evaluated by Codex. So the use of the term "extraneous" is itself misleading as it implies that the presence of POPs in food will be so small as to warrant no concern. Yet the fact that these EMRLs have to be set in the first place, and set so high, contradicts this intended assumption.

Nevertheless, EMRLs have been set for seven of the 12 original POPs banned by the Stockholm Convention and U.S. law. They include DDT, Endrin, Heptachlor, Chlordane, Aldrin, Dieldrin, and Hexachlorobenzene. Currently, the EMRL for each chemical has not been evaluated for every food substance that it might contaminate, yet the commodities that have been examined and the subsequent EMRLs established for them do not bode well. For instance, DDT EMRLs are set at .2 ppm for carrots, .1 for cereal grains, .3 for poultry meat and a

---

[440] Pesticide Residues In Food. Codex Alimentarius. www.codexalimentarius.net

whopping 5 for meat with the exception of marine mammals.[441] Similar levels are established for Endrin, which is 2-4 times more toxic than DDT.[442] Indeed, this is the pattern for six of the seven POPs allowed in food under Codex guidelines. Observe the charts below:

Please note: for the purpose of this discussion, the values of ppm (parts per million) will be used. Although Codex uses values in mg/kg, these values are easily converted to the equivalent of the mg/kg in terms of ppm.

DDT[443]	
Food Product	EMRL (ppm)
Carrot	0.2
Cereal Grains	0.1
Eggs	0.1
Meat (mammals other than marine mammals)	5
Milk	0.02
Poultry Meat	0.3

---

[441] Pesticide Residues In Food. www.codexalimentarius.net http://www.codexalimentarius.net/mrls/servlet/PesticideSer vlet?Pesticides=21&Items=0&out_style=by+substance&Doma in=PesticideMRLs&Language=english&query_form=%2Fmrls% 2Fpestdes%2Fpest_q-e.htm Accessed 4/5/2010.
[442] "Codex Allows Deadly Pesticides." Global Healing Center. http://www.globalhealingcenter.com/phpprint.php
[443] Codexalimentarius.net http://www.codexalimentarius.net/mrls/servlet/PesticideServlet?Pesticides=21 &Items=0&out_style=by+substance&Domain=PesticideMRLs&Language=englis h&query_form=%2Fmrls%2Fpestdes%2Fpest_q-e.htm Accessed April 6, 2010.

Endrin[444]	
Food Product	EMRL (ppm)
Fruiting vegetables, cucurbits	0.05
Poultry Meat	0.1

Aldrin[445]	
Food Product	EMRL (ppm)
Bulb Vegetables	0.05
Cereal Grains	0.02
Citrus Fruits	0.05
Eggs	0.1
Fruiting Vegetables, Cucurbits	0.1
Leafy Vegetables	0.05
Legume Vegetables	0.05
Meat (mammals other than marine mammals)	0.2
Milk	0.006
Pome Fruits	0.05
Poultry Meat	0.2
Pulses	0.05
Root and Tuber Vegetables	0.1

[444] Codexalimentarius.net.
http://www.codexalimentarius.net/mrls/servlet/PesticideServlet?Pesticides=33&Items=0&out_style=by+substance&Domain=PesticideMRLs&Language=english&query_form=%2Fmrls%2Fpestdes%2Fpest_q-e.htm Accessed April 6, 2010.
[445] Codexalimentarius.net
http://www.codexalimentarius.net/mrls/servlet/PesticideServlet?Pesticides=1&Items=0&out_style=by+substance&Domain=PesticideMRLs&Language=english&query_form=%2Fmrls%2Fpestdes%2Fpest_q-e.htm Accessed April 6, 2010.

Dieldrin[446]	
Food Product	EMRL (ppm)
Bulb Vegetables	0.05
Cereal Grains	0.02
Citrus Fruits	0.05
Eggs	0.1
Fruiting Vegetables, Cucurbits	0.1
Leafy Vegetables	0.05
Legume Vegetables	0.05
Meat (mammals other than marine mammals)	0.2
Milk	0.006
Pome Fruits	0.05
Poultry Meat	0.2
Pulses	0.05
Root and Tuber Vegetables	0.1

---

[446] Codexalimentarius.net
http://www.codexalimentarius.net/mrls/servlet/PesticideServlet?Pesticides=1&Items=0&out_style=by+substance&Domain=PesticideMRLs&Language=english&query_form=%2Fmrls%2Fpestdes%2Fpest_q-e.htm April 6, 2010.

Heptachlor[447]	
Food Product	EMRL (ppm)
Cereal Grains	0.02
Citrus Fruits	0.01
Cotton Seed	0.02
Eggs	0.05
Meat (mammals other than marine mammals)	0.2
Milk	0.006
Pineapple	0.01
Poultry Meat	0.2
Soya Bean (immature seeds)	0.02
Soya Bean Oil, Crude	0.5
Soya Bean Oil, Refined	0.02

[447] Codexalimentarius.net
http://www.codexalimentarius.net/mrls/servlet/PesticideServlet?Pesticides=43&Items=0&out_style=by+substance&Domain=PesticideMRLs&Language=english&query_form=%2Fmrls%2Fpestdes%2Fpest_q-e.htm Accessed April 6, 2010.

Chlordane[448]	
Food Products	EMRL (ppm)
Almonds	0.02
Cotton Seed Oil, Crude	0.05
Eggs	0.02
Fruits and Vegetables	0.02
Hazelnuts	0.02
Linseed Oil, Crude	0.05
Maize	0.02
Meat (mammals other than marine mammals)	0.05
Milk	0.002
Oats	0.02
Pecan	0.02
Poultry Meat	0.5
Rice, Polished	0.02
Rye	0.02
Sorghum	0.02
Soya Bean Oil, Crude	0.05
Soya Bean Oil, Refined	0.02
Walnuts	0.02
Wheat	0.02

While some might argue that the levels permitted for these substances by the CCPR are so low that they should warrant no concern, the fact is that there should be no levels of any of these substances in food at all. Setting EMRLs for these pesticides only serve to legitimize their consumption as well as their potential reintroduction to the food supply and the environment. However, what may cause more concern than accepting levels of POPs in food is the lack of an EMRL for certain substances among the establishment of EMRLs for others. Indeed, this is

[448] Codexalimentarius.net
http://www.codexalimentarius.net/mrls/servlet/PesticideServlet?Pesticides=12&Items=0&out_style=by+substance&Domain=PesticideMRLs&Language=english&query_form=%2Fmrls%2Fpestdes%2Fpest_q-e.htm Accessed April 6, 2010.

the case for many general pesticides as well as some POPs.[449] If Codex were to establish an EMRL for particular hazardous chemical such as Hexachlorobenzene, the situation would be bad enough. If it were to simply ignore the question of EMRLs for a whole group of substances and claim neutrality, one might be alarmed but at least it would be consistent. However, in a situation in which Codex sets EMRLs for at least one substance, the lack of an EMRL effectively lifts the ceiling on the levels that might be present in the food. For this reason, only an EMRL of 0 is acceptable. Indeed, it is only an EMRL of 0 that prohibits the contamination of food from pesticide residues.

Of course this concern is not isolated to POPs. As of 2007, Codex had assessed over 185 different pesticides and established over 3,275 MRLs[450] and this issue applies to many of these chemicals as well. Pesticides such as Bromophos, Carbon Disulphide, and many others have no MRLs set for them, even though many of their counterparts do.[451] For those that do have limits imposed upon them, they are often different from EPA limits, some being set much higher and some much lower. Ultimately, however, the MRLs set by the EPA will be irrelevant, as they are to be harmonized with the Codex limits. Such a goal is discussed in more detail elsewhere in this book. Yet it can be no more clear that harmonization with Codex guidelines is the intention of the U.S. government than in the statement provided by the EPA in their own Reregistration for Eligibility Decision documents for pesticides. As

---

[449] Pesticide Residues In Food. Codex Alimentarius. www.codexalimentarius.net Accessed May 20, 2010.

[450] "Codex Committee on Pesticide Residues (CCPR)" Consumers International. http://www.consumerinternational.org/templates/internal.asp?NodeID=94886 October 8, 2007. Accessed April 6, 2010.

[451] "Pesticide Residues In Food." Codexalimentarius.net http://www.codexalimentarius.net/mrls/pestdes/jsp/pest_q-e.jsp

an example, we will look at the Reregistration for Eligibility Decision for Acephate, as it is typical for the rest of the documents dealing with pesticides. It says,

> The Codex Alimentarius Commission has established several maximum residue limits (MRLs) for residues of acephate in/on various plant and animals commodities. The Codex MRLs are expressed in terms of acephate per se. Harmonization of expression/definition between Codex MRLs and U.S. tolerances will be achieved when the residue definition of the U.S. tolerances is changed from combined residues of acephate and the metabolite methamidophos to acephate per se. A numerical comparison of the Codex MRLs and the corresponding reassessed U.S. tolerances is presented in Table 16. Recommendations for compatibility are based on conclusions following reassessment of U.S. tolerances (see Table 15.)[452]

This statement of intended harmonization with Codex standards is included in virtually every one of the Reregistration for Eligibility Decision (RED) documents. Interestingly enough, these statements do not only openly announce their intentions of harmonization, but clearly state that the U.S. will amend its' standards to meet those of Codex Alimentarius. These pesticides are continually reassessed for these reasons. Indeed, the charts presented in the RED documents contain figures for the "reassessed" MRLs in comparison to those of Codex. But while changing scientific conclusions for political purposes is not only unscientific, it is highly deceptive and unethical. Yet this is what the EPA admits to doing in its own documents. Obviously, neither the science

---

[452] "Reregistration Eligibility Decision for Acephate." U.S. Environmental Protection Agency Office of Pesticide Programs. http://www.epa.gov/pesticides/reregistration/REDs/acephate_red.pdf p. 44. Accessed April 6, 2010. P.44

nor the evidence will change simply because governments have entered into an agreement. However, it appears that the methods used to achieve conclusions, as well as the conclusions themselves will do just that.

Continuing with Acephate as an example, one can see harmonization in action. When one looks at the MRLs set by Codex and those set by the EPA, two things are readily apparent. First, in this particular case, the MRLs of Codex are set much higher than those of the EPA. Second, many of the "reassessed" U.S. MRLs are compatible with those of Codex.

The following values are expressed in ppm. Once converted, ppm is the same value as the mg/kg designation that Codex uses.

Codex and EPA MRLs for Acephate		
Food Product	EPA MRL ("reassessed)	Codex MRL
Brussels sprouts	3.0	5
Cattle Fat	TBD	0.1
Cattle Meat	TBD	0.1
Cauliflower	2.0	5
Cotton Seed	0.5	2
Eggs	0.1	0.1
Lettuce, Head	10.0	5
Milks	TBD	0.1
Pig Fat	TBD	0.1
Pig Meat	TBD	0.1
Poultry Fats	0.1	0.1
Poultry Meat	0.1	0.1
Soya Bean (dry)	1.0	0.5

[453]

Here, compatibility exists in three categories (eggs, poultry fats, and

---

[453] "Reregistration Eligibility Decision for Acephate." U.S. Environmental Protection Agency Office of Pesticide Programs. http://www.epa.gov/pesticides/reregistration/REDs/acephate_red.pdf p. 44. Accessed April 6, 2010. P. 45

poultry meats). With the exception of lettuce, all Codex MRLs are higher than the EPA limits. All of the EPA limits have been "reassessed" after the introduction of Codex MRLs. The differences in the upper limits are attributed to "differences in agricultural practices in the U.S. upon which the residue data were developed."[454] This may be, but it is also a convenient excuse. As stated earlier, it appears that true scientific practice is taking a backseat to political considerations in the arena of pesticide MRLs and Codex harmonization.

Yet even with the stated goal of harmonization, it appears that the levels of "acceptable" pesticide residues in food will not go down. That is, at least from the EPA's standpoint. When one observes the MRL list for substances such as Dicofol, a pesticide in which the EPA's tolerances are generally higher than that of Codex's own, the EPA tends to remain resolute in its' position. For instance, Codex sets a Dicofol MRL of 0.1 while the EPA sets an MRL of 0.5.[455] However, whereas the EPA "reassesses" its tolerances for substances such as Acephate as demonstrated above, in this case it states, "Data do not support a lower US tolerance, with field trial residues as great as 0.4 ppm." For dry hops, Codex sets the MRL at 50 mg/kg. The EPA sets the value at 65 ppm.[456] In this case as well, the EPA remains firm saying, "Data indicate that the tolerance cannot be decreased."[457] Apparently, the EPA is capable of standing up to Codex when it comes to harmonizing its own standards to higher acceptable levels of contamination, but not for lower ones. As will be discussed later, this opens the door to the WTO dispute resolution mechanism to address pesticide MRL's. It may be in the WTO

---

[454] Ibid.

[455] Reregistration Eligibility Decision for Dicofol." U.S. Environmental Protection Agency Office of Pesticide Programs. http://www.epa.gov/oppsrrd1/REDs/0021red.pdf p. 120.

[456] Ibid.

[457] Ibid.

"court" that the issues of MRLs for pesticide residues are resolved.

While such disregard for the welfare and concerns of consumers is to be expected of Codex, it is nonetheless hypocritical. This is most evident by examining the procedures being followed for pesticide residues when compared to those used when assessing vitamin and mineral supplements. However, some telling comments were made by the FAO on its' own website regarding the Revised Guidelines for Predicting Dietary Intake of Pesticide Residues. In reference to these guidelines it states, "The use of these guidelines should significantly reduce the number of cases where exposure assessments cause unnecessary concern."[458] While few would argue that this statement is unreasonable, it is without doubt a completely different mindset than that guiding the CCNFSDU in regards to natural supplements. Indeed, it seems that the purpose of the CCNFSDU is to "cause unnecessary concern" regarding vitamins and minerals. When it comes to pesticides however, the standards are quite a bit looser.

Again, in regards to the Revised Guidelines for Predicting Dietary Intake of Pesticide Residues, the same document continues by saying,

> The Guidelines explicitly state that a worst-case estimate is a gross overestimate of true exposure and that more refined calculations should be performed using other relevant data. However, some Members of CCPR reject MRLs when this additional data is not available. Others rely, for instance, on monitoring data, which may demonstrate that no exposure

---

[458] "Current risk management practices in the codex alimentarius commission, its subsidiary bodies, and advisory expert committees." FAO.org http://www.fao.org/docrep/w4982e09.htm Accessed March 23, 2010.

problems are to be expected.[459]

This statement, taken on its own, might not seem like anything for consumers to be up in arms about. However, not only does it downplay what it considers to be the worst-case scenario but it also admits to a potential bias toward conclusions that determine there are no exposure problems. It is also quite misleading to suggest that a gross overestimate of true exposure of pesticides is a trivial matter. To overestimate the exposure of populations, such as in the Global Average Daily Intake for vitamins and minerals, is to overestimate the tolerances (depending on which scientific model is chosen) of those populations, possibly leading to even higher MRL and acceptable tolerances of pesticide residues in foods.

Brief Summary

Pesticides have been linked to many adverse health effects, particularly those affecting the brain such as Parkinson's disease as well as different forms of cancers and diabetes. The Codex Committee on Pesticide Residues has evaluated and established over 3,275 MRLs for pesticide residues in food. Although Persistent Organic Pollutants (POPs) were banned by the Stockholm Convention, Codex allows many of these chemicals to exist in food. Because some chemicals have no MRLs established for them, this could actually open the door to unlimited amounts of that specific chemical being allowed in food. In the FDAs' Reregistration for Eligibility Decision (RED) documents, the agency clearly and plainly states the goal of harmonization with Codex standards.

---

[459] Ibid.

Chapter 7
Codex Harmonization, Enforcement, and Implementation

Codex Harmonization, Enforcement and Implementation

The official public-ready position of Codex Alimentarius is that the standards created under its' guidance are not mandatory or legally binding. It states on its' own website, "Codex standards are voluntary and non-binding recommendations and their implementation is not controlled but many governments implement them because they see the benefit of it for their consumers and their trade."[460] Codex would have you believe that these standards are set only out of benevolence and scientific interest. According to this view, the nations that implement them do so only out of a desire to protect their citizens even further and facilitate trade. Yet one would be tempted to ask the question of why so much money and so much time is spent on creating guidelines for virtually every form of food that can be consumed by humans if there is no obligation for national governments to comply with them? The answer is simple – the claim that the guidelines will not become mandatory is false.

While Codex Alimentarius on its' own has no authority over trade or trade laws, the standards set by it are enforced by various treaties, agreements, and international trade organizations. The World Trade Organization (WTO), Sanitary and Phytosanitary Agreement (SPS), the Technical Barriers to Trade Agreement (TBT), the North American Free Trade Agreement (NAFTA), the Central American Free Trade Agreement (CAFTA), the General Agreement on Tariffs and Trade, and the Trilateral Cooperation Charter (TCC) are a few of the agreements that serve to enforce Codex Guidelines.[461]

---

[460] Codexalimentarius.net "FAQs – General Questions." Accessed May 3, 2010. http://www.codexalimentarius.net/web/faq_gen.jsp#G11
[461] "Codex Alimentarius: Global Food Imperialism." Ed. Scott C. Tips. FHR. 2007.

The World Trade Organization was created in 1995 when GATT was updated to include new requirements of the signatory nations. The original GATT was agreed to in 1947.[462] The stated purpose of the WTO is to provide

> a forum for negotiating agreements aimed at reducing obstacles to international trade and ensuring a level playing field for all, thus contributing to economic growth and development. The WTO also provides a legal and institutional framework for the implementation and monitoring of these agreements, as well as for settling disputes arising from their interpretation and application.[463]

Translating this statement into reality, the WTO acts as a judge whenever trade disputes arise between countries. Admittedly, although presented in flowery language, the goal of the WTO is to aid in the expansion of international trade. It is not merely tasked with clearing up disputes between nations, as much as it is to promote and facilitate globalism and eventually global government. While it is not explicitly mentioned in these terms, the goal of the WTO is to create ultimate harmonization of national laws into a single all-encompassing system.

The idea behind the WTO is by no means a new idea. An organization such as the WTO was envisioned officially long before 1994. The GATT itself is a product of an attempt to create an International Trade Organization under the auspices of the UN that

---

[462] "General Agreement on Tariffs and Trade 1994." http://www.wto.org/english/docs_e/legal_e/06-gatt_e.htm Accessed May 4, 2010.
[463] "About the WTO - A Statement by the Director General." http://www.wto.org/english/thewto_e/whatis_e/wto_dg_stat_e.htm Accessed May 4, 2010.

would deal with exactly the same issues as the WTO. Because the American public, as well as that of some other nations were not as open to the establishment of such an organization, the United States did not approve the treaty, other nations followed suit, and the ITO was abandoned. However, a slightly attenuated version of the ITO was created in 1947 and went into effect in 1948. This creation was in the form of a treaty and was called GATT.[464] As mentioned above, the ITO later resurfaced under GATT as the WTO served as an expansion of the treaty itself. The difference was simple. Whereas, under GATT, the losing party in a trade dispute had the possibility of being able to block the final decision of the GATT and maintain some semblance of national sovereignty, the WTO removes this opportunity. Under the WTO, decisions are final[465] and even enforceable by the levying of massive fines on those countries viewed as guilty of engaging in unfair trade practices.[466]

This is extremely important, not only for international trade, but also for domestic legislation. Those who foolishly claim that national laws like DSHEA will never be trumped by other interests should pay close attention to both the international organizations and treaties that are designed to do just that. Indeed, this type of movement has already begun in areas not directly related to health or food. An example of how international trade disputes handled by the WTO can have a lasting

---

[464] Fergusson, Ian F. "CRS Report For Congress – The World Trade Organization: Background and Issues." May 9, 2007. http://www.nationalaglawcenter.org/assets/crs/98-928.pdf

[465] Dybring, Alex.; Mosegaard, Tamara Theresa.; "Codex Alimentarius Information – an Introduction." Codex Alimentarius: Global Food Imperialism." Ed. Scott C. Tips. FHR. 2007. Pp. 17-18.

[466] Tips, Scott C. "Rearranging the Deck Chairs on the Titanic." Codex Alimentarius: Global Food Imperialism." Ed. Scott C. Tips. FHR. 2007. Pp. 79-80.

impact on domestic legislation can be seen in the Foreign Sales Corporation (FSC) tax laws. These laws essentially provided tax benefits for exports by foreign sales corporations. Foreign sales corporations are subsidiaries of corporations established offshore to handle foreign sales.[467] In 1997, the European Union challenged this law as an "illegal export subsidy" that gave U.S. exporters an "unfair competitive advantage."[468] This trade dispute had its' roots in the 1980's with a similar disagreement being dealt with under the GATT, which resulted in the previous law being found illegal by GATT. The WTO, however, had more teeth than its predecessor, and ruled the FSC law illegal. It determined that the law was a "subsidy contingent on exporting" and therefore violated the Agreement on Subsidies and Countervailing Measures. Although the United States appealed the determination, on February 22, 2000, the Appellate Body of the WTO, upheld its decision. As a result, Congress repealed the FSC law and replaced it with the Extraterritorial Income Benefit law passed into law in November 2000 and signed into law by President Clinton on November 15 of that same year.[469] The changing, or more appropriately labeled, harmonization of U.S. domestic law at the behest of an international organization would have been considered unbelievable to most Americans. This feeling is echoed by Scott Tips in his article entitled "International Law Trumps Domestic Law," written in January of 2001 dealing with this very issue

---

[467] Paulson, Michael. "WTO Case File: foreign sales corporations." Seattle Post-Intelligencer. November 22, 1999. www.seattlepi.com/pi/national/case4.shtml

[468] Ibid.

[469] Brumbaugh, David L. "A History of the Extraterritorial Income (ETI) and Foreign Sales Corporation (FSC) Export Tax-Benefit Controversy." Congressional Research Service Report Summarizes History of FSC/ETI Controversy. November 9, 2004. http://www.taxhistory.org/thp/readings.nsf/cf7c9c870b600b 9585256df80075b9dd/d1e0dcc337b8048385256f860068159 e?OpenDocument   Accessed May 4, 2010.

and warning of the dangers to come. He says, "Considered 'unthinkable' only a few months before, and despite clear constitutional prohibitions against its actions, Congress knuckled under to the World Trade Organization's (WTO's) dictate that the United States must change its tax law governing foreign sales corporations."[470] Yet this was only the beginning. After the inaction of the ETI provisions, the EU filed another grievance with the WTO that even these provisions were an unfair trade subsidy. After a series of appeals, the WTO ruled against the United States again. The EU subsequently gave the U.S. a 2004 deadline to repeal the ETI or face retaliatory tariffs, which it began to phase in eventually reaching 12% by October 2004. Therefore, on October 22, President Bush, signed H.R. 4520, which repealed the ETI provisions and gave businesses a paltry replacement for the breaks.[471]

The situation mentioned above is an example of how the WTO has been used and will continue to be used in the future to circumvent, change, and harmonize domestic legislation in accordance with globalist aims. Yet, whereas previously the harmonization of national law and direction of international agencies was maintained by stealth and secrecy, these actions have become more and more open in recent years. The international organizations that serve as the front groups for the controllers (i.e. the elites, banks, etc.) are now moving to the forefront of the political and legal scenes, replacing national

---

[470] Tips, Scott C. "International Law Trumps Domestic Law." Codex Alimentarius: Global Food Imperialism." Ed. Scott C. Tips. FHR. 2007.P. 37.
[471] Brumbaugh, David L. "A History of the Extraterritorial Income (ETI) and Foreign Sales Corporation (FSC) Export Tax-Benefit Controversy." Congressional Research Service Report Summarizes History of FSC/ETI Controversy. November 9, 2004.
http://www.taxhistory.org/thp/readings.nsf/cf7c9c870b600b9585256df80075b9dd/d1e0dcc337b8048385256f860068159e?OpenDocument   Accessed May 4, 2010.

governments as decision makers.

The way the WTO works is that it acts as an independent judge and facilitator of international trade by the WTO dispute settlement process. Essentially, the WTO agrees and decides upon a set of standards for trade, the standards differing with the subject of the trade. These are the standards used to judge whether or not a nation is engaging in unfair trade practices or not. As the WTO itself states, "the dispute settlement system works on contractual remedies."[472] When a nation brings a complaint to the WTO, the organization makes a determination as to the validity of the complaint and makes a ruling based on this analysis and international agreements signed regarding the acceptable standards.[473] Generally speaking, as in the case of U.S. tax laws discussed above, the decisions come down against any form of "protectionism" that may discourage outsourcing and international economic harmonization. While the WTO cannot levy fines or sanctions on its own, it can make rulings and approve such actions to be taken by the plaintiff. In the end, the decision to impose fines or sanctions is made by the nations themselves, yet clearly they are facilitated by the WTO.[474]

The relevance of the WTO to Codex Alimentarius in the context of this discussion is that Codex is one of the agreements/organizations referenced for international standards in the WTO dispute settlement process. Officially, the WTO recognizes Codex Guidelines as international standards for the purpose of facilitating trade and settling

---

[472] "Key Issues in WTO Dispute Settlement: The First Ten Years." Ed. Refus Yerxa and Bruce Wilson. Cambridge University Press. http://assets.cambridge.org/97805218/61595/excerpt/97805 21861595_excerpt.pdf
[473] Ibid.
[474] Ibid.

disputes. This is where the "Codex Guidelines are completely voluntary" claim falls apart. It is true that Codex Alimentarius itself lacks any enforcement mechanisms for their Guidelines. However, what is rarely mentioned is that the WTO is the enforcement mechanism. The WTO on its' own website describes Codex as a relevant organization in regards to the development of international standards, guidelines, and recommendations for the protection of human, animal, or plant life and health.[475] This is done through the Sanitary and Phytosanitary (SPS) Agreement, to which all WTO member countries are signatories.[476] As Scott Tips wrote after attending a CCNFSDU meeting,

> The Codex Chairman, a German named Dr. Rolf Grossklaus, kept insisting that these standards under discussion were only "guidelines" and "not standards," implying if not actually stating that no one need therefore be overly concerned. Guidelines are of course voluntary, but because of World Trade Organization (WTO) membership obligations prohibiting its members from engaging in unfair trade practices, member countries may be sued and heavily fined if their trade practices do not conform to adopted international standards. We have already witnessed at least one instance where the United States Congress was forced to rescind domestic American law governing international business corporations because of a WTO dictate. So, far from being "guidelines" as we might think of them, once adopted, these guidelines will have a very real bite and they will restrict

---

[475] "Agreement on the Application of Sanitary and Phytosanitary Measures." World Trade Organization. http://www.wto.org/english/tratop_E/sps_e/spsagr_e.htm Accessed May 5, 2010.

[476] Tips, Scott C. "The Maginot Mentality." Codex Alimentarius: Global Food Imperialism. Ed. Scott C. Tips. FHR. 2007. Pp. 221-222.

vitamin and mineral potencies at ridiculously low levels.[477]

Suzan Walter echoes this sentiment when she mentions the fact that many of the delegates sent by Codex member countries have little or no idea as to what they are actually engaging in. She writes,

> I initially focused on surveying delegates as to their understanding of how, once the Guidelines [Guidelines for Vitamin and Mineral Food Supplements] are finalized, this document would be enforced. Everyone I spoke with erroneously believed that individual countries would be free to use the Guidelines as suggestions and adapt them as they wished. Further, none were aware that the World Trade Organization (WTO) has the actual enforcement power, and the WTO does not view a "guideline" document as optional. I found this extremely disturbing, as this indicated to me that the people responsible for creating the document did not understand how it would be used.[478]

It is unfortunate, though unsurprising, that a large number of seemingly educated people would simply go along to get along and remain in virtual ignorance of something so large taking place directly in front of them with their active engagement.

When one examines the mechanism of the WTO and the historical precedent for changing domestic law, one begins to see how the organization can and will be used to implement Codex Alimentarius Guidelines. It is not a far-fetched notion to see the day when a Codex-

[477] Tips, Scott C. "Codex Gets One Step Closer to Control." Codex Alimentarius: Global Food Imperialism. Ed. Scott C. Tips. FHR. 2007. Pp. 48-49.
[478] Walter, Suzan. "AHHA Attends Berlin Codex Session: What Did We Learn?" Codex Alimentarius: Global Food Imperialism. Ed. Scott C. Tips. FHR. 2007. P. 61.

compliant country such as the EU sues a non-compliant country such as the U.S. over the use of "unfair trade practices" regarding the higher levels of nutrients allowed in dietary supplements. Clearly, in this situation, the EU would be victorious, as the compliant country automatically wins suit over the non-compliant one. This produces an incentive on two different fronts for a country to harmonize its own standards with Codex. Essentially, if a country wants any legal standing with the WTO, they must be compliant with the standards set or agreed upon by the WTO. If a dispute arises, the non-compliant would logically lose in the decision, regardless of their arguments or the merits of their case, because they have not lived up to their contractual obligations under international agreements such as GATT and the WTO in the first place. Therefore, if a country declines Codex compliance at the outset, it can be hauled into an international tribunal known as the WTO and be loaded with fines, sanctions, and tariffs until it does so.[479] This, however, is only one way in which Codex Alimentarius can be implemented.

Another method that will enable the implementation of Codex Alimentarius is the Sanitary and Phytosanitary Agreement. This agreement is one which all WTO members have signed on to and is heavily relied upon in the new globalist version of international trade.[480] It is also implemented under the authority of the WTO by means of the WTO Committee for SPS measures as well as the dispute settlement mechanism of the WTO mentioned above. Created in 1995, the SPS Agreement is even more open about its goals of harmonization and

---

[479] Minton, Barbara. "Codex Threatens Health of Billions." Naturalnews.com July 30, 2009. http://www.naturalnews.com/026731_CODEX_food_health.html

[480] Tips, Scott C. "The Maginot Mentality." Codex Alimentarius: Global Food Imperialism. Ed. Scott C. Tips. FHR. 2007. Pp. 221-222.

internationalization.[481] Specifically, the agreement is to deal with sanitation issues regarding food in the context of international trade and commerce. As the USDA's Foreign Agricultural Service states, "SPS measures refer to any measure, procedure, requirement, or regulation, taken by governments to protect human, animal, or plant life or health from the risk arising from the spread of pests, diseases, disease-causing organisms, or from additives, toxins, or contaminants found in food, beverages, or feedstuffs."[482] However, while the goal of the SPS Agreement might sound commendable at first, the true purpose of the agreement is international harmonization of laws. Reading over the SPS Agreement provides the reader with numerous references and calls for the blending together of national laws into a single worldwide system.

Within the agreement there is also specific mention of Codex Alimentarius as an international standard - setter for these purposes.[483] The SPS Agreement reads, "Desiring to further the use of harmonized sanitary and phytosanitary measures between Members, on the basis of international standards, guidelines and recommendations, developed by the relevant international organizations, including the Codex Alimentarius . . ."[484] The SPS agreement is full of such statements regarding harmonization and Codex in particular. While many national government agencies as well as the international organizations involved in the WTO claim that the SPS agreement allows for nations to "set their

---

[481] "FACT SHEET: Sanitary and Phytosanitary Measures and the World Trade Organization." USDA Foreign Agricultural Service. February 2006. http://www.fas.usda.gov/info/factsheets/sps.asp Accessed May 6, 2010.
[482] Ibid.
[483] "Agreement on the Application of Sanitary and Phytosanitary Measures." World Trade Oganization. http://www.wto.org/english/tratop_E/sps_e/spsagr_e.htm Accessed May 5, 2010.
[484] Ibid.

own standards,"[485] this is far from the truth. In fact, it is quite clever and deceptive language used to make such a statement. The fact is, when one examines the SPS Agreement, member nations are indeed allowed to make their own laws. However, these laws must be equivalent or even more restrictive than the standards determined by the international organizations tasked for the job. As is stated in section 3.1 of the SPS, "To harmonize sanitary and phytosanitary measures on as wide a basis as possible, Members shall base their sanitary and phytosanitary measures on international standards, guidelines or recommendations, where they exist, except as otherwise provided for in this Agreement, and in particular in paragraph 3."[486] In other words, nations have fully sovereign authority to pass domestic legislation that mirrors that of the SPS, WTO, and other international standard-setting organizations.

Not only is Codex specifically mentioned in the introduction to the SPS it is also mentioned elsewhere in the Agreement. In section 3.4 it states, "Members shall play a full part, within the limits of their resources, in the relevant international organizations and their subsidiary bodies, in particular the Codex Alimentarius Commission . . ."[487] Codex is mentioned in particular here because it will play a major role in the harmonization efforts achieved by the WTO dispute settlement mechanism. It is also mentioned specifically because it is the

---

[485] "FACT SHEET: Sanitary and Phytosanitary Measures and the World Trade Organization." USDA Foreign Agricultural Service. February 2006.
http://www.fas.usda.gov/info/factsheets/sps.asp Accessed May 6, 2010.
[486] "Agreement on the Application of Sanitary and Phytosanitary Measures." World Trade Oganization.
http://www.wto.org/english/tratop_E/sps_e/spsagr_e.htm Accessed May 5, 2010.
[487] Ibid.

leading organization dealing with food and, therefore, is extremely important in the battle for global control. Section 5.1 also mentions Codex in a more indirect fashion. It says, "Members shall ensure that their sanitary or phytosanitary measures are based on an assessment, as appropriate to the circumstances, of the risks to human, animal or plant life or health, taking into account risk assessment techniques developed by the relevant international organizations."[488] Indeed, the term "relevant international organization" is often a code-word for Codex Alimentarius. Examining this statement, however, reveals the already laid groundwork for the "risk assessment" trick used by Codex to falsely apply risks to vitamin and mineral supplements where they do not exist. Under the SPS, an international agreement, national governments are required to submit to the flawed process of risk assessment applied to vitamin and mineral supplements. Because of this agreement, the risk assessment would have to be applied even if it stood in opposition to the position of the national government.[489]

Another danger to domestic law in the United States is the Central American Free Trade Agreement (CAFTA). Modeled after the economically devastating North American Free Trade Agreement (NAFTA), CAFTA is essentially an expansion of the NAFTA principal to include Costa Rica, Dominican Republic, El Salvador, Guatemala, Honduras, and Nicaragua in a "free trade" bloc.[490] Beyond the obvious further danger to the economy and the move toward the solidification

---

[488] Ibid.

[489] "Agreement on the Application of Sanitary and Phytosanitary Measures." World Trade Oganization. http://www.wto.org/english/tratop_E/sps_e/spsagr_e.htm Accessed May 5, 2010.

[490] "U.S. – Central America Free Trade Agreement: Frequently Asked Questions." United States Embassy – San Jose, Costa Rica. http://sanjose.usembassy.gov/Cafta/faq.html Accessed May 6, 2010.

of a single regional territory known as the North American Union (NAU), CAFTA carries with it concerns that are specific to the discussion of this book. CAFTA contains an entire section regarding sanitary and phytosanitary measures and extensive mention of the Technical Barriers to Trade (TBT) Agreement,[491] an agreement whose purpose is to ensure that "technical regulations and standards, including packaging, marking and labeling requirements, and procedures for assessment of conformity with technical regulations and standards do not create unnecessary obstacles to international trade."[492] Section 6 of CAFTA requires that a Committee on Sanitary and Phytosanitary Measures be established within 30 days of the entry into the agreement. The purpose of the Committee is to ensure the continuation of international harmonization under the SPS Agreement. Both sections 6 and 7 combine to further secure participation and commitment in the WTO, SPS, and TBT. The term "harmonization" is conveniently left out of the text of CAFTA, yet the SPS agreement contains this word frequently and it should be noted that CAFTA frequently refers to the SPS agreement.[493] Many similar "trade agreements" such as the Free Trade

---

[491] "Central America – Dominican Republic – United States Free Trade (DR-CAFTA)." SICE: Foreign Trade Information System.
http://www.sice.oas.org/Trade/CAFTA/CAFTADR_e/CAFTADR in_e.asp Accessed May 6, 2010.
[492] "Agreement on Technical Barriers to Trade." World Trade Organization.
http://www.wto.org/english/docs_e/legal_e/17-tbt_e.htm Accessed May 6, 2010.
[493] "Central America – Dominican Republic – United States Free Trade (DR-CAFTA)." SICE: Foreign Trade Information System.
http://www.sice.oas.org/Trade/CAFTA/CAFTADR_e/CAFTADR in_e.asp Accessed May 6, 2010.
See Also,

Agreement of the Americas, Security and Prosperity Partnership of North America, and many others are serving to advance the agenda of one-world globalism at an ever widening pace and will have similar effects on the significance Codex Alimentarius will play on the global scene.

There is absolutely no reason to believe that globalist attacks on domestic laws such as DSHEA and even the Constitution itself will be stopped by American lawmakers or the courts. Both have shown antipathy toward the document in the past and the trend is only getting bigger. Presidents, cabinet members, appointees, judges, lawmakers, regularly violate and openly express a lack of concern for the provisions of the U.S. Constitution. An example of the brazenness in which the spirit of globalism is now espoused can be seen in a quote from U.S. Supreme Court Justice Ginsberg in her address to the Constitutional Court of South Africa. Scott Tips quotes her as stating the following,

> Judges in the United States, are free to consult all manner of commentary – restatements, treaties, what law professors or even law students write copiously in law reviews. For example, if we can count those writings, why not the analysis of a question similar to the one we confront contained in an opinion of the Supreme Court of Canada, the Constitutional Court, or the European Court of Human Rights? . . . The notion that it is improper to look beyond the borders of the United States in grappling with hard questions . . . is in line with the view of the US Constitution as a document

---

Tips, Scott C. "The Maginot Mentality." Codex Alimentarius: Global Food Imperialism. Ed. Scott C. Tips. FHR. 2007. Pp. 222-223.

essentially frozen.[494]

This statement is only one of thousands that have made by those in powerful positions in support of a globalist ideology. Being outside the scope of this book, the ancient or even recent goal of the creation of a one world government will not be discussed here. Information is widely available to anyone who wishes to investigate it for themselves. There are many powerful individuals who wish to see this New World Order come to pass. However, there are also many more who engage in its' implementation unwittingly. Many even believe that they are actually doing the right thing. Due to the intense brainwashing provided in the education system, television, popular culture, etc. even those who oppose such an order have been accustomed to some level of tyranny at the domestic and international level. Because of this situation, those who are actively working toward the goal of a New World Order are now confident enough to come out in the open with their plans, as the statement above demonstrates.

It is therefore necessary to understand how Codex Alimentarius, among other top down international mandates, are implemented on a national, state, and local level. In the case of Codex, the implementation of oppressive and unhealthy food and supplement standards will not likely be done all at once, as those who claimed an implementation date of December 31, 2009 would have believed. Such an implementation strategy just might provoke an open revolt, even among a brainwashed and domesticated public as exists now in the United States. It would serve no real purpose to do this at once as it would pull the curtain back much too early and allow the serfs to see who they were really working

---

[494] Tips, Scott C. "The Maginot Mentality." Codex Alimentarius: Global Food Imperialism. Ed. Scott C. Tips. FHR. 2007. Pp. 225-226.

for. It is far more likely that the implementation of Codex Alimentarius will come incrementally as tyranny often does. We have already discussed the possibility of Codex implementation as a result of a WTO dispute settlement. This is a distinct possibility, but there is another that is even more likely.

This scenario is one in which domestic laws are harmonized with Codex guidelines under the pretext of a grassroots movement, top down (Big Pharma sponsored) movement, or even lawmakers simply attempting to appear useful. In this case, harmonization with international mandates can be accomplished without exposing the globalist nature of the changes. The issue of national sovereignty will not be raised because it will never be seen as under threat. Law passed in Congress or policy enforced by regulatory agencies such as the FDA or the FTC will serve the purpose equally. Indeed, this method of harmonization is being already utilized in the United States. Although it would be almost impossible to include every attack through legislation or regulatory policy that has been launched against health freedom and DSHEA, this book will attempt to show several examples of domestic laws being used to implement Codex Alimentarius guidelines. It should be noted that these examples are more recent and only a small number of them will be mentioned. One only needs to conduct a brief Google search on the internet in order to discover volumes more.

One example is the Food Modernization Act of 2009. Submitted on February 4, 2009 by Representative Rosa DeLauro, a Democrat from Connecticut, whose husband had ties with Monsanto, the bill would have allowed for the complete takeover of farming in the United States by large agribusiness such as the aforementioned company. [495] The law

---

[495] Huff, Ethan. "Stop Federal Takeover of Food Regulation in H.R. 875." Naturalnews. March 11, 2009. http://www.naturalnews.com/z025824_food_safety.html

would have allowed for the creation of new bureaucracy, known as the Food Safety Administration,[496] which would deal specifically with food leaving the FDA to deal with drugs and devices.[497] The FSA would have appeared to be even less accountable to the public than the FDA.[498] A few of the requirements under the Food Modernization Act are as follows:

1.) The FSA would be designated as the sole regulator of food safety rather than any authority granted to the states.

2.) The authority would be granted to the FSA to create and implement a "national system for regular unannounced inspection of food establishments" based upon its' own dictates.

3.) Reclassification of all farms as "food production facilities." This would ensure that they fall under the regulatory authority of the FSA. The FSA would be able to enforce compliance with whatever it deems as legitimate and appropriate food safety requirements.

4.) Require farmers to comply with minimum safety standards set by the FSA for farming practices, including things such as establishing a Hazard Analysis Critical Control Point plan and numerous other written documentation.

5.) Grant the FSA the power to enact "preventative process controls to reduce adulteration of food" subject to the whims of the FSA.

6.) Gives the FSA designation as Food Safety law enforcement,

---

[496] Ibid.

[497] "DeLauro Assails Full-Scale Breakdown of Food Safety System and Introduces New FDA Reform Legislation." Press Release. Rosa L. DeLauro website. February 4, 2009. http://delauro.house.gov/release.cfm?id=1469 Accessed May 7, 2010.

[498] Huff, Ethan. "Stop Federal Takeover of Food Regulation in H.R. 875." Naturalnews. March 11, 2009. http://www.naturalnews.com/z025824_food_safety.html

with the authority to levy fines of up to $1 million for each
violation as well as other civil penalties.

7.) FSA would have authority to impose a ban on raw milk
distribution, even within a state.

8.) Expands the definition of the word "contaminant," allowing
the more liberal interpretation of what can be considered
"adulterated food." [499]

There were also concerns expressed about the ability of the bill to ban
the practice of seed cleaning, which is integral to organic farming.[500] By
allowing the U.S. government such unbridled authority, this bill would
allow the implementation of Codex Alimentarius guidelines at a national
level through stealth and total cover under the law. Also introduced in
2009, were the Food Safety and Tracking Improving Act, the Trace Act of
2009, and the Food and Drug Administration Globalization Act of 2009.
These bills were themselves very similar to H.R. 875. Much of the
language was similar and the content served to center more authority in
the hands of government regulatory agencies with emphasis being put
on "contaminants" or "traceability" concerns that would unfairly burden
small, local, and organic farmers. Obviously, as smaller farms disappear,
the larger GMO ridden agribusiness "farms" take their place. This is
exactly the point of the animal ID project which is being implemented as
we speak.[501] Small farms are overloaded with regulations such as
electronic identification systems while large agribusinesses are either

---

[499] Ibid.

[500] Lendman, Stephen. "Unsafe Genetically Modified Food:
GMO Proliferation Bills in the US Congress." Global Research.
April 3, 2009.
http://www.globalresearch.ca/index.php?context=va&aid=13
025 Accessed May 24, 2010.

[501] Stuter, Lynn. "The National Animal Indentification
System." Newswithviews. June 6, 2006.
http://www.newswithviews.com/Stuter/stuter91.htm
Accessed May 7, 2010.

able to absorb the cost or are exempted completely.[502] No doubt that the decisions made by the appropriate regulatory agencies would be similar to the guidelines spelled out in Codex documents.

Such was the case with H.R. 2749/S 510, known as the Food Safety Enhancement Act. This bill was much more open with its goal of harmonization than any previous attempts. Keep in mind, as some of the provisions are read, the relevant documents from Codex Alimentarius that deal with the same issues and the similarities between the two. Also, keep in mind that, under the WTO, SPS, and TBT agreements, the U.S. has agreed to accept Codex standards as the ultimate guidelines.

1.) Gives the FDA the authority to enforce penalties of up to ten years in jail and levy fines of up to $100,000 for individuals and $7.5 million for corporations, regardless of their size, for violation of FDA policy, even on the administrative levels.[503]

   This sets up the enforcement structure to compel harmonization from producers that would be most likely to oppose it – the small farmers. The more rebellious firms would be brought in line under this capability as well.

2.) Gives the FDA the authority to conduct warrantless searches of any and all records having to do with any aspect of a company's manufacture, production, or distribution mechanism. This would apply to small farms and restaurants as well.[504]

---

[502] "New Bill (HR2749) Gives FDA Unheard-of Power over Small Farmers, Food and Supplement Producers." American Association for Health Freedom. http://aahf.nonprofitsoapbox.com/index.php?option=com_content&task=view&id=825 Accessed May 7, 2010.
[503] Ibid.
[504] Ibid.

*See Codex's "Foods Derived From Biotechnology." This
authority would enhance "traceability" and control efforts.*

3.) With no judicial oversight, the FDA would have the authority
to recall, seize, detain, and quarantine any food or food
production facility if it has "any reason to believe that an
article of food is adulterated, misbranded, or otherwise in
violation of this Act." It also would have the authority to
quarantine an entire geographic area for the same reasons.[505]

*Given the Codex-friendly stance of the FDA, it is apparent that
this authority can and most likely will be used to shut down
the production of organic, local, or small farms. Given that
adulteration is essentially whatever the FDA says it is, this
should be very concerning. Keep in mind, the FDA does not
consider GMO, rBGH, irradiation, and most pesticides to be
contaminants.*

4.) Gives the FDA authority to set "scientific and risk-based
standards" for the use of various farming methods,
harvesting practices, and pesticides. The FDA would have the
authority to pronounce the standards that are to be
considered "scientific."[506]

*This should sound very familiar. See, "Foods Derived From
Biotechnology," "Guidelines for Vitamin and Mineral Food
Supplements," "Pesticide Residues in Food." Scientific risk-
based standards are, under the jurisdiction of either Codex or
the FDA, are almost always completely unscientific.*

5.) Would require all farms, food production facilities, and
restaurants to implement new hazard analysis and risk-based
preventive controls, extensive and detailed record
maintenance programs, food safety plans, and a very

---

[505] Ibid.
[506] Ibid.

expensive and detailed food tracing system. [507]

See, "Foods Derived From Modern Biotechnology," "General Standard for Irradiated Food," and "Pesticide Residues in Food." This relates to the "traceability" issues that are mentioned by Codex repeatedly. Also, this relates to the implementation of the National Animal ID system, another topic entirely.

6.) The requirements involving adulteration of misbranding of products applies not only to food, but to drugs, devices, and supplements. [508]

See "Guidelines for Vitamin and Mineral Food Supplements." Under this law, the already prohibitively restrictive labeling requirements set by the FDA would be expanded to include an even more open-ended set of guidelines that are, essentially, based upon nothing more than the whim of the FDA itself. Coupled with the enormous fines in this bill, this would serve as a major deterrent for new supplement manufacturers to enter the market. It would also provide an easy mechanism by which to eliminate those already in existence.

Although just one example of the implementation of Codex Alimentarius under the cover of domestic legislation, the Food Safety Enhancement Act is typical of these attempts. In terms of vitamin and mineral supplements, the proposed laws will generally give blanket authority to ban supplements over to compromised agencies like the FDA, classify herbal supplements as drugs, or reduce their nutritional content. As has already been demonstrated, Codex standards may come in the form of legislation written for that specific purpose. Such laws may be direct or they may be attached as an amendment to a much

---

[507] Ibid.
[508] Ibid.

larger bill and, thereby slip under the radar of health freedom advocates. These attacks may also come as governmental directives (usually from the executive branch) to regulatory agencies ordering them to enforce certain policies. Of course, the agencies might openly come out and establish their own policy as well. A perfect example of this was mentioned earlier in the discussion POPs. The EPA's own RED documents regarding acceptable MRLs of pesticide residues in food contain statements indicating the purpose of Codex harmonization.[509]

The most recent direct legislative assault on natural supplements and the DSHEA law came in the form of the "Dietary Supplement Safety Act of 2010," (DSSA) authored by Sen. John McCain and Sen. Byron Dorgan. Under the cover of preventing the abuse of anabolic steroids,[510] the DSSA would require the registration of "any business or operation engaged in manufacturing, packaging, holding, distributing, labeling, or licensing a dietary supplement for consumption in the United States."[511] As it is, this definition could include even small retail stores that sell herbal and nutritional products.[512] The bill also

---

[509] "Pesticide Registration Status." Environmental Protection Agency.
http://www.epa.gov/pesticides/reregistration/status.htm
Accessed May 21, 2010.
[510] "Bullet Points on McCain's Anti-Supplement Bill S. 3002."
National Health Federation.
http://www.thenhf.com/press_releases/pr_19_feb_2010.html Accessed February 24, 2010.
[511] "Dietary Supplement Safety Act of 2010." February 2, 2010.
http://mccain.senate.gov/public/index.cfm?Fuseaction=Files.View&Filestore_id=2fe2fa5d-636b-4705-97df-8318a24f718f
Accessed February 2, 2010.
[512] "Bullet Points on McCain's Anti-Supplement Bill S. 3002."
National Health Federation.
http://www.thenhf.com/press_releases/pr_19_feb_2010.html Accessed February 24, 2010.

changes the current practices of Serious Adverse Event Reporting to simply Adverse Event Reporting, allowing for the most ridiculous claims against supplements to be accepted such as the dislike of packaging or bad taste. The increase of adverse events in this manner would then be used to give credence to the banning of these particular supplements. Perhaps the most notable change however, is the fact that the legislation would change the current practice of allowing any supplement on the market previous to October 15, 1994 to remain on the market. [513] This bill would reverse this and define a "new dietary supplement" as "one that "is not included on the list of 'Accepted Dietary Ingredients', to be prepared, published, and maintained by the Secretary."[514] These "new" supplements will be considered "adulterated" unless "there is a history of use or other evidence of safety establishing that the dietary ingredient when used under the conditions recommended or suggested in the labeling of the dietary supplement . . ."[515] Notice the similarity to both Codex guidelines and the EU Food Supplements Directive. The language in this bill mandates the creation of what are effectively positive and negative lists, the addition or subtraction of supplements being completely subject to the whim of the FDA and/or the HHS Secretary. There are also provisions in the bill which would allow the cost of recalls to filter all the way down to the retailers themselves.[516]

The McCain-Dorgan bill is not the only recent attack on the natural supplement industry and DSHEA, however. Senator Henry

[513] Ibid.
[514] "Dietary Supplement Safety Act of 2010." February 2, 2010. http://mccain.senate.gov/public/index.cfm?Fuseaction=Files.View&Filestore_id=2fe2fa5d-636b-4705-97df-8318a24f718f Accessed February 2, 2010.
[515] Ibid. p.5
[516] Ibid. p. 11.

Waxman, one of the co-authors of the Climate Change bill, also in Congress, attached a provision to the Wall Street Reform and Consumer Protection Act of 2009 which will allow virtually the same authority as mentioned above, to be bestowed upon the FTC. These new rules would allow the FTC to ignore much of the DSHEA law and force supplement companies to undergo ridiculously expensive tests to prove what has been known for thousands of years – that vitamins and nutrients are safe. Unfortunately at the time of the writing of this book, for many reasons, the Wall Street Reform and Consumer Protections Act of 2009 has passed the House of Representatives with the provision intact.[517]

Legislative maneuvering is not the only method of attack launched against health freedom. Volumes of books could be filled with the tyranny enforced the FDA alone. A recent example is the declaration made by the FDA that pyridoxamine, a naturally-occurring form of vitamin B-6, to be a drug. Because of this, any supplement that contains pyridoxamine can now be labeled as adulterated and hence illegal. Vitamin companies now face the possibility of FDA raids on their facilities because of this position. Not only this, but pyrodoxamine occurs naturally in fish, chicken, and many other foods.[518] This possibly opens the door to confiscation and banning of these foods by regulatory agencies such as the FDA or the USDA. Similarly to the vitamin B6 issue,

---

[517] "Waxman Slips Obscure Anti-Supplement Measure into Wall St. 'Reform' Bill Passed by the House." Alliance for Natural Health. April 27, 2010. http://www.anh-usa.org/congressman-waxman-slips-obscure-anti-supplement-measure-into-wall-st-%E2%80%9Creform%E2%80%9D-bill-passed-by-the-house-please-take-action-to-prevent-same-thing-happening-in-the-senate/ Accessed May 7, 2010.
[518] Adams, Mike. "FDA Declares Form of Vitamin B6 a Drug." Naturalnews. February 12, 2009. http://www.naturalnews.com/025606_vitamin_B6_pyridoxamine.html

the FDA has also declared the natural molecule lovastatin contained in red yeast rice, as a drug. It then went after many producers of red yeast rice supplements that contained the molecule.[519] Vitamin B17, also known as Laetrile and a known cancer cure, has also been banned for use in the United States by regulatory authorities.[520] In respect to Codex Alimentarius Guidelines, it should be noted that the tendency of the FDA to try and regulate vitamins, minerals, and foods as drugs bears great resemblance to both the Codex front legislation known as the EU Food Supplements Directive as well as Codex guidelines themselves. Indeed, the authority to regulate nutrients as drugs is an important tool in the fight against open access to them.

Clearly, domestic legislation is the preferred method of Codex harmonization. As the constant attempts at its implementation through national laws demonstrates, the world government structure, using this method, is able to remain largely unseen by those it wishes to govern. But the people of these nations, Americans in particular, should not expect to see an abrupt change in natural supplement regulation when these laws are finally passed. Again, this would perhaps provoke large scale revolt against the national structure of administration. Rather, changes will be made incrementally such as the banning of particular types of vitamins and even vitamins themselves. Americans are much less likely to revolt en masse if they do not see a direct threat to all of their supplements at once. The majority of people are unbelievably shortsighted and non-confrontational. A threat to a particular version of

---

[519] Chappels, Bradley R. "FDA Moves to Shut Down Red Yeast Rice Distributors Online." Naturalnews. September 20, 2007. http://www.naturalnews.com/022046_red_yeast_the_FDA_health.html

[520] Black, Alexis. "World Without Cancer Author G. Edward Griffin Exposes How Corrupt Politics Prevent Real Cancer Cures From Reaching The Public." Naturalnews. November 3, 2005. http://www.naturalnews.com/012923.html

vitamin B as compared to an attack launched on all vitamins is much less likely to draw large scale criticism. The cover of domestic legislation and the process of incrementalism cannot be underestimated in the drive to implement of Codex Alimentarius in every nation on the face of the earth.

Chapter 8

What Can Be Done To Stop Codex Alimentarius

What Can Be Done To Stop The Implementation of Codex Alimentarius

The majority of this book has been dedicated to the discussion of what Codex is and the dangers of its implementation. However, one would rightly ask, for all the dangers facing the global population in regards to Codex standards, how can this juggernaut be stopped? If an international cabal of elite individuals have already created a structural framework for world government, and national governments seem to be complacent, even active, in the matter, what chance do we have? The answer to this question is not a simple one. The fact is, if we rely on the UN funded organizations, the ruling elite, the United States government, and our so-called leaders to aid us, we have no chance. Therefore, we must rely solely on ourselves for the change we need. This fight will not be an easy one and it will require a great deal of work from all of us. But change can come if we put forth a full effort. Below are some suggestions that will aid in the prevention of Codex guidelines being implemented in the United States.

Unfortunately, most of the action taken against Codex Alimentarius is virtually useless. This is not meant to denigrate the tireless efforts of health freedom advocates and organizations that have been fighting against nutritional tyranny for so long. However, begging those wish to destroy access to nutritional supplements for a change in the standards guiding the access to these supplements is by no means an effective strategy. Relying on the moral integrity or honesty of the FDA is laughable and Congress is quite open about its disdain for the concerns of the American people. Many congressmen, such as John McCain, Henry Waxman, and Byron Dorgan, stand in direct opposition to natural supplements. Those that do support supplement access are easily bought off by pharmaceutical companies or globalist foundations and organizations. But the American people do not have to continue to put up with such open disregard for their wishes. These individuals do not have to continue to occupy these posts. Likewise, participation in government should not be reserved for politicians and fools. Therefore, some suggestions for change are as follows and are listed in order of importance – the fourth being the most effective.

1.) Join the many natural health organizations and foundations that are fighting against Codex Alimentarius and for natural health freedom. There are many organizations such as the National Health Federation, the Alliance for Natural Health, and the Dr. Rath Health Foundation. Many more of these organizations exist but those listed are the most active and reliable. These organizations often carry petitions against Codex on their sites and often lobby governmental agencies and representatives. The National Health Federation (NHF) actually obtained observer status by Codex Alimentarius and is now able to attend CCNFSDU meetings and make their position known to delegates from the U.S. as well as other countries. The observer delegates from NHF try their best, mostly in vain, to inject some reason into the "debate" over natural supplements. These organizations need all the help they can get in this fight. Go their sites, join, donate, sign petitions, and get active.

2.) Educate yourself and others as to the dangers of Codex. Simply by reading this book, you are a million times more informed than most Americans about Codex Alimentarius. However, numbers are important. It is true that one person can change the world, but not by keeping silent. Knowledge is only powerful when put to use. Talk to your friends, your family, your co-workers, and even people you don't know about the dangers of

Codex Alimentarius. Tell them about this book, tell them about the health freedom websites, and tell them what you know. There is strength in numbers and we outnumber the globalists by at least a million to one. The more people who are educated as to the danger of Codex, the more chances we have that one of those individuals will be the one to spark the end of Codex and globalism.

3.) Pressure and elect representatives, presidents, and senators that support health freedom, clean food, and national sovereignty and remove those that do not. We must be increasingly vigilant as to domestic legislation that would implement Codex Alimentarius guidelines in the United States. We should then pressure our elected officials to vote against such legislation at the peril of their career. The United States is not a kingship. There is no reason that a Senator should remain in his/her position for 50 years if he/she is not satisfying the needs of his/her constituency. These people can be removed. Vote them out, campaign against them, and even run against them yourself. Also remember that Democrats and Republicans are not the only options. In turn, elect representatives to government offices that do support true American values.

4.) Pull out of the WTO and repeal unfair, un-American trade policies. The WTO, GATT, NAFTA, CAFTA, SAFTA, and the Chinese Trade Agreement all serve the purpose of destroying the economies of the developed world, the United States in particular, and ensuring the creation of an eventual world government. No sane individual would have supported any of these agreements for any other purpose. All of these agreements are creating a "global market" which not only harmonizes standards, but laws and cultures. While this is a frightening thought to say the least, it presents a unique opportunity for the U.S. to stop the global government tyranny in its tracks. Indeed, this is the most important solution to Codex guidelines. Pulling out of the WTO would remove any enforcement ability for Codex guidelines. Pulling out of GATT, NAFTA, CAFTA, SAFTA, and Chinese trade would remove obligations for the nation to be involved with the WTO. Not to mention the economic revival the United States would see from repeal of these agreements. Being the most powerful nation on earth and saying no to Codex Alimentarius guidelines and global governance would send shockwaves through the plans of the globalists.

Although the focus of this book has been on Codex Alimentarius, it is important to remember that Codex is not the heart of the problem but a symptom of it. It is merely another useful tool being used to set up a one-world government where no one has access to natural supplements or clean food. Therefore, ironically, the effort to defeat Codex should not focus solely on Codex. We must treat it for what it is and focus on the disease, not the symptom. Then, and only then, can we be free of its' tyranny.

Bibliography

"Dietary Supplement Safety Act of 2010." February 2, 2010.
http://mccain.senate.gov/public/index.cfm?Fuseaction=Files.View&Files
tore_id=2fe2fa5d-636b-4705-97df-8318a24f718f

"Use of Vitamins in Foods: Toxicological and nutritional-physiological
aspects." Domke, A., Grossklaus R., Niemann B., Przyrembel H., Richter
K., Schimdt E., WeiBenborn B., Worner B., Ziegenhagen R., Federal
Institute for Risk Assessment, BfR, 2005.

"About the WTO - A Statement by the Director General."
http://www.wto.org/english/thewto_e/whatis_e/wto_dg_stat_e.htm
Accessed May 4, 2010.

"Agreement on Technical Barriers to Trade." World Trade Organization.
http://www.wto.org/english/docs_e/legal_e/17-tbt_e.htm Accessed
May 6, 2010.

"Agricultural Pesticide Use May Be Associated With Increased Risk of
Prostate Cancer." National Cancer Institute. May 1, 2003.
http://www.cancer.gov/newscenter/pressreleases/agriculturehealthstu
dy

"All Herbs and Supplements." Medline Plus Website.
http://www.nlm.nih.gov/medlineplus/druginfo/herb_All.html#V
Accessed April 15, 2010.

"Birth Control or Race Control?" Margaret Sanger Papers Project #28,
Fall 2001. New York University.
http://www.nyu.edu/projects/sanger/secure/newsletter/articles/bc_or
_race_control.html

"Birth Control Organizations – American Birth Control League – About
Margaret Sanger." New York University.
http://www.nyu.edu/projects/sanger/secure/aboutms/organization_ab
cl.html

"Birth Control Organizations – American Birth Control League – About Margaret Sanger." New York University. http://www.nyu.edu/projects/sanger/secure/aboutms/organization_ab cl.html

"Bullet Points on McCain's Anti-Supplement Bill S. 3002." National Health Federation. http://www.thenhf.com/press_releases/pr_19_feb_2010.html Accessed February 24, 2010

"Canadians Deserve To Know What They Are Eating: Food Safety Must Come Before Trade." Canadian Health Coalition, Media Advisory, May 1-4, 2001. http://www.healthcoalition.ca/codex.html

"Central America – Dominican Republic – United States Free Trade (DR-CAFTA)." SICE: Foreign Trade Information System. http://www.sice.oas.org/Trade/CAFTA/CAFTADR_e/CAFTADRin_e.asp Accessed May 6, 2010

"Chipotle Mexican Grill is Nation's First Chain to go Entirely rBGH-Free," Chipotle Mexican Grill, November 5, 2007. Organic Consumers Association, http://www.organicconsumers.org/articles/article_8847.cfm

"Claims That Can Be Made For Conventional Foods and Dietary Supplements." FDA.gov September 2003. http://www.fda.gov/Food/LabelingNutrition/LabelClaims/ucm111447.h tm

"Codex Alimentarius Commission: New Standards, old concerns," July 14, 2008. http://www.freshplaza.com/print.asp?id=25392

"Codex Alimentarius: Codex – government and corporate control of our food supply." Alliance for Natural Health Europe. http://www.anhcampaign.org/campaigns/codex Accessed May 24, 2010.

"Codex Allows Deadly Pesticides." Global Healing Center.
http://www.globalhealingcenter.com/phpprint.php

"Codex Committee on Pesticide Residues (CCPR)" Consumers International.
http://www.consumerinternational.org/templates/internal.asp?NodeID=94886 October 8, 2007. Accessed April 6, 2010.

"Council Decision of 28 June 1999 laying down the procedures for the exercise of implementing powers conferred on the Commission (*) (1999/468/EC)"
http://www.ena.lu/council_decision_1999_468_ec_laying_down_procedures_exercise_implementing_powers_june_1999-02-4941 Accessed April 21, 2010.

"Current risk management practices in the codex alimentarius commission, its subsidiary bodies, and advisory expert committees." FAO.org http://www.fao.org/docrep/w4982e09.htm Accessed March 23, 2010.

"DeLauro Assails Full-Scale Breakdown of Food Safety System and Introduces New FDA Reform Legislation." Press Release. Rosa L. DeLauro website. February 4, 2009.
http://delauro.house.gov/release.cfm?id=1469 Accessed May 7, 2010.

"Dietary Supplement Health and Education Act of 1994," Food and Drug Administration.
http://www.fda.gov/RegulatoryInformation/Legislation/FederalFoodDrugandCosmeticActFDCAct/SignificantAmendmentstotheFDCAct/ucm148003.htm Accessed May 24, 2010.

"Dietary Supplement Health and Education Act of 1994." Food and Drug Administration. http://vm.cfsan.fda.gov/~dms/dietsupp.html

"Dietary Supplement Safety Act of 2010." February 2, 2010.
http://mccain.senate.gov/public/index.cfm?Fuseaction=Files.View&Files

tore_id=2fe2fa5d-636b-4705-97df-8318a24f718f   Accessed February 2, 2010.

"EU food authorities say genetically modified maize is safe." AFP. June 30, 2009. http://www.france24.com/en/20090630-eu-food-authorities-say-genetically-modified-maize-safe-   Accessed May 24, 2010.

"Europe balks at GE corn in NZ," Stuff.co.nz, Feb. 11, 2009. http://www.stuff.co.nz/national/3020246/Europe-balks-at-GE-corn-in-NZ

"Fact Sheet: History, Background, and Status of Labeling of Irradiated Foods" 8/25/2008. http://www.organicconsumers.org/irrad/labelingstatus.cfm   Accessed May 24, 2010.

"FACT SHEET: Sanitary and Phytosanitary Measures and the World Trade Organization." USDA Foreign Agricultural Service. February 2006. http://www.fas.usda.gov/info/factsheets/sps.asp   Accessed May 6, 2010

"FAO/WHO Training Package – Section Two: Understanding the Organization of Codex" CodexEurope. http://webcache.googleusercontent.com/search?q=cache:eqkOscOnYG MJ:codexeurope.ch/ppt/Section%2520Two%2520-%25202.6%2520How%2520does%2520Codex%2BEC.ppt+%E2%80%9CF AO/WHO+Training+Package+%E2%80%93+Section+Two:+Understandin g+the+Organization+of+Codex%E2%80%9D&cd=3&hl=en&ct=clnk&gl=u s   (this is the html format).

"FAQs – Rumours" CodexAlimentarius.net http://www.codexalimentarius.net/web/faq_rum.jsp#R1   Accessed April 26, 2010

"FDA Responds to Citizen Petition on BST." Food and Drug Administration. April 21, 2000.

http://www.fda.gov/AnimalVeterinary/NewsEvents/CVMUpdates/ucm1 30325.htm Accessed May 24, 2010.

"Food and Drug Administration, 21 CFR Parts 111 and 112 Current Good Manufacturing Practice in Manufacturing, Packing, or Holding Dietary Ingredients and Dietary Supplements; Proposed Rule." Part 2. March 13, 2003. http://www.fda.gov/OHRMS/DOCKETS/98fr/03-5401.pdf

"Food Derived From Modern Biotechnology." Codex Alimentarius 2nd Edition. ftp://ftp.fao.org/codex/Publications/Booklets/Biotech/Biotech_2009e.p df

"Food Irradiation." University of Minnesota. http://www.cidrap.umn.edu/cidrap/content/fs/irradiation/biofacts/irra d-bkgd.html

"Foods Derived From Modern Biotechnology." 2nd edition. Codex Alimentarius. ftp://ftp.fao.org/docrep/fao/011/a1554e/a1554e00.pdf Accessed May 24, 2010.

"Further 'Rubberstamp' GMO Approvals In The Pipeline In Europe." Bridges Trade BioRes October 5, 2007. Vol. 7 No. 17. http://ictsd.org/i/news/biores/60002/ Accessed May 24, 2010.

"Gene Altered Giant Salmon Cannibals." Mercola.com. June 23, 2004. http://articles.mercola.com/sites/articles/archive/2004/06/23/gene-altered-salmon.aspx

"General Agreement on Tariffs and Trade 1994." http://www.wto.org/english/docs_e/legal_e/06-gatt_e.htm Accessed May 4, 2010.

"Genetically Modified Fish: A Disaster Waiting To Happen." www.mercola.com. February 01, 2003. http://articles.mercola.com/sites/articles/archive/2003/02/01/gm-fish.aspx

"Genetically Modified Ingredients Overview." Seedsofdeception.com
http://www.seedsofdeception.com/Public/BuyingNon-GMO/index.cfm.

"GM Salmon Muscle In on Wild Fish When Food Is Scarce." Scientific American. June 8, 2004.
http://www.scientificamerican.com/article.cfm?id=gm-salmon-muscle-in-on-wi   Accessed May 24, 2010.

"Guidance For Industry: Voluntary Labeling Indicating Whether Foods Have or Have Not Been Developed Using Biotengineering: Draft Guidance." Food and Drug Administration. January 2001.
http://www.fda.gov/Food/GuidanceComplianceRegulatoryInformation/GuidanceDocuments/FoodLabelingNutrition/ucm059098.htm

"Guidelines for Vitamin and Mineral Food Supplements." Codexalimentarius.net
www.codexalimentarius.net/download/standards/.../cxg_055e.pdf

"Health Canada rejects bovine growth hormone in Canada," Health Canada. January 14, 1999. http://www.hc-sc.gc.ca/index-eng.php

"Health Canada rejects bovine growth hormone in Canada," News Release, January 14, 1999.
http://www.springerlink.com/content/h875812u334m2g01/

"Health Fraud." FDA.gov September 10, 2001.
http://www.fda.gov/NewsEvents/Testimony/ucm115204.htm

"Heavy Pesticide exposure linked to brain cancer." Reuters. June 12, 2007. http://www.reuters.com/article/idUSTON27410120070612

"Household pesticide link to cancer." The Ecologist. July 30, 2009.
http://www.theecologist.org/news/news_round_up/294917/household_pesticide_link_to_cancer.html

"India Fast-Tracks Imports Of Non-Living GM Material." Bridges Trade BioRes October 5, 2007. Vol. 7 No. 17. http://ictsd.org/i/news/biores/59999/ Accessed May 24, 2010.

"Individuals Who Apply Pesticides Are Found to Have Double the Risk of Blood Disorder." American Society of Hematology." June 12, 2009. http://www.hematology.org/news/2009/4171.aspx

"Joint FAO/WHO Food Standards Programme: Codex Alimentarius Commission(Thirty-Second Session)" FAO Headquarters, Rome, Italy, June 29 – July 4, 2009. P. 15. www.codexalimentarius.net/download/report/710/al32_26e.pdf Accessed May 24, 2010.

"Key Issues in WTO Dispute Settlement: The First Ten Years." Ed. Refus Yerxa and Bruce Wilson. Cambridge University Press. http://assets.cambridge.org/97805218/61595/excerpt/9780521861595_excerpt.pdf

"Mastitis in Beef Cows – Frequently Asked Questions" Government of Alberta, Ministry of Agriculture and Rural Development. http://www1.agric.gov.ab.ca/$department/deptdocs.nsf/all/faq8106

"Medisin." Whitaker, Scott; Fleming, Jose. Divine Protection Publications. 2007.

"Monsanto pulls GM corn amid serious food safety concerns," GM Free CYMRU. http://gmfreecymru.org/Press_Notice9Nov2009.htm

"Monsanto pulls GM corn amid serious food safety concerns," GM Free CYMRU. http://gmfreecymru.org/Press_Notice9Nov2009.htm

"Monsanto's Genetically Modified Milk Ruled Unsafe By The United Nations," PR Newswire. August 18, 1999. Archived on GENET-News as "1-Hormones: Codex Alimentarius voted in favor for EU ban on rBST." http://www.gene.ch/genet/1999/Aug/msg00054.html

"New Attack on GM Food Safety Testing Standards," Centre for Integrated Research in Biosafety, University of Canterbury. February 2007.
http://www.sustainabilitynz.org/docs/Backgrounder_NewAttackonGMFoodSafetyStandards.pdf Accessed May 24, 2010.

"New Bill (HR2749) Gives FDA Unheard-of Power over Small Farmers, Food and Supplement Producers." American Association for Health Freedom.
http://aahf.nonprofitsoapbox.com/index.php?option=com_content&task=view&id=825 Accessed May 7, 2010.

"Persistant Organic Pollutants: A Global Issue, A Global Response." Environmental Protection Agency. December 17, 2009.
http://www.epa.gov/international/toxics/pop.htm

"Pesticide Registration Status." Environmental Protection Agency.
http://www.epa.gov/pesticides/reregistration/status.htm Accessed May 21, 2010.

"Pesticide Residues In Food." Codexalimentarius.net
http://www.codexalimentarius.net/mrls/pestdes/jsp/pest_q-e.jsp

"rBGH: How Artificial Hormones Damage the Dairy Industry and Endanger Public Health." Food and Water Watch.
http://www.foodandwaterwatch.org/food/report/rbgh-how-artificial-hormones-damage-the-dairy-industry-and-endanger-public-health-2/rbgh-how-artificial-hormones-damage-the-dairy-industry-and-endanger-public-health-1/ Accessed May 24, 2010.

"Recombinant Bovine Growth Hormone: FDA Approval Should Be Withheld Until the Mastitis Issue Is Resolved." U.S. GAO, August 6, 1992.
http://www.gao.gov/products/PEMD-92-26 Accessed May 24, 2010.

"Report of Codex Alimentarius Commission: 23rd Session, FAO Headquarters, Rome, June 28-July 3, 1999. P. 13-14.

www.codexalimentarius.net/download/report/518/Al99_37e.pdf
Accessed May 24, 2010.

"Report of the Canadian Veterinary Medical Association Expert Panel on rBST." Conclusions and Recommendations. Health Canada. November 1998. http://www.hc-sc.gc.ca/dhp-mps/vet/issues-enjeux/rbst-stbr/rep_cvma-rap_acdv_14-eng.php Accessed May 17, 2010.

"Report on the Food and Drug Administration's Review of the Safety of Recombinant Bovine Somatropin." Food and Drug Administration. April 23, 2009. http://www.fda.gov/AnimalVeterinary/SafetyHealth/ProductSafetyInformation/ucm130321.htm Accessed May 24, 2010.

"Reregistration Eligibility Decision for Acephate." U.S. Environmental Protection Agency Office of Pesticide Programs. http://www.epa.gov/pesticides/reregistration/REDs/acephate_red.pdf p. 44. Accessed April 6, 2010.

"Safe Milk," The Council of Canadians. 1998. http://www.canadians.org/archive/documents/safe_milk.pdf

"Safety aspects of genetically modified foods of plant origin, a joint FAO/WHO consultation on foods derived from biotechnology, Geneva, Switzerland 29 May – 2 June 2000". World Health Organization. http://www.who.int/foodsafety/publications/biotech/ec_june2000/en/index.html

"Settlement Protects Illinois Consumers From Misleading Food Labels," Illinois Department of Health News Release. August 14, 1997. http://www.idph.state.il.us/public/press97/ben.htm

"Statement of Food Policy – Foods Derived From New Plant Varieties," FDA Federal Register Vol. 57. 1992. http://www.fda.gov/Food/GuidanceComplianceRegulatoryInformation/GuidanceDocuments/Biotechnology/ucm096095.htm Accessed May 24, 2010.

"Statement of Michael Hansen, Ph.D., Research Associate Consumer Policy Institute, Consumers Union On FDA's Safety Assessment of Recombinant Bovine Growth Hormone December 15, 1998." http://www.cosumersunion.org/pub/1998/12/002269print.html

"Statement of Michael Hansen, Ph.D., Research Associate Consumer Policy Institute, Consumers Union On FDA's Safety Assessment of Recombinant Bovine Growth Hormone December 15, 1998." http://www.cosumersunion.org/pub/1998/12/002269print.html

"The Documentation About 'Codex Alimentarius.'" Dr. Rath Health Foundation. http://www4.drrathfoundation.org/PHARMACEUTICAL_BUSINESS/health_movement_against_codex/health_movement24.htm   Accessed April 26, 2010.

"The History of the 'Business With Disease.'" Dr. Rath Health Foundation. http://www4.dr-rath-foundation.org/PHARMACEUTICAL_BUSINESS/history_of_the_pharmaceutical_industry.htm Accessed April 26, 2010.

"The Issues: Artificial Hormones." Sustainabletable.org http://www.sustainabletable.org/issues/hormones/   Accessed May 24, 2010.

"Transgenic high-lysine corn LY038 withdrawn after EU raises safety questions," The Bioscience Resource Project, Nov. 10, 2009. http://www.bioscienceresource.org/news/article.php?id=43   Accessed May 24, 2010.

"U.S. – Central America Free Trade Agreement: Frequently Asked Questions." United States Embassy – San Jose, Costa Rica. http://sanjose.usembassy.gov/Cafta/faq.html   Accessed May 6, 2010.

"Understanding the Codex Alimentarius." World Health Organization. Food and Agricultural Organization. 2006.

http://www.scribd.com/doc/25710873/WHO-Understanding-the-Codex-Alimentarius   Accessed April 23, 2010.

"Vitamin C." Medline Plus website.
http://www.nlm.nih.gov/medlineplus/druginfo/natural/patient-vitaminc.html   Accessed April 15, 2010.

"Vitamin C." Oregon State University. Linus Pauling Institute.
http://lpi.oregonstate.edu/infocenter/vitamins/vitaminC/   Accessed April 15, 2010.

"Vitamin D." Medline Plus Website.
http://www.nlm.nih.gov/medlineplus/druginfo/natural/patient-vitamind.html   Accessed April 15, 2010.

"Voluntary Labeling of Milk and Milk Products From Cows That Have Not Been Treated With Recombinant Bovine Somatotropin." Federal Register, 59 FR 6279, February 10, 1994.
http://www.fda.gov/Food/GuidanceComplianceRegulatoryInformation/GuidanceDocuments/FoodLabelingNutrition/ucm059036.htm Accessed May 24, 2010.

"Waxman Slips Obscure Anti-Supplement Measure into Wall St. 'Reform' Bill Passed by the House." Alliance for Natural Health. April 27, 2010. http://www.anh-usa.org/congressman-waxman-slips-obscure-anti-supplement-measure-into-wall-st-%E2%80%9Creform%E2%80%9D-bill-passed-by-the-house-please-take-action-to-prevent-same-thing-happening-in-the-senate/   Accessed May 7, 2010.

"What are POPs?" Stockholm Convention on persistent organic pollutants. Accessed March 23, 2010.
http://chm.pops.int/Convention/ThePOPs/tabid/673/language/en-US/Default.aspx

"What Do Scientists Say About the Dangers of Genetic Engineering?" Mothers for Natural Law. http://www.safe-food.org/-issue/scientists.html

"What has happened to high lysine corn?" Biosafety Information Centre.
http://www.biosafety-info.net/bioart.php?bid=583&ac=st

"What is Codex?" American Holistic Health Association,
http://ahha.org/codex1.htm

"WTO Codex to Allow Dangerous Levels of Food Irradiation," Organic
Consumers Association. July 10, 2003
http://www.organicconsumers.org/corp/071403_wto_irradiation.cfm
Accessed May 24, 2010

A Model for Establishing Upper Levels of Intake for Nutrients and
Related Substances, WHO/FAO.
http://www.who.int/ipcs/highlights/full_report.pdf   Accessed May 24,
2010.

Abelsohn, Alan., Gibson, Brian L., Sanborn, Margaret D., Weir, Erica.
"Identifying andmanaging adverse environmental health effects:5.
Persistent Organic Pollutants." Canadian Medical Association Journal.
June 11, 2002. 166 (12).
http://www.cmaj.ca/cgi/content/full/166/12/1549 Accessed May 24,
2010.

Adams, Mike. "FDA Declares Form of Vitamin B6 a Drug." Naturalnews.
February 12, 2009.
http://www.naturalnews.com/025606_vitamin_B6_pyridoxamine.html

Adams, Mike. "FDA Declares Forms of Vitamin B6 a Drug, Effectively
Banning Pyridoxamine from Dietary Supplements." Naturalnews.com
February 12, 2009.
http://www.naturalnews.com/025606_vitamin_B6_pyridoxamine.html

Baker, S.L. "On-the-job pesticide exposure is linked to Parkinson's
disease." Naturalnews.com October 9, 2009.
http://www.naturalnews.com/027202_Parkinsons_pesticides_disease.h
tml

Beers, Allison. "Billy Re-elected Chairman of Codex." Food Chemical News. July 9, 2001. http://www.accessmylibrary.com/article-1G1-76444795/billy-re-elected-chairman.html Accessed May 13, 2010.

Behreandt, Dennis. "The crimes of I.G. Farben: during WWII, I.G. Farben, a synthetic-fuels manufacturer for the German war machine, was a major supporter of the Nazi regime and a willing co-conspirator in the Holocaust." The New American. November 27, 2006. http://findarticles.com/p/articles/mi_m0JZS/is_24_22/ai_n24996865/ Accessed April 26, 2010.

Black, Alexis. "World Without Cancer Author G. Edward Griffin Exposes How Corrupt Politics Prevent Real Cancer Cures From Reaching The Public." Naturalnews. November 3, 2005. http://www.naturalnews.com/012923.html

Black, Edwin. "The Horrifying American Roots of Nazi Eugenics." History News Network, GeorgeMason University. November 11, 2003. http://hnn.us/articles/1796.html

Brown, Colin. "Suppressed report shows cancer link to GM potatoes." The Independent. February 17, 2007. http://www.independent.co.uk/life-style/health-and-families/health-news/suppressed-report-shows-cancer-link-to-gm-potatoes-436673.html May 24, 2010

Brumbaugh, David L. "A History of the Extraterritorial Income (ETI) and Foreign Sales Corporation (FSC) Export Tax-Benefit Controversy." Congressional Research Service Report Summarizes History of FSC/ETI Controversy. November 9, 2004. http://www.taxhistory.org/thp/readings.nsf/cf7c9c870b600b9585256df80075b9dd/d1e0dcc337b8048385256f860068159e?OpenDocument Accessed May 4, 2010.

Chaitkin, Anton. "Population Control, Nazis, and the U.N.!" Tetrahedron.com. 2002

http://www.tetrahedron.org/articles/new_world_order/UN_Rockefelle
r_Genocide.html

Chappels, Bradley R. "FDA Moves to Shut Down Red Yeast Rice
Distributors Online." Naturalnews. September 20, 2007.
http://www.naturalnews.com/022046_red_yeast_rice_the_FDA_health
.html

Codex Alimentarius - USDA Food Safety and Inspection Service.
http://www.fsis.usda.gov/Codex_Alimentarius/index.asp   Accessed
April 30, 2010.

Codex Alimentarius: Committees and Task Forces – ad hoc
Intergovernmental Task Forces. USDA Food Safety and Inspection
Service.
http://www.fsis.usda.gov/codex_alimentarius/Ad_Hoc_International_T
ask_Forces/index.asp   Accessed on April 30, 2010.

Codex Alimentarius: Committees and Task Forces – Commodity
Committees. USDA Food Safety and Inspection Service.
http://www.fsis.usda.gov/codex_alimentarius/Commodity_Committees
/index.asp   Accessed on April 30, 2010.

Codex Alimentarius: Committees and Task Forces – General Subject
Committees. USDA Food Safety and Inspection Service.
http://www.fsis.usda.gov/codex_alimentarius/General_Subject_Commi
ttees/index.asp   Accessed April 29, 2010.

Codex Committee On Nutrition and Foods For Special Dietary Uses.
https://www.ccnfsdu.de/index.php?id=493

Codexalimentarius.net "FAQs – General Questions." Accessed May 3,
2010. http://www.codexalimentarius.net/web/faq_gen.jsp#G11

Codexalimentarius.net
http://www.codexalimentarius.net/mrls/servlet/PesticideServlet?Pestic

ides=1&Items=0&out_style=by+substance&Domain=PesticideMRLs&Language=english&query_form=%2Fmrls%2Fpestdes%2Fpest_q-e.htm

Codexalimentarius.net
http://www.codexalimentarius.net/mrls/servlet/PesticideServlet?Pesticides=1&Items=0&out_style=by+substance&Domain=PesticideMRLs&Language=english&query_form=%2Fmrls%2Fpestdes%2Fpest_q-e.htm
Accessed April 6, 2010.

Codexalimentarius.net
http://www.codexalimentarius.net/mrls/servlet/PesticideServlet?Pesticides=12&Items=0&out_style=by+substance&Domain=PesticideMRLs&Language=english&query_form=%2Fmrls%2Fpestdes%2Fpest_q-e.htm
Accessed April 6, 2010.

Codexalimentarius.net
http://www.codexalimentarius.net/mrls/servlet/PesticideServlet?Pesticides=21&Items=0&out_style=by+substance&Domain=PesticideMRLs&Language=english&query_form=%2Fmrls%2Fpestdes%2Fpest_q-e.htm
Accessed April 6, 2010.

Codexalimentarius.net
http://www.codexalimentarius.net/mrls/servlet/PesticideServlet?Pesticides=21&Items=0&out_style=by+substance&Domain=PesticideMRLs&Language=english&query_form=%2Fmrls%2Fpestdes%2Fpest_q-e.htm
Accessed April 6, 2010.

Codexalimentarius.net
http://www.codexalimentarius.net/mrls/servlet/PesticideServlet?Pesticides=43&Items=0&out_style=by+substance&Domain=PesticideMRLs&Language=english&query_form=%2Fmrls%2Fpestdes%2Fpest_q-e.htm
Accessed April 6, 2010.

Codexalimentarius.net.
http://www.codexalimentarius.net/mrls/servlet/PesticideServlet?Pesticides=33&Items=0&out_style=by+substance&Domain=PesticideMRLs&La

nguage=english&query_form=%2Fmrls%2Fpestdes%2Fpest_q-e.htm
Accessed April 6, 2010.

Costa, LG., Giodano, G., Guizzetti, M., Vitalone, A., "Neurotoxicity of
pesticides: a brief review." Frontiers of Bioscience. January 1, 2008. 13.
Pp. 1240-1249. http://www.ncbi.nlm.nih.gov/pubmed/17981626
Accessed May 24, 2010.

Council on Foreign Relations.
http://www.cfr.org/about/people/international_advisory_board.html
Accessed on April 28, 2010.

Damato, Gregory. "Codex Alimentarius: Population Control Under the
Guise of Consumer Protection." September 10, 2008. Naturalnews.
http://www.naturalnews.com/024128_CODEX_food_health.html
Accessed May 17, 2010.

Directive 2002/46/EC Of The European Parliament And Of The Council
of 10 June 2002 on the approximation of the laws of the member states
relating to food supplements. "Codex Alimentarius: Global Food
Imperialism." Ed. Scott C. Tips. FHR. 2007.

Doughton, Sandi. "Research fuels fear of gene-altered fish." The Seattle
Times. June 08, 2004.
http://seattletimes.nwsource.com/html/localnews/2001950789_genefi
sh08m

Dybring, Alex.; Mosegaard, Tamara Theresa.; "Codex Alimentarius
Information – an Introduction." Codex Alimentarius: Global Food
Imperialism." Ed. Scott C. Tips. FHR. 2007.

Eggertson, Laura. "Expert Worked For Drug Firm: Nutritionist Now
Examining Safety Of BST Hormone," The Toronto Star September 21,
1998. http://archives.foodsafety.ksu.edu/fsnet/1998/9-1998/fs-09-21-
98-01.txt

Evans, Kim. "Pesticides Cause Parkinson's Disease." Naturalnews.com September 25, 2009.
http://www.naturalnews.com/027098_pesticides_disease_Parkinsons.html

Fact Sheet: History, Background, and Status of Labeling of Irradiated Foods." Organic Consumers Association. 8/25/2008
http://www.organicconsumers.org/Irrad/LabelingStatus.cfm Accessed on May 13 2010.

Fassa, Paul. "A Fluoride-Free Pineal Gland is More Important than Ever," Natural News, June 2, 2009.
http://www.naturalnews.com/026364_fluoride_pineal_gland_sodium.html Accessed May 24, 2010.

Fassa, Paul. "How To Detox Fluorides From Your Body," Natural News, July 13, 2009. P.1
http://www.naturalnews.com/026605_fluoride_fluorides_detox.html Accessed May 24, 2010.

FDA.gov, "Dietary Supplement Health and Education Act of 1994." Food and Drug Administration.
http://www.fda.gov/RegulatoryInformation/Legislation/FederalFoodDrugandCosmeticActFDCAct/SignificantAmendmentstotheFDCAct/ucm148003.htm Accessed May 24, 2010.

Federal Register Proposed Rule – 72 FR 16291 April 4, 2007: Irradiation in the Production, Processing, and Handling of Food p.1
http://www.fda.gov/Food/LabelingNutrition/FoodLabelingGuidanceRegulatoryInformation/RegulationsFederalRegisterDocuments/ucm077977.htm Accessed May 24, 2010.

Fergusson, Ian F. "CRS Report For Congress – The World Trade Organization: Background and Issues." May 9, 2007.
http://www.nationalaglawcenter.org/assets/crs/98-928.pdf

Ferrara, Jennifer. "Revolving Doors: Monsanto and the Regulators." The Ecologist, Vol. 28, No. 5, September/October 1998.

Food and Agricultural Organization. "Codex Alimentarius: how it all began." Food and Agricultural Organization. http://www.fao.org/docrep/v7700t/v7700t09.htm Accessed April 23, 2010.

Food and Agricultural Organization."Opening Statement by Dr. B.P. Dutia Assistant Director-General Economic and Social Policy Department, FAO to the Nineteenth Session of the Codex Alimentarius Commission." Food and Agricultural Organization. July 1, 1991. http://www.fao.org/docrep/meeting/005/t0490e/T0490E04.htm

Franzon, Ingrid. "Report from the Thai Codex Meeting." Codex Alimentarius: Global Food Imperialism. Ed. Scott C. Tips. FHR 2007.

General Standard For Irradiated Foods Codex Stan 106-1983, REV.1-2003. Codexalimentarius.net. www.codexalimentarius.net/download/standards/16/CXS_106e.pdf Accessed May 24, 2010.

Griffin, G. Edward. "World Without Cancer." 2nd edition. American Media. 1997.

Guitierrez, David. "Chemicals Pass Through Breast Milk to Cause Testicular Cancer." www.naturalnews.com February 9, 2010. http://www.naturalnews.com/z028124_brst_milk_testicular_cancer.html

Gutierrez, David. "Consumer Outrage May Reverse Pennsylvania's rBGH-Free Dairy Label Censorship Sham." Naturalnews.com. http://www.naturalnews.com/023575.html Accessed May 24, 2010.

Gutierrez, David. "Pesticides Cause Childhood Brain Cancers." www.naturalnews.com September 29, 2009.

http://www.naturalnews.com/z027121_pesticides_cancer_brain_cance r.html

Hamlin, Heather. "Pesticides blamed for some childhood brain cancers." Enviromental Health News. April 7, 2009. http://www.environmentalhealthnews.org/ehs/newscience/pesticides-linked-to-child-brain-cancer

Hansen, Michael Ph.D., Halloran, Jean M., Groth, Edward III, Ph.D., Lefferts, Lisa Y. "Potential Public Health Impacts Of The Use Of Recombinant Bovine Somatropin In Dairy Production." September 1997

Hansen, Michael, Ph.D., Halloran, Jean M., Groth, Edward III, Ph.D., Lefferts, Lisa Y."Potential Public Health Impacts Of The Use of Recombinant Bovine Somatotropin In Dairy Production." ConsumersUnion.org. September 1997. http://www.consumersunion.org/pub/core_food_safety/002272.html Accessed May 24, 2010.

Hickman, Martin; Roberts, Genevieve. "Fury as EU approves GM potato." The Independent. March 4, 2010. http://www.independent.co.uk/environment/green-living/fury-as-eu-approves-gm-potato-1915833.html

Ho, Mae-Wan; Ryan, Angela; Cummins, Joe; "Cauliflower Mosaic Viral Promoter-A Recipe for Disaster?" Institute of Science in Society. http://www.i-sis.org.uk/camvrecdis.php

Hoebben, D. Burvenich, C. Heyneman, R. "Antibiotics Commonly Used To Treat Mastitis and Respiratory Burst of Bovine Polymorphonuclear Leukocytes." Journal of Dairy Science, 81: 403 – 410. 1998. http://jds.fass.org/cgi/reprint/81/2/403.pdf   Accessed May 24, 2010.

http://www.iaea.org/About/index.html   Accessed May 24, 2010.

http://www.iaea.org/About/index.html   Accessed May 24, 2010.

Huff, Ethan. "Stop Federal Takeover of Food Regulation in H.R. 875." Naturalnews. March 11, 2009.
http://www.naturalnews.com/z025824_food_safety.html

Huff, Ethan. "Stop Federal Takeover of Food Regulation in H.R. 875." Naturalnews. March 11, 2009.
http://www.naturalnews.com/z025824_food_safety.html

Joint FAO/WHO Expert Committee on Food Additives.
http://www.who.int/ipcs/food/jecfa/en/

Kaufman, Marc. "Biotech Corn Is The Test Case For Industry: Engineered Food's Future Hinges on Allergy Study." Washington Post. March 19, 2001. http://www.gmfoodnews.com/wp190301.txt

Krebs, Al. "WTO Codex To Allow Dangerous Levels of Food Irradiation." Organic Consumers Association. July 10, 2003.
http://www.organicconsumers.org/corp/071403_wto_irradiation.cfm
Accessed May 24, 2010.

Lahm, H; Suardet, L; Laurent, PL; Fischer, JR; Ceyhan, A; Givel, JC; Odartchenko, N. "Growth regulation and co-stimulation of human colorectal cancer cell lines by insulin-like growth factor I, II and transforming growth factor." British Journal of Cancer, 65, 341-346. 1992. http://www.ncbi.nlm.nih.gov/pubmed/1558785 Accessed May 24, 2010.

Laibow, Rima. "'Nutraceuticide' and Codex Alimentarius." Alternative and Complementary Therapies, October 2005.

Lazaris, Lous. "Residential Pesticides Linked to Childhood Brain Cancer." April 29, 2009.
http://www.naturalnews.com/z026155_brain_pesticides_exposure.html

Lee, Duk-Hee., Lee, In-Kyu. Song, Kyungeun. Steffes, Michael. Toscano, William. Baker, Beth A., Jacobs, David R. Jr., "A Strong Dose-Response

Relation Between Serum Concentrations of Persistent Organic Pollutants and Diabetes." Diabetes Care. Vol. 29. Number 7. July 2006. American Diabetes Association. http://care.diabetesjournals.org/content/29/7/1638.abstract Accessed May 24, 2010.

Lendman, Stephen. "Unsafe Genetically Modified Food: GMO Proliferation Bills in the US Congress." Global Research. April 3, 2009. http://www.globalresearch.ca/index.php?context=va&aid=13025 Accessed May 24, 2010.

LeRoith, Derek; Baserga, Renato; Helman, Lee; Roberts, Charles T. "Insulin-like Growth Factors and Cancer." Annals of Internal Medicine. January 1, 1995. Vol. 122. No.1. Pp. 54-59. http://www.annals.org/content/122/1/54.full   Accessed May 24, 2010.

MacKenzie, Anne. A. "The Process of Developing Labeling Standards For GM Foods In The Codex Alimentarius." AgBioForum, Vol.3, Number 4, 2000. http://www.agbioforum.org/v3n4/v3n4a04-mackenzie.htm Accessed May 24, 2010.

Marrs, Jim. "Rule By Secrecy." Harper. 2000.

McCauley, V.M. "Insulin-like growth factors and cancer." British Journal of Cancer 65, 311-320. 1992. http://www.ncbi.nlm.nih.gov/pmc/articles/PMC1977607/ Accessed May 24, 2010.

Mellon, Margaret, Benbrook, Charles and Benbrook, Karen. "Hogging It: Estimates of Antimicrobial Abuse in Livestock." Union of Concerned Scientists. January 2001

Minton, Barbara. "Billions of People Expected to Die Under Current Codex Alimentarius Guidelines." Natural News. July 21, 2009. http://www.naturalnews.com/026731_CODEX_food_health.html

278

Minton, Barbara. "Codex Threatens Health of Billions."
Naturalnews.com. July 30, 2009.
http://www.naturalnews.com/026731_CODEX_food_health.html
Accessed May 24, 2010

Morehouse, Kim M., Komolprasert, Vanee. "Irradiation of Food and
Packaging: An Overview." Food and Drug Administration.
http://www.fda.gov/Food/FoodIngredientsPackaging/IrradiatedFoodPa
ckaging/ucm081050.htm   Accessed May 24, 2010.

Morris, Owen. "New Kansas Bill Restricts rBGH Labeling." The Pitch.
3/23/09. Reprinted by Organic Consumers Association.
http://www.organicconsumers.org/articles/article_17366.cfm
Accessed May 24, 2010.

National Park Service: Biographical Vignettes – John D. Rockefeller.
http://www.nps.gov/history/history/online_books/sontag/rockefeller.h
tm

National Park Service: Biographical Vignettes – John D. Rockefeller.
http://www.nps.gov/history/history/online_books/sontag/rockefeller.h
tm

Nausoulas, Andrianna. "Codex Alimentarius and the International
Politics of Food Irradiation." Toronto Food Policy Council, July 2003.
http://www.publiccitizen.org/documents/codextoronto.pdf   Accessed
May 24, 2010.

Nield, Michael. "The Police State Road Map." March 2005.
http://www.bibliotecapleyades.net/sociopolitica/policestate_roadmap/
policestate_roadmap.htm#Contents

Paulson, Michael. "WTO Case File: foreign sales corporations." Seattle
Post-Intelligencer. November 22, 1999.
www.seattlepi.com/pi/national/case4.shtml

Pesticide Residues In Food. Codex Alimentarius.
www.codexalimentarius.net

Pesticide Residues In Food. Codex Alimentarius.
www.codexalimentarius.net   Accessed May 20, 2010.

Pesticide Residues In Food. www.codexalimentarius.net
http://www.codexalimentarius.net/mrls/servlet/PesticideServlet?Pestic
ides=21&Items=0&out_style=by+substance&Domain=PesticideMRLs&La
nguage=english&query_form=%2Fmrls%2Fpestdes%2Fpest_q-e.htm
Accessed 4/5/2010

Press Release: National Health Federation. "December 31, 2009 –
Where Were You When The Earth Ended?" January 4, 2010.
http://www.thenhf.com/press_releases/pr_04_jan_2010.html

Press Release: National Health Federation. "December 31, 2009 –
Where Were You When The Earth Ended?" January 4, 2010.
http://www.thenhf.com/press_releases/pr_04_jan_2010.html

Pus, Sores, Tumors, & Filth: USDA's Deregulation of the Meat Industry
Draws Public Criticism," The Agribusiness Examiner. Issue # 82, July 27,
2000. http://www.organicconsumers.org/toxic/chixpus.cfm   Cited from
Organicconsumers.org website. Accessed May 24, 2010.

Rathke, Lisa. "Ben & Jerry's Opposes Monsanto's Move in Several States
to Ban rBGH-Free Labels." Associated Press, February 5, 2008. Reprinted
by Organic Consumer's Association.
http://www.organicconsumers.org/articles/article_10095.cfm

Reinberg, Steven. "FDA Issues Final Regulations for Genetically
Engineered Animals." US News And World Report. January 15, 2009.
http://health.usnews.com/health-news/managing-your-
healthcare/policy/articles/2009/01/15/fda-issues-final-regulations-for-
genetically.html   Accessed May 24, 2010.

Reregistration Eligibility Decision for Dicofol." U.S. Environmental Protection Agency Office of Pesticide Programs.
http://www.epa.gov/oppsrrd1/REDs/0021red.pdf

Rockwell, Llewellyn Jr. "Medical Control, Medical Corruption." www.lewrockwell.com
http://www.lewrockwell.com/rockwell/medical.html

Rohan, Thomas, Yu, Herbert. "Role of the Insulin-like Growth Factor Family in Cancer Development and Progression." Journal of the National Cancer Institute. September 20, 2000. 92 (18). 1472-1489.
http://www.ncbi.nlm.nih.gov/pubmed/10995803   Accessed May 24, 2010.

Ryberg, William. "Growers of biotech corn say they weren't warned." Des Moines Register. August 20, 2000.
http://www.gmfoodnews.com/dm251000.txt

Schneider, Andrew. "Harmful pesticides found everyday food products." Seattle Post Intelligencer. January 30, 2008.
http://www.seattlepi.com/local/349263_pesticide30.html

Section 7.2 "Report of the Canadian Veterinary Medical Association Expert Panel on rBST." http://www.hc-sc.gc.ca/dhp-mps/vet/issues-enjeux/rbst-stbr/rep_cvma-rap_acdv_tc-tm-eng.php

Shim, Youn K., Mlynarek, Steven P., van Wijngaarden, Edwin., "Parental Exposures to Pesticides and Childhood Brain Cancer: U.S. Atlantic Coast Childhood Brain Cancer Study." Enviromental Health Perspectives. Vol. 117 Number 6. June 2009.
http://www.ncbi.nlm.nih.gov/pmc/articles/pmc2702394/pdf/ehp-117-1002.pdf

Smith, David L., Harris, Anthony D., Johnson, Judith A., Silbergeld, Ellen K., Morris, Glen Jr., "Animal antibiotic use has an early but important impact on the emergence of antibiotic resistance in human commensal bacteria." Proceedings of the National Academy of Sciences, Vol. 99. No. 9, April 30, 2002.

Smith, Jeffrey. "Seeds Of Deception." YES Books, 2003.

Smith, Jeffrey. "You're Appointing Who? Please Obama, Say It's Not So!" July 23, 2009. http://www.huffingtonpost.com/jeffrey-smith/youre-appointing-who-plea_b_243810.html Accessed May 24, 2010.

South, James. "Vitamin Safety, RDAs and the Assault on Vitamin Freedom." National Health Federation. March 2004. http://www.thenhf.com/articles_19.htm

Starling, Shane. "Food Supplements Directive: Stay positive (or bans may follow)." Nutraingredients.com January 8, 2010. http://www.nutraingredients.com/Regulation/Food-Supplements-Directive-Stay-positive-or-bans-may-follow

Stuter, Lynn. "The National Animal Identification System." Newswithviews. June 6, 2006. http://www.newswithviews.com/Stuter/stuter91.htm Accessed May 7, 2010.

Takeuchi, Aiko. "The Transnational Politics of Public Health and Population Control: The Rockefeller Foundation's Role in Japan, 1920's – 1950's." Rockefeller Archives. 2009. http://www.rockarch.org/publications/resrep/takeuchi.pdf

Tanner, CM, Ross GW, Jewell SA, Hauser RA, Jankovic J., Factor SA, Bressman S. Deligtisch A., Marras C, Lyons KE,Bhudhikanok GS, Roucoux DF, Meng C., Abbott RD, Langston JW. "Occupation and risk of parkinsonism: a multicenter case-control study." Archives of Neurology. September 2009. 66(9): 1106-13. http://www.ncbi.nlm.nih.gov/pubmed/19752299 (link to abstract)

Tape, N.W. Dr. "International Consultative Group on Food Irradiation: Role, Achievements, and Impacts, 1984-88."

http://www.iaea.org/Publications/Magazines/Bulletin/Bull311/3110578
3538.pdf

Taylor, Paul Anthony, "The Growing Threats To DSHEA," Page1
http://www4.dr-rath-foundation.org/us/growing_threats.html

Taylor, Paul Anthony. "Codex Guidelines for Vitamins and Minerals –
Optional or Mandatory?" Dr.Rath Health Foundation. http://www4.dr-
rath-foundation.org/features/codex_wto.html

Taylor, Paul Anthony. "Nutrient Risk Assessment: What You're Not
Being Told." http://www4.dr-rath-
foundation.org/features/risk_assessment.html

The Trilateral Commission: Membership.
http://www.trilateral.org/memb.htm   Accessed on April 28, 2010.

Tips, Scott C. "A Meeting Of Two." Codex Alimentarius: Global Food
Imperialism. Ed. Scott C. Tips. FHR. 2007.

Tips, Scott C. "Breathe Easier – Codex Adjourns." Codex Alimentarius:
Global Food Imperialism. Ed. Scott C. Tips. FHR. 2007.

Tips, Scott C. "Codex Alimentarius: Global Food Imperialism." FHR. 2007.

Tips, Scott C. "Codex Gets One Step Closer to Control." Codex
Alimentarius: Global Food Imperialism. Ed. Scott C. Tips. FHR. 2007.

Tips, Scott C. ""Foreword – Codex Alimentarius: Global Food
Imperialism – What is Codex?" Ed. Scott C. Tipps. FHR. 2007

Tips, Scott C. "International Law Trumps Domestic Law." Codex
Alimentarius: Global Food Imperialism." Ed. Scott C. Tips. FHR. 2007.

Tips, Scott C. "Rearranging the Deck Chairs on the Titanic." Codex
Alimentarius: Global Food Imperialism." Ed. Scott C. Tips. FHR. 2007.

Tips, Scott C. "The Maginot Mentality." Codex Alimentarius: Global Food Imperialism. Ed. Scott C. Tips. FHR. 2007.

Tomlinson, Nick. "Joint FAO/WHO Expert Consultation on Foods Derived from Biotechnology." 2003. ftp://ftp.fao.org/es/esn/food/Bio-03.pdf Accessed May 24, 2010.

Tricoli, James V; Rall, Leslie B; Karakousis, Constantine P; Herrera, Lemuel; Petrelli, Nicholas J; Bell, Graeme I; Shows, Thomas B. "Enhanced Levels of Insulin-like Growth Factor Messenger RNA in Human Colon Carcinomas and Liposarcomas." Cancer Research 46, 6169-6173, December 1986.
http://cancerres.aacrjournals.org/cgi/content/abstract/46/12_Part_1/6169 Accessed May 24, 2010.

United Nations Population Fund website.
http://www.unfpa.org/public/about Accessed April 29, 2010.

Walter, Suzan. "AHHA Attends Berlin Codex Session: What Did We Learn?" Codex Alimentarius: Global Food Imperialism. Ed. Scott C. Tips. FHR. 2007

Walter, Suzan. "Important News from Bonn." Codex Alimentarius: Global Food Imperialism. Ed. Scott C. Tips. FHR. 2007.

Watson, Steve; Watson, Paul Joseph; Jones, Alex. "Professor's 'Kill 90% of Population' Comments Echo UN, Elite NGO Policies." www.prisonplanet.com April 4, 2006.
http://www.prisonplanet.com/articles/april2006/040406_b_depopulation.htm

Weimbs Lab: Molecular, Cellular and Developmental Biology University of California, Santa Barbra.
http://www.lifesci.ucsb.edu/mcdb/labs/weimbs/people/weimbs/index.html Accessed April 27, 2010. Dr. Thomas Weimbs received a scholarship from the Fritz ter Meer Foundation in 1988.

Weiss, Rick. "Biotech Food Raises a Crop of Questions." Washington Post. August 15, 1999.
http://www.organicconsumers.org/ge/biotechfood.cfm

www.IAEA.org

Yoon, Carol Kaesuk. "News Analysis; What's Next for Biotech Crops? Questions." New York Times. December 19, 2000.
http://nytimes.com/2000/12/19/science/news-analysis-what-s-next-for-biotech-crops-questions-.htm?pagewanted=1&pagewanted=print

About The Author

Brandon Turbeville is a writer from Florence, South Carolina. He is the author of seven books including Seven Real Conspiracies, The Road To Damascus: The Anglo-American Assault On Syria, Dispatches From A Dissident, and The Difference It Makes: 36 Reasons Why Hillary Clinton Should Never Be President. He has published over 600 articles dealing with a variety of issues including health, banking, politics, environment, and civil liberties.. Formerly a member of the Board of Directors of South Carolina Health Freedom Coalition, Turbeville is a regular writer for Activist Post, Natural Blaze, and the Anti Media. He also hosts a weekly radio show on the UCY radio network called Truth on the Tracks, broadcast every Monday night at 9pm EST. His website is BrandonTurbeville.com

To contact the author, send all correspondence to anticodex@yahoo.com

Printed in Poland
by Amazon Fulfillment
Poland Sp. z o.o., Wrocław